The Age of Illusion

ENGLAND IN THE TWENTIES
AND THIRTIES

1919-1940

By the same Author

A TREASONABLE GROWTH

IMMEDIATE POSSESSION

RONALD BLYTHE

The Age of Illusion

ENGLAND IN THE TWENTIES AND THIRTIES

1919–1940

Illustrated

HAMISH HAMILTON

LONDON

FOR MY BROTHER
H. E. S. BLYTHE

CONTENTS

LIST OF ILLUSTRATIONS

ACKNOWLEDGMENTS

AMONG all those who have assisted me so generously in writing this book I would like particularly to acknowledge the great help given me by Mr. A. T. Austing and his staff at Colchester Public Library, Mrs. Denis Burroughs, Mr. Robert Collison and the Staff of the B.B.C. Library, Miss Livia Gollancz, Mr. Thomas Frankland, Mr. John Nash, R.A., Mr. John Penn, Sir Osbert Sitwell, Bt., Mr. Lawrence Tanner and the Staff of Westminster Abbey Library, The Librarian and Staff of the Westminster City Library, and Miss Dorothy White and the Staff of Ipswich Public Library.

My publishers and I would also like to thank the following for generously granting permission to quote copyright material in this book:

W. H. Auden and Louis MacNeice for lines from *Letters from Iceland* (1937).

Basil Blackwell Ltd. for extracts from *The Home Letters of T. E. Lawrence and His Brothers*.

Jonathan Cape Ltd. and the Executors of the T. E. Lawrence Estate for extracts from *The Mint* by T. E. Lawrence and *The Letters of T. E. Lawrence* edited by David Garnett and for the Dedication Poem to *Seven Pillars of Wisdom* by T. E. Lawrence.

Chatto & Windus Ltd. and Harcourt, Brace & World Inc. for 'Just a Smack at Auden' by William Empson (1940).

Faber & Faber Ltd. and Random House Inc. for the Dedication Poem to *Poems* (1930) by W. H. Auden, an extract from 'Spain' in *Collected Poems* by the same author, and for an extract from 'From all these events' from *Collected Poems* by Stephen Spender (1945).

William Heinemann Ltd. for extracts from *I Believed* by Douglas Hyde.

Sir Alan Herbert, the Proprietors of *Punch*, and Ernest Benn Ltd. for 'Come to Britain and lead the gay life' from *A Book of Ballads*.

James Laver for three verses from *The Woman of 1926*.

Punch for two verses 'Where all the waking birds sing Heil!' from *The Way of a Dove* by 'Evoe' (E. V. Knox) (21 September 1938).

The Times Publishing Company for an extract from their fourth leader of 19 January 1933.

R.B.

1*

CHAPTER ONE

A Great Day for Westminster Abbey

IT HAS become the custom to say that the old world died when the shots were fired in Sarajevo, but a world doesn't die as easily as all that. Certainly it doesn't collapse and vanish with the neat poignancy of a murdered archduke. All that is certain is that the bullet which entered Franz Ferdinand's throat ricocheted on for thirty-seven days like a comet to announce the end of the cosmos. Engineering the actual destruction of the cosmos, however, was a very different matter. It required the apprentice virtues of perseverance and blind devotion, and it got them. The lights went out all over Europe and in the fifty-one months of darkness which followed the heirs of the West were marched, like the Tollund man, to a vast quagmire on the Belgian border and suffocated. Altogether, eight and a half millions were slaughtered and twenty-one millions were hurt. It was a world which ended with a bang and without a whimper. In what Wilfred Owen called 'carnage incomparable and human squander' encumbered with a morality which no longer worked but which, like Christian's load, couldn't be jettisoned, and with a fine naïve patriotism, an immense company of the young was immolated in the dark arterial trenches. No more innocent generation was ever destroyed so ignorantly or so thoroughly. The particulars of its destruction were disgusting and were bowdlerized by the official obituarists. They had to be; the truth was obscene. A popular print which found its way into thousands of British homes showed a handsome Tommy sprawling at the foot of the Cross. It was called 'The Great Sacrifice' and it invited comparison. Neither body of God nor man exhibited outrage or indecency, and so it was with all the official written and spoken references to what was happening. Sons and lovers simply 'fell' like cut flowers and the tireless scything of young life went on.

The trench system of the 1914–1918 War was based on certain

1

primitive military ideas stretched out on a vast scale. Besides trap-
ping the armies of the Allies and their opponents in a complex
muddy grid which made them virtually immovable, the trenches
defiled the spirit as well as the flesh of the ordinary civilian-soldier.
The main trench line stretched from Switzerland to the Channel
coast just above Ypres in a great double artery which was so close
together in certain places that friend and foe could hear each other's
conversation. From the main trenches there reached back an enormous network of ramified capillaries which veined off to the supply
depots and troop trains. The prizes, stark, ruined and coveted by
both sides to an insane degree, were between the two fronts. No
price was deemed too great for the smallest advance. In the spring of
1915 the shattered hamlets round Neuve Chapelle were captured by
the Allies at a cost of a quarter of a million lives. These agonizing
losses were received in both Britain and Germany with a noble
stoicism which convinced their Governments that they had a moral
mandate to prosecute the war in every way possible. After 1915 there
is little evidence on either side to show that consideration for human
expenditure, or thought for human misery, was to influence military
experiments or military ambition. The front had become a rite, a
mystery to which all young male Europe was committed. Recruiting
offices were besieged. Jobs, families and personal identity were discarded. Kitchener's manic gaze and pointing finger solicited the
youth of England from every hoarding, and soon the rich, heady
fatalism of the age reached out and took command above that of the
rival politicians and generals. A few voices were raised to check the
death-rush but they could not be heard above the ritual music-hall
singing and uproarious patriotic cheerfulness which deafened reason.
By the end of 1915 the vast trench system was choked and throm-
botic with new blood and early in 1916 Falkenhayn, the German
Chief-of-Staff, began to put into practice his belief in military attrition. This was simply to inflict more casualties than one suffers
oneself and the spread of this doctrine to the Allied Command
marked a new phase of moral recklessness. It justified the deaths of
ten men for the deaths of twelve. *Je les grignote*, as Joffre used to say.

Falkenhayn's first application of his attrition tactics was very much
more than a nibble, however. He lured great masses of French
troops to Verdun, where they were massacred over a period of six
months and in this way the fate of Kitchener's Army—perhaps the

noblest fighting force ever mobilized—was sealed. Because, before Verdun, the French and the British had worked out a grand attack on the Somme. It was to be the first genuinely all-out attempt by the two touchily chauvinistic powers at military brotherhood, and much depended upon it. But the shocking Verdun losses made it impossible for the French to take up their full commitments in the Somme offensive, and the whole plan should have been halted and revised.

But the entire history of the First World War is an itinerary of compulsive fatalism. On July 1st, 1916, the Somme attack began. The Allies attempted to move forward and lost a hundred thousand men on the first day. Eventually they did move forward—for three miles. It took three months to achieve this and it was here, within sight of Crécy and Agincourt, that the old world died. British losses alone were more than half a million. They included nearly all the promise and what was best of the nation, and the wild patriotic gallimaufrey of the brave and the brainless pouring through the recruiting stations was momentarily checked. The casualty lists broke all the bounds and precedents of private and public grief, and Edith Cavell's 'Patriotism is not enough' began to be vaguely comprehended.

Kitchener and Rupert Brooke, the Zeus and Adonais of the old order, were gone too. Public mourning for Kitchener did not entirely conceal the long thankful sigh of official relief at his passing. Brooke's death evoked a wave of passionate sadness which was genuinely and perfectly attuned to the clean patriotism of his elegiacs. He was buried on St. George's Day on the Greek island of Skyros, where Achilles once lived as a girl in order to escape the Trojan war. He died with his Anglo-Hellenism intact, his beautiful image inviolable.

Lloyd George succeeded Kitchener at the War Office and the conflict entered its second stage. The whole mood of the nation had changed. The glittering, exciting and, beyond all reckoning, extravagant party was over and an incoherent misery took its place. 'Why are we fighting . . . ?' sang the troops ironically to the tune of *Adeste Fideles*. There was a great Press campaign to unseat Asquith. On December 4th, 1916, Lloyd George resigned from the Cabinet. Then Asquith himself resigned and the King sent for Bonar Law. Bonar Law had arranged to 'fail to form a Cabinet' and this being formally announced, the King sent for Lloyd George. He went to Downing Street when almost every family in the country had been bereaved and at a moment when the old civilized continuity had been severed. The hour called for a realist and a vulgarian, and in the tricky, talkative Welshman it got both. By what was little less than a miracle of persuasive oratory Lloyd George brought back, if not the one hundred per cent 1914 mood, a good working model of it.

There were difficulties, of course, and most of them were named Haig. When Lloyd George was still at the War Office he had induced Haig to place himself under the French General Nivelle. It was disastrous. Both men were arrogant and proud to a pathological degree, and neither allowed himself to be in the full confidence of the other. Nor did they believe it to be their duty to allow their immediate inferiors to know their complete plans. Nivelle's plan was not only very bad, but it had been captured by the Germans. This, however, did not deter him from putting it into action. For three long weeks he flung wave after wave of helpless *poilus* against an intractable barrier of barbed wire, where they hung in brief crucifixion for just sufficient time for them to be given the *coup de grâce* by German machine-guns. And this in spite of the fact that he had given his word not to pursue the plan if a break-through had not been achieved in a single day. At last the *poilus* mutinied. They expected agony—for this had always been a recognizable ingredient of *la gloire*—but the sheer illogicality of what they were being asked to do was intolerable. Nivelle was dismissed and Pétain succeeded him.

Though on the face of it to give Pétain a breathing space in which to soothe and tidy up his army after this carnage, Haig, as though not to be outdone in recalcitrance and in spite of all warnings about field drains and autumn rain, decided to attack in Flanders. What followed was three months of such extreme horror that nothing which either preceded them or came afterwards was comparable. This was Passchendaele.

The Haig-Lloyd George relationship was based less on mutual distrust than on total incomprehension of each other's natures. After Passchendaele the Prime Minister began to withhold the reserves, fearing that if they crossed the Channel they would be wasted by Haig. There was a noticeable decline in the recruiting figures and an obvious reticence among males to march singing into the insatiable Flanders bog. This produced a strong resentment among the newly emancipated women against any man who, although legally exempted by the National Service Act of 1915 from military service because he was essential to war industry, still did not volunteer. A white feather in a game-bird's tail was a sign of inferior breeding in sporting circles and the symbol had been given a wider application in 1902 with the publication of A. E. W. Mason's popular novel, *The Four Feathers*. Between the numbing effects of Passchendaele and Lloyd George's miraculous fillip the streets were regularly prowled by women with handbags stuffed with feathers which they thrust into the lapel of any man still out of uniform and not actually on crutches. There was, too, a note of undisguised accusation in the song 'We don't want to lose you but we think you ought to go. . . .'

By 1917 both the mysterious lyricism and the nerve-shattering shock of the war had disappeared. Its origins had been forgotten by the common man—if he had ever known them—and he was in energetic agreement with the Government that the whole thing must be stopped. Winston Churchill had noticed that farm tractors fitted with caterpillar treads rode ruts and ditches with ease. If the tractor was encased in armour and had men inside it . . . The War Office dismissed the idea, though this did not invalidate it as Churchill was Minister of Munitions. He made tanks and was rewarded by deep advances into the enemy lines. The static nature of the war made any advance extraordinarily thrilling and these elephantine advances, made without the customary massacres, lifted the spirit and elated the heart of the ordinary soldier. The very novelty and lively innovation of the grotesque weapon caught the imagination of men, not the least of whose sufferings had been caused by the sacred inflexibility of the military mind and the strict observance of antiquated regimental snobbery.

And so the end approached. On March 21st, 1918, Ludendorff launched his titanic offensive. Germany was starving and there was open talk of 'peace without conquests' in Berlin. Hindenburg was in a great passion of rage at such talk and an all-or-nothing plan for a swift and terrible advance, a vast final flood-tide of might, was set in action. The violence and immensity of the attack surpassed anything known previously. In three days the Fifth Army commanded by General Gough was destroyed and the German avalanche rolled through the gap for forty miles in the direction of Paris. If this overwhelming onslaught lacerated the Allied line it also, at long last,

unified the Allied Command. Haig and Pétain put themselves under
Foch. At home the recruiting depots were besieged with volunteers
and the quite incredible losses on the battlefields were made up time
and time again with hurriedly trained men, some of them only boys
who had lied about their age. The river lands of the Somme, the
Aisne and the Marne were a delta of blood.

The final scenes were orgasmic and when the shuddering armies
at last disengaged there was an enfeebled, confused and ignoble
approach to an armistice which proved to be nothing more than a
respite. Just before eleven o'clock on the morning of November 11th,
1918, the British troops marched into Mons and the war ended.

*

1919 was Boom Year. Inflated war industries absorbed the returning
heroes. There were gratuities to be spent, homes and love and
whoopee to make. Life, dear life, was seen to be so precious, so enchanting, that people experienced the conscious living of it hour by
hour and day by day. In spite of the fact that few families were out
of mourning there was a near-delirious happiness. This continued
until the first anniversary of the Armistice, which took the country
by surprise and was acknowledged with a mixture of embarrassed
dignity and resentment. Families that had been decimated now began to feel the sharp ache of their loss, besides which, the world fit
for heroes to live in was noticeably being run up on the cheap by a
new type of hard-faced men. These were the war profiteers. In
America Henry Ford handed *his* twenty-nine million dollars war
profit back to the United States Government, though history, being
bunk, seems hardly to have recorded the fact. There is no record of
any such gesture in this country. The fortunes from swords were
soon ploughed back into shares and honours. The truth didn't bear
thinking about, yet the official Armistice anniversary plans were such
as to make thought inevitable.

Sir Percy Fitzgerald, a South African, had told Lord Milner that
there had been a daily observance in Cape Town all through the
war called the 'Two Minutes Pause' as a salute to the dead. King
George V liked this idea and at eleven o'clock on November 11th,
1919, the dancing and the shouting and the spending stopped. They
never quite got going again. The crippling silence, like Prospero's
island, turned out to be full of noises. It was all over, not only the

fighting but the old familiar order of things. Somehow this had not been allowed for in the jubilation estimates. Life would go on, but without the ancient spiritual certainty. *Tous les jours, à tous points de vue, je vais de mieux en mieux* was seen to be the formula of a faith-cure which would never work again.

While sculptors worked overtime on the great stream of commissions which flowed from regiments, schools, corporations, parish councils, colleges, railway stations and every hamlet, village, town and city in the country, carving in stone the names of a million dead, adding always that their lives had been given and not taken, there was a growing sense of the inadequacy of it all. Sir Edward Lutyens' design for an empty tomb to stand in Whitehall was approved and was a step in the right emotional direction, though its triumphant analogy could not be carried—like the lines of its stone—to a point in the sky because this must constitute a blasphemy. The ordinary man took his cap off to it, motor-cars perceptibly slowed in passing it, but its full significance never really touched the average heart. And in less than a year of its erection there was to be a poetic, macabre and brilliant rite which would cancel its whole meaning and leave it to function as a reflective architectural centrepiece for an annual ceremony.

In France the battlefields were being tidied up. Wire parties strolled in No Man's Land cutting and baling the terrible mesh. Scarcely any of the millions of victims had been brought home and most of them lay shallowly just beneath the soil. The trenches were filled in and the grim shell-pollarded trees were levelled. At home the national economy began to shrink back to its peace-time dimensions and wages shrivelled up accordingly. Between 1919 and 1920 there were upwards of 2,000 strikes. As the second anniversary of the war drew near a moral and material shabbiness enveloped everything.

The Cenotaph was completed and the King was to unveil it on Armistice Day. It was very much more like an altar than a tomb but it was refreshingly pure in concept and quite different to any other monument in the capital. The idea had been cool, correct and adequate, and the King had liked it from the beginning. But in October a letter arrived at Buckingham Palace from the Dean of Westminster suggesting a sensational pendant to the carefully arranged Cenotaph unveiling. The body of an unidentified soldier should be dug up, the writer suggested, brought to England and buried in the Abbey. Classless, nameless, rankless and ageless, this man would be the silent ambassador of the legion dead to the courts of the living.

The King shrank from the idea; it was novel, it was emotional and it was poised most precariously on the tightrope of taste. One false move and there would be a morbid sideshow in the national shrine. Lord Stamfordham replied for him on October 7th, 1920.

'His Majesty is inclined to think that nearly two years after the last shot was fired on the battlefields of France and Flanders is so long ago that a funeral now might be regarded as belated, and almost, as it were, reopen the war wound which time is gradually healing. . . .'

The dean then approached Lloyd George and Sir Henry Wilson, who were immediately enthusiastic. The King then added his some-what subdued approval. Lord Curzon, who had disliked the Two Minutes Silence idea, was made chairman of the Cabinet committee responsible for the ceremonial of this extraordinary funeral. He— who had stopped to observe a platoon of naked Tommies bathing in the sea and had remarked, 'How is it that I have never been informed that the lower orders had such white skins?'—was to stage state obsequies for a farm labourer, an apprentice, a clerk—though just possibly a peer.

Armistice Day was very near and the funeral arrangements were forced to move at far from a funeral pace. To make lack of identity absolute the military authorities in France were asked to exhume the bodies of six anonymous soldiers who, so far as it could be judged, had been killed in the early fighting. On the early afternoon of November 9th, six small working parties, each carrying tools and a plain deal coffin, and each commanded by a subaltern, set out for the six main battlefields. A nameless corpse was chosen from the forest of rough crosses marked 'Unknown' which sprouted from the sour earth of Ypres, the Marne, Cambrai, Arras, the Somme and the Aisne. The bodies were sealed in the coffins near the spots where they were found and driven back separately in six motor ambu-lances to an army hut not far from Ypres. Here they were received by a clergyman, the Rev. George Kendall.

After they had been laid side by side, everybody concerned with the operation up until this stage retired to a distance and an officer who had never been inside the hut previously was blindfolded and led to the door. He entered and his groping hand touched a coffin. And so was chosen the poor nameless flesh which would be followed through the streets of London by the King-Emperor on foot and interred with every pomp and dignity known to the State in Westminster Abbey.

Immediately after its selection the body was taken to Boulogne. Its apotheosis had barely begun and its companions at this stage were humble enough—a sergeant-major of the R.A.S.C., an R.E. sergeant, two ranker gunners, an Australian and a Canadian private, a private from the 21st London Regiment and a member of the R.A.M.C. But once at Boulogne, the superb elevation began. H.M.S. *Verdun* had been sent to receive the corpse and bring it to England. The ship had brought a great coffin made of oak from a tree from Hampton Court and specially designed and constructed by the British Undertakers' Association. The deal coffin was placed inside the massive oak casket without being opened and the whole thing was locked by two wrought-iron straps which went round it like string round a parcel. Where the straps crossed on the lid there was a great seal on which was inscribed in Gothic letters,

A British Warrior
Who fell in the Great War
1914–1918
For King and Country

Under this was clipped an antique sword which was the King's own idea and which he had selected from his private collection, for he was now absorbed by the plan.

The *Verdun* set sail with her strange burden, the man who had been nothing and who was now to be everything. A funeral convoy of six destroyers waited in mid-Channel. At Dover there was a field-marshal's salute of nineteen guns from the castle. From Dover it travelled in a specially fitted saloon carriage to London and rested overnight in a temporary chapel at Victoria Station. The next morning, November 11th, pallbearers arrived to attend the corpse on its journey across the city, Admirals Meux, Beatty, Jackson, Sturdee and Madden; Field-Marshals French, Haig, Methuen, Wilson and Generals Horne and Byng. Air-Marshal Trenchard followed alone.

The day was gentle and fair. The soot-encrusted buildings were rimmed in thin gold sunlight and late leaves rustled in the gutters. It was curiously quiet everywhere, not so much silent as hushed and muted. Although the West End pavements were packed with a vast multitude it was a subtly different crowd from any that the authorities had seen before. What had happened was that this most stately public show was being observed with an intensely private emotion. The dead man who had set out without a name, a voice, or a face only a few hours before was being invested with a hundred thousand likenesses, and for those who could not resist a temptation to strip the symbol there was the possibility that one of the likenesses fitted. The affair *was* morbid, but grandly and supremely so, like the morbidity of Sir Thomas Browne or John Donne, and those who had received War Office telegrams with only a little less stoicism than that with which they had been sent were moved and grateful for this chance to express grief and personal loss.

The British have a flair for elegiacs and, once this unprecedented funeral had been approved, the entire ceremonial genius of the country was put into action. The authorities were taken by surprise by the success of the idea. They had made certain that it would be dignified; they never dreamt it would be overwhelming. They had intended to honour the average soldier and instead they had produced the perfect catharsis. As the coffin was carried into the Abbey there was a sense of release, a conviction that what was happening belonged to honour in its absolute state. The reckless destruction of young life over four mad years and the platitudes which sought to justify it were momentarily engulfed by the tenderness flooding into the tomb of this most mysterious individual. The formal programme broke down into a great act of compassion and love. The King and his family crowded the coffin as though it literally did contain a son and brother. The King's wreath bore a card affectionately crammed with his own scratchy, rather uneducated handwriting. It was the moment of truth.

The congregation was chiefly composed of private mourners. There was no foreign representation. A hundred V.C.s lined the nave. The service was brief and, *The Times* said, 'the most beautiful, the most touching and the most impressive . . . this island has ever seen. . . .' Gramophone records were obtained of it by Major Lionel Guest and Captain Merriman and sold later at seven-and-sixpence each. These were the first recordings ever made in the Abbey.

The grave had been dug just inside the west entrance and at the feet of Chatham. It was dug deep into the sand of Thorney Island and there was no trace of any previous burial. After the committal the grave was filled in with a hundred sandbags of earth brought from the main battlefields and a very large slab of Tournai marble was laid over it. For a brief time it was simply inscribed 'An Unknown Warrior' but the Dean of Westminster could not leave it at this because, he said, 'In fifty years' time they will want to know who the Unknown Warrior was.' So he drew up the inscription for the present word-packed memorial.

After the funeral came the homage. In five days over a million people visited the grave and left a hundred thousand wreaths at the Cenotaph, which became almost obscured by flowers. The popular Press, titillated beyond endurance by the exquisitely suppressed sensational aspects of the whole procedure, speculated fancifully on the identity of the warrior. Some anxiety was also felt that the ghostly rags-to-riches romance of these pitiful bones might make their grave a place of unhealthy pilgrimage. Though in fact this did not happen and even the King said that he was relieved to admit that his original apprehensions were unjustified.

The French buried their Unknown Warrior on the same day. They had lost one and a quarter million men and, unlike Britain, had had great tracts of their country reduced to a shambles. They chose their nameless hero from one of nine graves uncovered at Lille, Amiens, Chalons, Belfort, Nancy, Epinal, Alsace, Lorraine and a vague spot called simply 'Belgium'. There was much argument whether he should rest in the Pantheon or beneath the Arc de Triomphe and finally, with considerably more military panache than his British comrade, and preceded by the heart of Gambetta in an urn through the streets of Paris, the soldier was buried under the fine classical arch and a significantly enduring flame. The French gesture, perhaps because it had been so hurriedly copied from the British original, or because French militarism is so surrounded by its own mystique that any honour beyond that of dying for France is thought superfluous, did not quite touch popular feeling with the same poignancy as the Westminster Abbey burial.

In 1921 the present gravestone of black marble from Belgium, crowded with texts by Dean Ryle, was laid over the grave. 'A great day,' the dean wrote in his diary, 'for Westminster Abbey.' But hardly had this stone been put in position than the dean ran into trouble. The Principal of the Liverpool Hebrew Schools wrote him the following letter.

November 22nd 1921

Very Rev. Sir,

At the foot of the new stone over the Unknown Warrior's grave in Westminster Abbey there is the line, 'In Christ shall all be made alive'. Beneath the stone rests the body of a British warrior unknown by name or rank. Unknown also was the faith of the Unknown Warrior. Heavy was the toll of Jewish life on the battlefields of France. In many Jewish homes today the missing warrior son is mourned. The line 'In Christ shall all be made alive' does not meet the spiritual destinies of both Jew and Gentile.

Amid the unbounded wealth of biblical inspiration a line could have been selected which would not have offended the living religious susceptibilities of the unknown warrior, whatever his faith may have been. None of those who remain behind to mourn their beloved ones should be disturbed in their meditations. . . . It is not too late to make the amendment and I await your kind reply.

S. I. Levy

The dean's reply, marked Private, was to the point. The Abbey was a Christian Church and in it one would expect to find Christian texts. 'On a gravestone containing *five* texts it is not unreasonable that one of those texts should contain the Christian resurrection hope. . . .' When Mr. Levy persisted the dean answered tartly that it was not outside the bounds of possibility that the Unknown Warrior might have been a Moslem . . . or a Mormon. 'We cannot hope to please everybody.' Mr. Levy returned to the attack and also demanded that their correspondence should be published in a Jewish newspaper. But it all came to nothing; High Anglican tact is a weapon that would reduce firmer arguments than Mr. Levy's to silence.

The most famous text on the grave, 'They buried him among the Kings because he had done good toward God and towards His house', had already been in use on an Abbey tomb for close on

600 years, though the dean did not seem to realize it and he told people that he was indebted to a North-Country archdeacon for the suggestion. But Richard II had it inscribed on the tomb of his friend the Bishop of Salisbury in 1395.

The anonymous grave swiftly assumed precedence over all the mortuary magnificence which crammed the great building. Its pathos was irresistible and the dean himself became mesmerized by it. Every day he was to be found walking and watching by the dark marble slab upon which single flowers, rosaries, the United States Congressional Medal and small, private talismanic things had been dropped. Besides receiving a constant procession of foreign dignitaries, for protocol made a visit to the tomb as essential as writing one's name in the Visitors' Book at Buckingham Palace, the dean would go out of his way to talk about the soldier with the humblest sightseer. It was therefore curious that the dean's official biographer, Maurice Fitzgerald, should write,

> 'Of all the special services none laid a deeper hold upon the popular imagination than the burial of the Unknown Warrior on November 11th 1920. It is not possible to say to whom the credit is due for the original idea of such a service. . . .'

But it was very possible to say to whom the credit was due, and it was not the dean. The Vicar of Margate, the Rev. David Railton, had spent the war years as a young padre and one evening in 1916 he said,

'I came back from the line at dusk. We had just laid to rest the mortal remains of a comrade. I went to a billet in front of Erkingham, near Armentieres. At the back of the billet was a small garden, and in the garden only six paces from the house, there was a grave. At the head of the grave there stood a rough cross of white wood. On the cross was written in deep black-pencilled letters, "An Unknown British Soldier" and in brackets beneath, "of the Black Watch". It was dusk and no one was near, except some officers in the billet playing cards. I remember how still it was. Even the guns seemed to be resting.

'How that grave caused me to think. Later on I nearly wrote to Sir Douglas Haig to ask if the body of an "unknown" comrade might be sent home. I returned to Folkestone in 1919. The mind of the world was in a fever. Eventually I wrote to Bishop Ryle, then

Dean of Westminster . . . the only request that the noble Dean did
not see his way to grant was the suggestion I gave him—from a
relative of mine—that the tomb should be inscribed as that of the
Unknown Comrade—rather than Warrior. . . .'

CHAPTER TWO

The Salutary Tale of Jix

Mother's advice, and Father's fears
Alike are voted—just a bore
There's negro music in our ears,
The world is one huge dancing floor.
We mean to tread the Primrose Path,
In spite of Mr. Joynson-Hicks.
We're People of the Aftermath
We're girls of 1926.

In greedy haste, on pleasure bent,
We have no time to think, or feel,
What need is there for sentiment,
Now we've invented Sex-Appeal?
We've silken legs and scarlet lips,
We're young and hungry, wild and free,
Our waists are round about the hips,
Our skirts are well above the knee.

We've boyish busts and Eton crops,
We quiver to the saxophone,
Come, dance before the music stops,
And who can bear to be alone?
Come drink your gin, or sniff your snow,
Since Youth is brief, and Love has wings,
And time will tarnish, ere we know
The brightness of the Bright Young Things.

Come all you birds
And sing a roundelay,
Now Mrs. Meyrick's
Out of Holloway . . .

THE motif for the Chelsea Arts Ball of 1922 was 'Brighter London One Hundred Years Hence', for as things stood no one dared to prophesy deliverance from D.O.R.A. a day earlier than this. D.O.R.A. was the Defence of the Realm Act, though the rather grand patriotic title and its spinsterly abbreviation seemed to have nothing in common, the one suggesting halberds and the other pins. In 1922 D.O.R.A. was enthroned as the Big Auntie of England. The politicians, the bishops and the sermonizing generals all declared that they regretted having to trouble her, particularly so soon after her untiring and selfless labours during the war to end all wars, but they had no option. The country was going to pot. There were official estimates for post-war disillusionment and cynicism, but not for all this *enjoyment*. To be grateful for still being alive was one thing, to be *glad* to be alive was another. And so, although there was the glaring reality of over two million unemployed, a quite extraordinary percentage of the energy of state and Church was directed to moral reform.

The break with Victorian ethics, both moral and cultural, would have happened even if there had been no war. What the war did most was to expose the fearful hollow of 'authority'. It had put a premium on obedience. Obedience was the king's mystical due, the country's right, the generals' demand, the Church's everlasting exhortation and Lord Northcliffe's constant clamour. It became a phobia. Deafened by so much journalistic patriotism, violated by slogans and hypnotized by death and claptrap, a great population had resigned itself to the ecclesiastical political and Press manipulators. When, after the war, these leaders continued to ask for blind obedience and didn't get it, there was at first consternation and then an intense fury. A new morality campaign was put in action. The forces of reaction swept to the colours. The police were alerted, vigilance committees sprang up and the popular Press gave a great rich sigh of pure pleasure as it saw stretching before it a decade of state-subsidized prurience. Distinguished bigots like James Douglas forked over the week's misdemeanours each Sunday and screamed about licence and laxity and ancient Rome, so setting a precedent for Scottish columnists. The clergy, although somewhat handicapped in their endeavours by lack of facts to make hell-fire and perdition sound anything like as frightful as most people's well-documented experiences in France, prayed that England, to whom, as it was well known, God had given the victory, would mend her ways. Behind this stern uproar there was a less hysterical and far more menacing rumble of anger as the *ancien régime* massed to defend the *status quo*.

The young people listened to all this with amazement. It was like being lectured on the preciousness of one's pearl of greatest price by one's rapist. Very soon they found that they were not able to listen to such talk any more, partly because they found it indecent and partly because they were too busy dancing.

Dancing in Britain and America, and sunbathing in Germany were the catharses by which the young of the twenties cleansed their souls of the sediment left behind by the war. The girls, as near naked as women have been at any time in Europe since the *Directoire*, and the young men in wrinkled jackets and trousers so wide that they looked like split skirts, tangoed, waltzed, one-stepped, black-bottomed, fox-trotted and, pre-eminently, Charlestonned. The Charleston was as indigenous to the twenties as the *pavane* was to the Escorial. To dance it well required a subtly disciplined mixture of energy, style and uninhibition. It arrived in London from the United States during the summer of 1925 and was received in state by sixty dancing instructors reverently amassed by the *Dancing Times* at the Carnival Club in Dean Street. There was a slight pause in order that no single twitch of its flamboyantly angular rules should be misinterpreted and then it swept the country, causing the Vicar of St. Aidan's, Bristol, to thump the pulpit and declare, 'Any lover of the beautiful will die rather than be associated with the Charleston. It is neurotic! It is rotten! It stinks! Phew, open the windows!' This did not deter the Prince of Wales from learning to Charleston exceedingly well and being seen doing it in the most unlikely places, a fair, animated story-book royalty sparklingly alive at the heart of a decade in whose meaningless afterglow he was later to be trapped, like a dragonfly in amber.

The twenties was not a drunken decade as decades go but a revolution in drinking habits, plus the existence of Lady Astor, caused it to sound as though it was. The alcoholic emphasis in much twenties writing (drinking is easily the most boring subject in all literature and it defies sympathetic interpretation by any except the rarest drunkard poets, such as Li Po or Verlaine) is really nothing more than the Briton's eternal plea to have a drink when he feels like it. Before the war it was exceptional to be offered a drink before luncheon or dinner and sherry would be served with the soup. The immediate post-war years found people entering the dining-room very jolly indeed and ever so slightly sick, the reason being the cocktail boom. A great queasy river of manhattans, bronxes and martinis flowing from countless all-too-amateur sources savaged the taste buds and jarred the nervous systems of the middle and upper classes. 'Cocktails,' maintained M. Boulestin, the distinguished restaurateur, 'are the most romantic expression of modern life, . . . but the cocktail habit as practised in England now is a vice. . . .' This, meant as a criticism, was accepted as a compliment by a generation intent on outraging the old order.

Their experiences on the Continent during the war had given many young people an appetite for café society which came into strong conflict with polite evenings with Mrs. Amy Woodforde-Finden's

> *Pale hands, pink-tipped, like Lotus buds that float*
> *On those cool waters where we used to dwell,*
> *I would have rather felt you round my throat*
> *Crushing out life, than waving me farewell!*

round the family piano. The moralists saw in this the inevitable break-up of family life, not being clairvoyant and so able to foresee the result of Baird's exciting invention which would unite brother to sister, mother to son and grandparents to a close-locked dynastic group which would only temporarily disintegrate for sleep, food and other natural functions. There was the gramophone, of course. Its charm and fascination then can hardly be imagined now. It blared, gaily and a trifle wildly like the age itself, from a smart portable box or from a tall cabinet. The silver sound-box undulated on the thick wax record and there was a particular moment when the steel needle susurrated in the first virgin grooves which was like the first motion of the curtains at the theatre. But nothing could keep the new generation at home for long. The 'modern', as it was called, home was O.K. but it could not satisfy the driving restlessness, the plan-less and ubiquitous activity which, except in a few professionally depraved instances, meant little more than drifting from pub to club to party—in that order if one was lucky.

The genesis of London's night-club boom is lost somewhere between the 'Shades' so brilliantly described in Michael Sadleir's *Forlorn Sunset* and something less reprehensible in the shape of a revue-bar. One of the first night-clubs was opened in 1913 by Strindberg's second wife, a beautiful ex-actress with a Viennese reputation. It was called the Cave of the Golden Calf and Epstein and Wyndham Lewis decorated its walls and columns. It was haunted by artists, the *demi-monde* and guardsmen who went there, so they said, to listen to the accordions of Galician gypsies and hear Lilian Shelley singing 'Popsie-wopsie'. During the war there was a spread of murkily discreet 'clubs' which were little more than military brothels catering for the officer class on leave. But by 1923 sex taboos were falling like fig-leaves and the majority of those who crowded the noisy, stifling backrooms and cellars called night-clubs, often did so because these places represented a kind of healthily ribald answer to the soul-sickening platitudes of the 'as you were' faction.

The Establishment did not take these lewd gestures lying down. The constabulary, armed by D.O.R.A., was able to spend an enormous proportion of its time and energy vetting private morals. A kiss in the park, a look in the street or bringing back a French translation of *The Hunting of the Snark* in one's luggage could easily land one, if not in Queer Street, at least in some equally desperate address. The post-war writers reacted towards this new puritanism with the highly profitable flippancy of Michael Arlen's *The Green Hat* or with D. H. Lawrence's derision and bitterness. Ronald Firbank, who contrived to link the decade with the nineties by a string of lilac-coloured postcards, found it bizarre even for him, and told Aldous Huxley that he felt he would have to go to the West Indies to live among the negroes to collect material for a novel about Mayfair. To add to the general ethical turmoil, Dr. Marie Stopes was addressing large mixed audiences at the Queen's Hall on contraception and claiming that her work was divinely inspired. Her message was a great comfort to a country which now had many hundreds of thousands more women than men.

There was a miraculous element in this return to life. Only the dullest and most grudging of minds could have escaped seeing that courage was not the prerogative of the trenches and that this wild upsurge of art and literature, absurd clothes and tireless fun were reflections of a new kind of human gallantry. Yet the truth was that the middle class, still punch-drunk with 'patriotism', and the lower middle class, still smugly wrapped round Lord Northcliffe's vulgar little finger, took fright. They imagined a strong link between Bolshevism abroad and what they called 'lack of respect' at home. They found the hundreds of thousands of working-class unemployed hanging round the streets, their medals sardonically clinking on their thin chests, menacing. Because they feared the gaiety of the young they mocked the validity of those exciting developments in personal freedom, painting, writing and music which helped to establish this gaiety. Nearly every new work of art was met with a guffaw, though some artists, the Sitwells in particular, met this philistinism with some very sharp answers. And because they felt guilty about the misery of the unemployed ex-servicemen and their families, these hordes of shabby young men and women made spiritless, drab and ugly by broken promises, malnutrition and loss of hope, the lower middle and middle classes forced themselves to regard the prole-tariat as something not quite human, and therefore not subject to an entirely human reaction to its wretched condition. In this way a contempt for working-class people of a kind quite unknown before the war began to develop.

The incredible reality of the first Labour Government in January, 1924, provided another terrifying seismic jolt to those who had long believed that Britain was 'above' the earthquakes which shook lesser social systems. Fortunately the Scottish ex-board school boy who went to Downing Street wasn't in any way encumbered with the common touch and could walk quite comfortably with kings, which he frequently did. Ramsay MacDonald was a most remarkable man. He could speak for an hour and say nothing. He was extremely hand-some and tremendously snobbish, and he managed to convince the country that Labour and the Soviet Union had nothing in common. This was quite a feat in 1924. But some of the people who were kissing hands at Buckingham Palace hadn't taken nearly as much trouble as 'Gentleman Mac' with their p's and q's, not to mention their h's, and again the moribund cry went up, 'where will it all end?'. There was now a solid longing for a return to the dear dead days which were not entirely beyond recall, to late Victorian security and scenes which were already beginning to glow dangerously with golden thoughts. The clock must be put back. The monstrous years, 1914–1918, would have to be cut out of the body politic in a piece of relentless social surgery, so that healthy nineteenth-century doctrines and standards could surge through the national heart and purge it of its ills. As Lord Carson had said, 'There is nothing England likes better than forgetting. . . .' And who better to put down his foot, put on the brake, put back the clock, than Jix, to whom the term die-hard could scarcely apply since no out-dated political idea which had come *his* way had ever been known to perish? Jix would stop the rot. Jix would lead them back. But where was Jix?

The story of England is the story of national saviours waiting for their hour. It is a constant tale of heroes being urgently interrupted at bowls, at building walls; at making love. When the first notes of the retreat from the present began to make themselves heard above the saxophones Jix was in Norfolk breeding Suffolk Punches. His hour had come so late that anyone other than Jix would have doubted whether it would ever come at all. But Jix had no doubts, nor modesty, nor indeed anything to prevent his jumping into the air with pleasure whenever he thought of himself. He was irrepressible, self-satisfied and shallow. At his mother's knee he had learnt a great truth—that black was black and white was white. Guided by this truth he was able, like God, to pronounce with finality on the failings of mankind. He knew what was good for them —white. Which meant that he had only to deny them black for the world to be the best of all possible worlds. That the world had come to such a beastly pass was entirely because it had invented a lot of silly shades of behaviour between black and white. All these were quite imaginary—the inventions of artists whose pictures were ridiculous and of writers with dirty minds and of mad rich women like Dr. Stopes. He and his very good friends the policemen would soon put things right. Ladies would return to their pedestals, gentlemen to their frock coats and those who dared ever to mention black again, be they Mrs. Kate Meyrick or D. H. Lawrence, would discover that Jix would rout them out to the limits of his prejudice.

Sir William Joynson-Hicks, alias Jix, eventually Viscount Brentford, arrived at the Home Office towards the close of 1924, when he was fifty-eight years old. His extraordinary appointment was in its way the greatest compliment the forces of reaction could pay to the progressive spirit of the twenties. Jix was a challenge. If art and life could endure in spite of Jix, then surely they had earned their right to exist.

Jix was born in 1865, the year Palmerston died, a coincidence which moved him greatly and which he never forgot for one moment. 'If I believed in the transmigration of souls,' said Jix, 'I should indeed like to think that some of his spirit had entered into me. . . .' And there is something not unmoving in the thought of two such die-hard stars so fatefully, though momentarily, in conjunction, Pam's on the wane and Jix's in the ascendant. Jix, then simply Hicks, differed from most men in that he was born with a full set of small ideas, none of which he outgrew, though whether out of deference to his Maker or to his mother it is not certain.

When he was fourteen he signed the pledge—his first refusal in a long career of professional negation. His father, a London merchant, sent him to Merchant Taylors' School, where his smugness and piety brought him fame but few friends, and where he successfully defended the school's debating society's motion 'That Capital Punishment Should Be Retained'. He was a charming-looking boy whose presence behind the offertory bag at church or on temperance platforms produced a decided appeal. His delight in public speaking caused him to join, among many other organizations, the Highbury Debating Society, which was run in the form of a Conservative Government. Hicks became 'Prime Minister' and the Society immediately collapsed, laid low by Tory ideas and teetotal haranguings so antiquated and so fierce that debate seemed out of the question. This was in the eighties, but when Jix got close to being the real Prime Minister during the twenties there was no evidence to support the hope that his prejudices had shrunk or that his understanding had matured. Though by this time his static mentality was seen to be a form of genius.

Hicks was now an articled clerk to a firm of City solicitors, where he roused the staff to violence by practising on it his debating society speeches. Sometimes they threw him physically into the street, but even as Hicks Jix was jaunty and neither then nor later was he ever to know discouragement. He became a mason and the Master of his Lodge at twenty-five. But before this, when he was only twenty-three, he set up as a one-man firm of solicitors in Old Jewry. Business did not go too well at first in spite of Hicks's twin dictums of 'never make a friend into a client' and 'always assume when writing

Photo: Radio Times Hulton Picture Library

Jix—'It is I who am the ruler of England!'—with his monarch at the Richmond Horse Show, June 1923.

Photo: Radio Times Hulton Picture Library

A poignant moment in Park Square. Mrs. Kate Meyrick welcomed home on her release from Holloway, January 27th, 1930

a letter that it may be read before you on the Day of Judgement'. But then his father, Henry Hicks, became a deputy chairman of the London General Omnibus Company, which owned a thousand omnibuses and eleven thousand horses. The Claims Agent of the Company was swift in recognizing the value of this angelic-looking little solicitor and soon, between the two of them, they began to save the Omnibus Company a small fortune. As a writer in the *Motor Weekly* was to remark, 'He [Hicks] steered the ship of the L.G.O.C. through many troubled financial waters from 1905 to 1912, when it was successfully brought into harbour'—which was no mean feat when one considers those eleven thousand horses. But here, whether on the knife-board of early London transport or the *Motor Weekly*'s metaphorical ship-board, was young Hicks's first leg up in the world, and he never forgot it. Later, whenever he heard of a bus accident he would cry, 'Hurrah! there's a day at the Zoo for my wife and family!'

This was perhaps the left leg up. The right leg followed it in the time-honoured manner by means of a useful rather than a brilliant marriage. When he was twenty-nine Hicks, in a rare moment of self-examination, saw that gloss had little connection with polish and realized that he must obtain a little of each if he was to succeed. So he set off for Italy with a rigid itinerary of churches, museums and galleries in his pocket. At Mentone he met the Joynsons, a well-to-do, right wing, evangelical family from Manchester. Grace Joynson, the daughter, was twenty-one. William Hicks loved her at once but as he had not included courtship in his holiday plans he was seriously perturbed about the possibility of having to cut his cathedral schedule. Miss Joynson had a preview of the kind of man she was to marry when William found time to win her heart without losing a single date with his Baedeker. On his wedding morning he worked in the office until the carriage called to take him to St. Margaret's, Westminster.

This marriage was William Hicks's *entrée* to the fascinating political North, in those days almost another kingdom. Manchester itself was more cosmopolitan than London. The rich Jews it attracted from all over the Continent veneered its money-grubbing soul with music and art, and as both immigrant millionaire and native tycoon relished conformity and ostentation, the great industrial city at the turn of the century glittered like a slag-heap stuck with brilliants. Hicks arrived at this fabulous place with his father-in-law's name nailed firmly before his own. It was the sesame he needed. The well-oiled doors gaped before him. He was entranced. He became an Oddfellow, a Forester, a Good Templar and a diner at Manchester's Carlton Club. In 1898, after much pushing on his part and some shoving on Mr. Joynson's, he was adopted by the North Manchester Conservative Association. It was a triumph and it would have gone to his head if there had been room for it there. Instead it went to his tongue. His first speech was such a tintinnabulation of jingoism that even the cotton kings blanched. It was short and far from the point. It throbbed like the drums themselves with Majuba Hill, The Royal Navy, Khartoum, Omdurman, the speaker's unique fitness for office, Mr. Balfour's equally unique fitness for being great, John Morley's total lack of fitness for being anything and scores of other things. He was hardly a man, he was the Flag incarnate. Wrapped securely in its folds he could be part of the semi-divine patriotism of the age. Could they deny the Union Jack? Then how could they deny him? This heady nonsense sent blood pressures up in the cotton lands, but not the poll itself, for the Radical Mr. Schwann (later Sir Charles Swan) swept home with a majority of twenty-six. As Joynson-Hicks's biographer was mournfully to remark, 'Just two more carriages working for a few hours. . . .' Even when Jix was at the height of his glory, doctoring the gaiety of nations at the Home Office, this first narrow reversal still left its aloe flavour behind whenever he thought of it.

It was not in Jix's nature to give up, self-inquire or worry. He couldn't stay down—any more than a weighted Chinese doll can stay down. It seemed to the electors of North-West Manchester a perfect quality for a candidate who would have to struggle with the terribly self-confident Tory-turned-Liberal the Radicals were putting up. Winston Churchill was nine years younger than Jix but the smooth, blandly dimpled faces of both men contrasted most strikingly with the shaggy city fathers who crowded their respective platforms, making both candidates look like a couple of talkative lads. Winston's effrontery at their first meeting would have staggered Jix, had he not been constitutionally unstaggerable. 'I am sorry I have come to Manchester to queer your pitch,' said Winston. Which he did with ease.

The true-blue Jix was this time not so much disappointed as out-raged. He lashed Winston with dreadful prophecies. 'There is between him and our party a gulf fixed . . . which enables me to declare that, while there is seedtime and harvest we will never have him back.' Winston said nothing; he went straight from Manchester into an under-secretaryship.

During this campaign Jix had revealed a disquieting facet of his nature and something rare in British politics, a distaste for all aliens and for Jewish aliens in particular. This touched a nerve deep down under the tough hide of Manchester and disturbed the gross good health of the city.

Towards the end of 1907, Sir Henry Campbell-Bannerman became very ill and all through the winter of 1908, although he continued to struggle through his duties, it became clear that he must soon resign. The Manchester electors thought that, should the Prime Minister's illness entail another general election, it would be sheer bad luck for their delightful new member, particularly as Winston had just been made President of the Board of Trade. Soon voices were heard questioning the propriety of forcing him to defend his seat in the circumstances. People—Tories and Liberals— were openly saying that Winston should go back unopposed. When Jix was told this he was amazed. He'd never heard of such a thing! Shedding fat crocodile tears, he declared, in what was a very moderate speech for him, that the Government 'had alienated our colonies, thrown away the fruits of the Transvaal War, weakened our Navy, attempted to jerrymander our Constitution, increased taxation, flouted our religious convictions, let loose chaos and bloodshed in Ireland' and much else.

After this it was war to the knife, as Jix would have said. The contest which need never have taken place at all became the most brilliant, entertaining and hilarious electoral fight of the century. Lloyd George (for Winston's opportunist step across the floor of the House had landed him with exotic company) whipped up the vast sermon-tasting Northern audiences with glittering oratory. In the *Daily News*, H. G. Wells, unhinged obviously by the fact that he was putting in a good word for a duke's grandson, wrote of Jix, 'I know nothing and I want to know nothing about his social standing or his private quality, and I do not suppose that I should ever have heard his name . . . if it were not that I keep myself informed by means of Press cuttings.' Sir Walter Elliot of Kellynch Hall could hardly have done better.

The whole election got more and more topsy-turvy as polling day grew near. The Liberals had brought about changes in the Licensing Bill and the blushing Winston was embarrassed by ardent temperance support, while Countess Markievicz's Barmaids' Political Defence League rallied to the one-sip-and-you're-damned Jix. Countess Markievicz, getting into practice for her subsequent career as a Sinn Feiner, was a marvellous sight as she whipped her own coach and four through the Manchester streets. When things began to get tough, Winston indulged his flair for scurrility. 'Bill Hicks . . .' cried Winston, 'a petty provincial politician engaged in a contest far beyond his abilities!' It was rude but it was percipient. What Jix did when he came to power was to treat a great nation as if it were a troublesome village and he was its benevolently despotic squarson.

On polling day Manchester was in a state of near-hysteria. Then whole of the centre of the city was a locked mass of carriages, early motor-cars and multitudes. And at nine-thirty it was announced that Jix had beaten Winston. It was the death-knell of the old radicalism. Manchester was ecstatic. Winston was dumbfounded. When the news reached London, George Alexander stopped the performance at the St. James's Theatre and announced it from the stage to a cheering audience, which later stood as the orchestra played 'God Save the King'. The next morning the *Daily Telegraph* bawled, 'Winston Churchill is out-*out*-OUT. We have all been yearning for this to happen with a yearning beyond utterance.'

Jix, smarting all over from the physical nature of North Country congratulations ('I won't be banged about like a football') and with his head turned so completely that from henceforth he always found it more comfortable to look backwards, went to Court to be presented to King Edward. Then the great day came for his maiden speech. The House was packed. Rarely had Parliament so honoured a new member. Lloyd George, Balfour, Asquith—all were there, for Jix was now by way of being a national miracle, like Old Parr or Queen Elizabeth's hymen. Jix rose and the astonished Commons listened to a speech of such staggering immodesty, such a use of the royal 'we', such Jixian pomp and assurance as to leave it stupefied. The *Daily Express* summed the whole thing up when it said, 'It was good of Mr. Joynson-Hicks to come and speak to the House this week.'

But Jix didn't care. That same evening he went to a dinner given in his honour by the Maccabeans, a distinguished Jewish society, where he told his hosts, in a speech of quite incredible insensitivity and insolence, what he thought of them.

'I could say you were a delightful people, that Jews were delightful opponents, that I am very pleased to receive the opposition of the Jewish community, and that I am, in spite of all, your humble and obedient servant. I could say that, but it wouldn't be true in the slightest degree. I have beaten you thoroughly and soundly and I am no longer your servant!'

The Press received the news of this with amazement. The *Manchester Evening News* called it a breach of the elementary rules of good manners and the *Jewish Chronicle* marvelled that a public man could commit such a solecism.

But Jix took no notice. He never took notice. The bubble of complacency in which his ego floated protected his nerve centres from criticism. He rejoiced in the limitations of his vision. His policy was, when in doubt, talk. All the hundreds of evangelical, temperance, masonic, debating club and chamber of commerce platforms which he had haunted since the days of his extreme youth had given him a great wealth of experience. 'He has,' said A. G. Gardiner, 'a thoughtless fluency of speech, and the suppressed enthusiasms of his Puritan upbringing find vent in a caricature of patriotism that makes him the easy prey to any wave of folly. It is much easier to cut a knot than to untie it, and he always takes the easy way. He is a Die-hard, not because he is a sanguinary man, but because to his childish and romantic vision no Englishman ever surrenders, right or wrong, to anything or anybody. His mind responds to the short-sighted view and the popular expedient. He thinks, not as a statesman, but as a talkative man in a suburban train who has just read the headlines in his favourite paper.'

His contemporaries were thus often driven to such charitable views of Jix as seeing him as a phenomenon, for otherwise how could speeches like the following be explained?

'We did not conquer India for the benefit of the Indians. I know it is said at missionary meetings that we conquered it to raise the level of the Indians. That is cant. We conquered India as the outlet for the goods of Great Britain. We conquered India by the sword and by the sword we should hold it. ("Shame.") Call shame if you like. I am stating facts . . . but I am not such a hypocrite as to say we hold India for the Indians. We hold it as the finest outlet for British goods in general, and for Lancashire cotton goods in particular.'

In 1913, when the Ulster question was at its most delicate phase, Jix rushed in with, 'The people of Ulster have behind them the Unionist [Conservative] party. Behind them is the God of Battles. In His name and their name I say to the Prime Minister, "Let your armies and your batteries fire! Fire if you dare! Fire and be damned!" '

Jix's terrible fluency of speech, plus the actor-like pleasure he got from platform appearances, led him into the most appalling predicaments. But he never cared. 'If there is one town in England that is drink-sodden it is Portsmouth,' he said. There was uproar and then statistics to prove him wrong. Jix accepted the uproar as his due, but not the statistics. 'I am not interested in establishing facts by figures,' he said. 'I have been told that Portsmouth is not a sober town and that is that.' Smiling cheerily, impeccably turned out, his features as endurably youthful as those of a musical comedy male lead, he vented his prejudices wherever there happened to be a rostrum. After advocating civil war in Ireland—'There are worse things than civil war. England has known civil war before today and has risen from it stronger and purer'—he went straight on to an engagement at the Church of England Scripture Readers' Association.

When war of a very different kind came, Jix dashed nimbly from ministry to ministry in his great anxiety for leadership. He soon discovered that he was the sort of luxury his party was apt to give up during a real crisis. Abandoned mournfully to his own devices, with even his bellicosity drowned in the general jingo, Jix interested himself in aviation and in raising a regiment entirely composed of footballers. When the war was over he was fifty-three and that dazzling moment in Manchester when he had slain Winston now seemed a very long time ago. He, like everybody else, was very tired. Lack of office had not kept him idle. He had gone from platform to platform putting heart into the lads, silencing the critical with rivers of true-blue invective and rousing the timid to heroism.

In 1919 King George made Jix a baronet. It was the only thing which ever happened to him which pierced his complacency. He interpreted the honour as an indication that, while his *ex-officio* war-mongering had not been entirely unwelcome, the need for both it and Jix was over. Jix took his title gloomily. It was the end of all things. He had tried to get into Parliament for twenty years, had been in it for eleven years, and that was that. So he went to India to have a holiday, all unconscious of the heady prospect before him.

Jix and Lady Jix arrived in India in the turmoil which followed the extraordinary Amritsar massacre and being Jix he could not resist going to the scene of the trouble. There he found a situation which held the greatest piquancy for him, a perfect example of the ridiculous fuss which occurred when God's chosen race was obliged to exercise its prerogative.

The extreme right element of the British administration in India were known as men of the Punjab school, because of their affection for the Punjabi's simple, manly, sporting way of life, and his un-complaining acceptance of rough justice. The men of the Punjab believed, quietly and implicitly, that God had sent them to civilize the savage, of whom they saw Indians as a superior form. A good clean flogging or hanging, they thought, was the medicine which both doctor and patient understood. Few details of the men of Punjab's rule ever left India. The attitude at New Delhi was that they would all one day die out.

But on April 10–12th, 1919, the good, clean actions of a General Dyer were too much, even for India, and hit London for six. For General Dyer, not getting the law and order he required, had opened fire in the Jallianwala Bagh in Amritsar on an unarmed crowd and had killed 379 people. Having done this, the General then proceeded to order that all Indians using a certain street in Amritsar where a woman missionary had been insulted should only do so in a crawling position. When the news reached England, Asquith spoke of it in Parliament as one of the worst outrages in the whole of our history. But to the men of the Punjab the indignation in London had no relevance whatsoever. So they gave him promo-tion. When this became known there was uproar at Westminster and to appease it an investigatory committee went to India to see the situation for itself. It found that General Dyer's action had made racial tension worse than at any time since the mutiny and that more than half a century's carefully built-up goodwill had been for-feited, and recommended that the general should be relieved of his new post. Eventually Dyer returned to England, where he was much vilified.

All this would have had no relevance at all where Jix was concerned had it not been for his insistence on seeing Amritsar. As one of nature's Punjabi and a great believer in the doctrine which divided mankind into the chastened and the chastizers, Jix was drawn, not to the scene of the crime, but to the scene of General Dyer's martyrdom. At Amritsar he asked scores of questions and he returned to London with the opinion that the general was right. He rallied the die-hards and helped to collect an enormous consolation prize of £27,000 for General Dyer. But the long term result of Amritsar, both on Jix and on India, was hardly to be guessed in 1919, for it was to convert Gandhi into a revolutionary and Jix into an admirer of Mussolini.

The Amritsar publicity reminded the extremists in his party that Jix was still bouncingly alive and a sound Empire man. Lloyd George was toppling; there was a delicious whiff of the old stuffiness in the air and a searching around for new men with old ideas. There had not been a pure Tory Government since 1905 and Jix, more hopeful than at any time since his Manchester triumph and ever-mindful of his brush with the great god Pam, waited on destiny.

When his chance came it was a terrible anti-climax. Bonar Law offered him the Parliamentary Secretaryship to the Department of Overseas Trade. Jix took it and lumped it, bitterly aware of the absence of glory. Then he became Postmaster General and then Financial Secretary to the Treasury—all in a few months. Destiny, it seemed, was giving him the once-over. It seemed to Jix but a single step from the Treasury to the Exchequer and he could hardly contain himself when the Prime Minister sent for him once more to tell him that he was about to offer the Exchequer—to Neville Chamberlain—and that he was to go to the Ministry of Health.

For all that, this leapiest leap of all from the back bench to an entire suite of Cabinet seats, all in a few months, heartened Jix and inflamed Home Counties Punjabi with dreams of their hero skipping into Number Ten itself. Jix became rather wild. 'Attack! attack! attack!' he cried to the astonished Primrose League. He preached what he termed 'a new belief in old principles'. He rushed about, talking, talking, talking. He praised Stanley Baldwin when others forgot to, and in the Conservative Government of 1924 his perky little craft sailed into harbour at last—the Home Office was his.

The Home Office could have been invented for Jix and he for it. His nature and its function closed with each other in inseparable embrace. Here was the seat of awe, if not of majesty. Here were the brakes, the cold douches, the wet blankets, the Great Book of Don't, the little cane and the big stick, the king's ear, the dear old codes all laid out in lavender, the Union Jacks and the succulent rubber stamps, all of them, though dusty from disgraceful neglect, in splendid working order. Jix entered upon his heritage with undisguised joy.

'But what do you *do* there?' somebody asked, mystified by so much delight. Jix hesitated until the truth dawned on him. 'It is I who am the ruler of England!' he said. And, in a way, for the rest of the twenties he was just that. The Home Office, he soon discovered, was stuffed with everything a person such as he could ever wish for. There was no need to seek new legislation for police powers, cleaning up London, keeping foreigners out, suppressing nasty modern books, raiding art galleries, saving the Church of England from its bishops and vetting sexual behaviour at all levels—it was there, in his exciting Home Office. His power, if he cared to use it, was dazzling. And as nothing upset Jix so much as an unenforced law, the country woke up to find itself infamous. In vain it protested.

> *Come to Britain and lead the gay life!*
> *As a rule it's illegal to bathe with your wife;*
> *There's a Councillor watching to see you behave,*
> *But still you may stand at the window and wave;*
> *You mustn't buy choc'late, you mustn't buy ale,*
> *But come to Britain and see our new jail.*
>
> *Come to Britain! We've done what we could*
> *To make the place healthy and wholesome and good.*
> *Your whisky may cost you much less in the States,*
> *And here between drinks we have tedious waits,*
> *But Ivor Novello is always on show,*
> *So come to Britain and let yourselves go!*

wrote A. P. Herbert but Jix only smiled.

2*

His table piled with tea and toast,
Death Warrants and the Morning Post,

He knew himself to be the chosen one, the saviour of England, and
that saviours do not shrink from unpopular remedies. He knew that
some were born to rule and some were born to obey, and that
democracy was the mercifully unworkable invention of an immoral
race. All the same, it occasionally worried him that his impeccable
Toryism was so often out of step with that of his colleagues. In the
Liberal Press it didn't worry him in the least, even when criticism
like the following appeared:

> 'Since he cannot round up the brewers, he will round up the
> abominable alien, and if the Communists become troublesome his
> mind incontinently leaps to Fascism as the corrective, and he has
> to be reminded by his Prime Minister that this is a constitutional
> country, that it is the function of the Government, and not of
> Black Shirts to protect the community, and that a Mussolini is not
> wanted. If he should emerge, it will not be Sir William Joynson-
> Hicks who will fill the part. He does not belong to the serious
> drama of affairs, but to the comedy stage, and his rôle has been
> allotted to him in the genial and festive name which the public
> has, not without affection as well as derision, bestowed upon
> him.'

Jix's first attentions were directed towards aliens. He found to his
horror, for he detested all foreigners, that there were 272,000
registered aliens in Britain. Jix stared at the figure hysterically and
then began to do something about it. He went to the ports. He
snooped through all the arrangements for detaining immigrants and
worked up an anti-alien campaign which shocked a country which
had always prided itself on its hospitality towards the oppressed of
all nations. His interference with individual liberty was somewhat
of a novelty to the England of the twenties, but when a great many
respectable foreigners began to be chivvied around in London by the
police and Jix's rabid anti-communism began to be made the excuse
for any action he cared to take, a deputation of immigrants went to
the Home Office to get things straight. Jix was furious. 'It is rather
remarkable,' he lectured his visitors, 'that while our socialist friends
declaim against the conditions of working men in this country their

friends the socialists from Eastern Europe are pouring in to secure better conditions than can be obtained in their own lands.'

Gradually, the mid-Victorian busybody was evolving into a familiar twentieth-century leader. He used hypnotic catch phrases. For instance, he never said aliens, he always said *undesirable* aliens, and he said it so often that stupid people began to hate foreigners for reasons they couldn't express. His worship of visas helped to turn a document of convenience into a prized possession. He saw himself as the watchdog of the sceptred isle and anyone he didn't care for he dubbed Bolshevist and shipped back home. All this seemed irrelevant to the ordinary working-class Englishman in the dole-queue, and tasteless to the ordinary middle-class Englishman with his war-widened horizon. To the intellectual he was plain anathema. He was satirized, caricatured and lampooned with a virulence rarely seen in the popular Press since the Regency. When Jix turned to suppressing literature on moral grounds, a particularly sharp lampoon appeared called *Policeman of the Lord*. Its authors were P. R. Stephenson and Beresford Egan, and it set the pace for further criticism of the Home Secretary.

> *In* 1865,
> *When Little Jix was born, or came alive,*
> *The Great Queen ruled, and everyone was good.*
> *Since then the times have changed, the clock has clicked.*
> *Jix does not think so, Jix was brought up strict.* . . .

Soon Jix's features, a twinkling edition of von Ribbentrop's, were as familiar to the country as those of the two bombazined old harpies who accompanied him everywhere, Mrs. Gamp and Dora. Jix, like all pilloried politicians, let it be known that he thoroughly enjoyed this. Was it not proof of the public's affection? He would never, he said, interfere with the time-honoured license of the political caricaturist. No one really believed this. The fact that certain men are not despots is because they are not allowed to be despots. Jix, who had thrilled to the utter despotism of the Nizam of Hyderabad when he had been the prince's guest in 1919, found his way blocked by strange figures like A. P. Herbert and David Low when he made despotic moves in Whitehall.

After his anti-alien campaign, Jix moved towards his second objective, sex. Sex was a beastly invention which was fast turning

London into a sewer, but he would destroy it. The police agreed with Jix. They assured the Home Secretary of their utmost loyalty to his mission. They would not flinch from helping him mop up all the sex in London, even if it meant their coming into contact with the disgusting thing. Jix was troubled that such a decent, clean-limbed body of men should have to concern itself with so unspeakable a task and as a reward he promised the police an affection and loyalty such as no Home Secretary had shown the Force in all its existence. The beautiful friendship which grew up between the Home Office and Scotland Yard brought fresh gusts of laughter, but now the mockery did not entirely conceal an underlying vein of anxiety.

Jix's conception of a policeman was rather like that of a dear old lady's, big, jolly chaps in blue, always willing to lend a helping hand. It was only right that such men should receive society's mandate for enforcing society's protection. Jix enjoyed the residual power of the Force and used it unsparingly to interpret his own Puritanism. The lengths of 'reform' to which he might legitimately go fascinated him and the vision of an austere metropolis rose before his eyes as wistfully and as enticing as the heavenly city of the popular drawing-room song. It was this profound inner assurance that he was right which allowed him to take his extraordinary action in matters which were often academically or emotionally quite outside his experience, but it was plain conceit which enabled him to shrug off mockery and ridicule which would have destroyed an ordinarily sensitive man.

All through the twenties Jix's appearance offered some kind of evidence that prohibition had paid off where he personally was concerned. He looked years younger and jollier than his Cabinet friends, dressed with a pre-war garden party elegance and faced a whole series of calamities with a dreadful cheerfulness. He looked as happy as a sandboy as he emptied the stews, wagged his finger in Hyde Park, leafed through a packet of erotic poems D. H. Lawrence had rashly put in the post unsealed, and sent the town to bed by ten. His gaiety as he suppressed the virtue in others was particularly offensive and soon people wondered what was the worse, his policy or the enjoyment he got from enforcing it. There was a perverse element in his obsession with sexual morality and something immature in his neurotic ideas about drink.

He set out to destroy London's night-clubs immediately he took office. This, on the whole, was all right. Only like all little tyrants, Jix had to justify his ruthlessness by a colourfully exaggerated denunciation of the evil he intended to crush. A reasonable man would have seen that night-clubs were rather shame-faced versions of ordinary café and revue-bar life such as could be found in any major Continental city, and in most instances the haunts of people who merely didn't happen to want to go to bed early. Jix's preoccupation with them gave them a reputation for orgiastic activities and the raids made headlines in the Sunday newspapers. The smuttiness of the latter at this time always amazed foreign visitors. Nearly all the raids concerned drinking out of hours, that strange sin whose enormity is only exceeded by paederasty in Anglo-Saxon countries. The police would arrive, everyone's name would be taken, the club would be closed down—and the following evening it would open up in the house next door under a new name.

One club resisted these attentions. It was called the Cecil Club but was known as the '43' to its members and to a great many others as well, because of the number on its door. It was run by the notorious Mrs. Kate Meyrick. This fact and the fact that no policeman had got his boot inside the door for four whole years during Jix's reign of terror mystified everybody, not least Jix himself. While Ma Meyrick lived, Babylon would never perish. While vigilantes of all kinds prowled around outside, Ma flourished. How? It was a mystery. The months passed and then the years, and still the police reports on the '43' made it sound like a coaching inn where the weary traveller in Gerrard Street might call for home-baked bread and porter. As the travellers included such people as the King of Roumania, Tallulah Bankhead and Steve Donoghue, the mystery deepened. Jix and the Commissioner for Police were at their wits' end how to nab Ma.

Mrs. Kate Meyrick began her life as respectably as even Jix could wish. She was the daughter of an Irish doctor and the wife of a medical student. The Meyricks resided at Sylvan Hall, Brighton, where they produced a number of good-looking children. The boys were sent to Harrow and the girls to Roedean. Having achieved all this, Mrs. Meyrick and Mr. Meyrick parted. Finding herself with only £50 in the world and with all these boys and girls at Harrow and Roedean, Mrs. Meyrick came to London to seek her fortune.

Instead of going to the Distressed Gentlefolk's Association, she went to a Mr. Murray Dalton, who ran a tea-dance club in Leicester Square. And one can imagine her shock when, a little later, the police broke in and arrested all the cockney geishas. In court Mrs. Meyrick heard for the first time that official description of her business premises which was to become a cliché in her ears. Calling the club a sink of iniquity, the beak fined Ma £25.

Mrs. Meyrick's next venture was Brett's Club in the Charing Cross Road, which she sold as a going concern for £1,000. In 1921 she started the Cecil Club—the famous '43'—and by 1924 she was the undisputed night-club queen of London, with a string of sister clubs all over town. All these clubs were, of course, purely for the convenience of those who required early breakfast. 'What time did breakfast begin?' asked Mr. Justice Avory at her trial. 'Ten p.m.,' said Ma.

The '43' had *chic*. At the beginning of its life, when it was raided in the conventional manner, the police returned to their head-quarters with notebooks like the Almanac de Gotha. Those who suffered most were not the socialites, for whom this ritual name-taking added a certain *frisson* to the rather dull crime of drinking in the small hours, but to highly respectable provincials on the occasional spree in Soho, whose entire small town universe could come tumbling down if their names got into the papers. The older section of the upper class was less shocked. It had always accepted an un-spoken convention of wild oats. When, in *Brideshead Revisited*, Lord Sebastian and 'Boy' Mulcaster get picked up by the police after a visit to Ma's, Sebastian in particular is worried stiff about what his mother, the saintly Lady Marchmain, is going to say. She says very little. Her experience of men is that they are partly animals and that only religion can crush their animality. Only by being a saint would a man not want to do what she thought Sebastian had done. To be *frightened* into not doing it by the Jixes of this world would have been a particularly vulgar kind of cowardice in her eyes. Jix himself was more bewildered than perturbed by the attitude of aristocratic and intellectual acquaintances (he failed consistently at actual friendship all through his life) towards the social evils he was trying to stamp out. If they supported him at all it was 'for the good of the masses' and they made it plain that they wouldn't be seen dead with his ideas themselves. One of the things which astonished him about night-clubs was that he expected them to be filled with whores and found them crammed with 'society'.

The '43' was very smart indeed when the blow finally fell. A well-wisher had written to Scotland Yard telling them that he thought they ought to know that Station-Sergeant Goddard, whose pay was £6 a week, owned a freehold house at Streatham, a motor-car and two safe accounts. The police were shattered at this news. Their popularity was at the lowest ebb ever known. Jix's purity campaign had reduced them in the public's regard from a decent lot of men with a difficult job to do to a lot of Paul Prys. All through 1928, when Jix's battle was at its climax, there had been a series of incidents which had caused great damage to the good name of the Force, and had culminated in the uproar over the Savage case.

Miss Savage, an entirely respectable girl, had been charged by the police with immorality, that is, she had been seen sitting talking to Sir Leo Money, in Hyde Park, but the evidence offered was so hopeless that the court stopped the case and Miss Savage was released. But immediately after this trial, in which she was proved innocent, two police officers came to the office where she worked, forced her to accompany them to Scotland Yard and there grilled her for five hours. The matter was raised in a shocked House and Jix tried to bluff his way out by saying that it was all being looked into by the Director of Public Prosecutions. This didn't wash at all and over a hundred supplementary questions about the affair were entered on the order paper, and Jix was forced to set up an inquiry into police methods, which was the last thing he wanted to do.

In 1927 there had been the sensational case of police bribery by bookmakers at Liverpool. On May 23rd, 1928, a young stillroom maid was arrested as a prostitute and then found to be *virgo intacta*. Her compensation for this outrage was two guineas. On May 31st, 1928, a Major Murray was arrested for drunkenness in Piccadilly. He was cleared and awarded £500 and the police were severely censured. All over the country it was the same.

Male inversion also came under the fullest persecution by the police at this time. Homosexuality was something scarcely comprehensible and never mentioned before 1914. 'I thought that men like that shot themselves,' said George V with astonishment when he was told that someone he knew quite well was homosexual. It was believed to be infectious like leprosy and any instance of it which

came to light was treated with a vindictiveness far greater than that
which attended most other crimes. No man ever socially survived
such a prosecution and many, rather than risk such a very great
disaster, made their homes abroad. Freud, Jung, Havelock Ellis and
gentle humanists like Edward Carpenter then began to state the
truth readably. The result was that, after the war, many homosexuals of both sexes, who now had some understanding of their
inversion, were unwilling to take on the furtive respectability of the
'confirmed bachelor' and the 'born old maid'. They, too, demanded
to 'live their lives'—it was a great period for 'living one's life'—
and to the horror of the Jixites they came out into the open. Male
homosexuals, with their brittle elegance and humour, broke cover,
as it were and began to be seen openly and without apology. They
tended to congregate together in certain pubs and were driven from
bar to bar across the capital like pheasants before the beaters as
each new haunt was discovered and raided. There were endless
prosecutions and it was believed that Scotland Yard kept a register
of male homosexuals in which much of *Who's Who* was duplicated,
and running to many thousands of names.

Female homosexuals, who tend to take their pleasures sadly, found
their spokesman in Radclyffe Hall, whose bathetic though utterly
sincere novel *The Well of Loneliness* became the apologia of modern
Lesbia. There being no law against female transvestism, the author
was seen at the best restaurants and at first nights dressed in an
immaculate black tie, starched shirt, monocle, dinner-jacket—and
skirt. Her hair was cut like a boy's, but as a great many heterosexual
girls' heads were cropped as severely, this did not seem exceptional.
Gradually it dawned on the Bright Young Things that many a
jolly aunt and her 'companion' who bred dogs in Gloucestershire
or helped the vicar at Little Tilling were lovers.

Jix was absolutely incapable of seeing an element of *outré* honesty
in all this. All he saw was a country stripped of its whalebone and
showing its sores. He gave the police *carte blanche* to stem 'the flood
of filth'. The police raided the Warren Gallery where D. H.
Lawrence's paintings were on view. 'Stephen', the heroine of *The
Well*, as it was called, went to court like Lady Chatterley and was
defended by a great many distinguished people. But all to no purpose. *The Well* was tucked away with other porn behind a screen of
Sappers and Dornford Yateses in the Charing Cross Road. Quite a

few prosecutions of this nature occurred, though when the police seized the drawings of William Blake it was almost too much and indignation was drowned in laughter.

Jix rode the storm of derision smilingly as ever. 'I am not a literary censor,' he declared. 'I have no qualifications for the post. My duty is to see that the law is carried out, and when the law says that obscenities and indecencies are not permitted . . . it is my duty to carry out the law. . . .' His policy had a great effect on the Lord Chamberlain, though Jix emphatically denied that he was against the theatre. It was true, he said, that he was against 'problem plays'. 'But no one enjoyed an evening's entertainment by Mr. Tom Walls and Mr. Ralph Lynn more than he.'

Jix's philistinism was supported by certain sections of the Press, which found it an excuse for being simultaneously sensational while appearing to be moral at the same time. The effect of such journalism on the semi-educated of all classes was to produce a hatred of art which expended itself in insulting great artists like Epstein, and in any creativity which wasn't immediately apparent to the lowest common denominator. The *Daily Mail* worked itself up into a fury of jeering about Edith Sitwell's and William Walton's *Façade* and James Douglas inveighed against the 'blasphemies' of *Antic Hay*. Jix was pleased with this state of affairs. He believed the country was healthy while it could be dominated by men with 'standards', by which he meant limitations. All progress shocked him and he regarded anything imaginative as being vaguely absurd. Art and sex, he vaguely comprehended, had some kind of connection, so art needed watching.

Such was the position in the country when Station-Sergeant Goddard confronted the dream of Sir William Joynson-Hicks with his shabby realism. Goddard was the bluest-eyed boy in the vice squad. He had been in the police force for twenty-eight years and had specialized in raiding night-clubs since 1918. The fervour he brought to his task and the success by which he had been rewarded had taken the station-sergeant out of the ordinary chap-with-a-job-to-do class and put him among the vocationists. His nose was so keen that he could pick up the chypre-and-bubbly scent of a new club almost before the first member had sidled past its chucker-out. He had been involved in the raiding of 234 premises. The Force had commended him over and over again, and had paid him £6 a week. Life was good for the station-sergeant, though not good enough as it proved. An anonymous letter set dog on to dog. The safe deposits were unlocked and in one of them was found £12,000—all the nice crisp notes which had been pressed into his simple hand by Ma and a Mr. Ribuffi, who ran a club called Uncle's in Albemarle Street, for letting them know when there would be a raid. The station-sergeant defended himself topically. He told the judge that his fortune was the profits from selling rock at the Wembley Exhibition in his spare time. The judge was quite unable to believe this and sent the sergeant down for eighteen months' hard labour and fined him £2,000. Ma and Mr. Ribuffi each got fifteen months' hard labour, and Soho went into half-mourning. It was then revealed that a Sergeant Josling had been forced to resign from the police seven years earlier for bringing a false charge of corruption against Goddard. It was now proved that Josling had been right and he was given £1,500 compensation.

Ma Meyrick went to prison twice more, but when she looked as though she might be going there for a fourth time a kindly judge persuaded her to give him an honourable undertaking that she would have nothing more to do with night-clubs. Ma kept her word, though she knew what she had promised would be the death of her. In 1933 she passed away, leaving £58 and any number of well-frisked friends, to the quite genuine sorrow of many distinguished people, not quite a Magdalen but always a lady. She had run through half a million, placed two daughters in the peerage and had challenged Jixery. And all in a decade.

Those who argue from immovable prejudices which they believe to be convictions can rarely be defeated. This was proved when Jix, almost single-handed, routed all the proposed changes in the Book of Common Prayer which came before Parliament in the autumn of 1927. It was madness to have even contemplated such changes while Jix was in office. Eighty years had passed since Newman went over to Rome but to Jix the whole Oxford Movement was still a very real menace to the national Church. When the patient work of all these years, every letter of it undertaken with scrupulous spiritual thought and scholarship, was presented, as it was legally bound to be, to Parliament for its approval, the Whips were withdrawn and it was expected that the Revised Prayer Book would be quietly and formally made law. Jix was aghast. Change the Prayer Book?

Change *anything*? In a great sweep of oratory he turned the quiet affair into something which brought the pungent smoke of Smithfield drifting into the House. Hypnotized by Jix's fervour, nonconformists and even non-Christians all found themselves crowding into the Noes lobby. The Book was defeated and withdrawn. Six months later the bishops tried another Revised Version on the House and once again Jix flung it out. Only this time the criticism of his behaviour was more marked. Many M.P.s found his holy thunder and his opinions on the Real Presence somewhat grotesque, coming as it did, from one whose main business was with death warrants and night-clubs. Jix's performance, brilliant in its way, brought anti-puritans and humanists together regardless of party. George Lansbury and Churchill both attacked Jix. Lord Hugh Cecil, in *The Times*, wrote what a great many people had been feeling.

'Clearly he thinks the Bishops are incompetent. But suppose he were right; is this an argument against the measure? There is no sense in complaining about the Bishops. The government of the Church is episcopal . . . and what may be done in the Church is what its Bishops can and will do. The House of Commons is not going to govern the Church. Nor is the Home Secretary. He is indeed fully occupied in enforcing the law upon motorists. . . . And then there is Hyde Park, which seems to be in its way almost as disorderly as the Church of England. . . .'

There were still a few months left before Jix and the rebellious decade parted company, months in which poor Jix was to get a nasty savaging from his own pampered die-hards and in which he was to hear the cat-calls from his own Tory Press. During the war D.O.R.A. had forced the shops to close at eight all the week and at nine on Saturdays. This didn't suit the Gradgrinds, who wanted to close when they felt like it, and they asked Jix to lift the restrictions. Jix, to universal amazement, refused the request. He said that eight o'clock was quite late enough for shop assistants to work. The Tories could hardly believe their ears but Jix said he meant it and that was that.

His next gaffe was more serious, if gaffe it was. The matter has never been adequately explained. For a man like Jix, who talked incessantly, it was inevitable that there should be a certain wastage in what he said. This time it concerned what came to be known as the 'Flapper Vote'. Up until 1929 only women aged thirty and over were allowed to vote. Suddenly, in the middle of a debate about something quite different, Jix was alleged to have said that at the next election the Conservatives would give the vote to women of twenty-one. The extraordinary business is best described in an article by Winston Churchill in the *Sunday Pictorial* of August 9th, 1931.

> 'Here was a private Member's Bill, debated on a Friday. No one took it very seriously. Interrupted by Lady Astor, he [Jix] quite unexpectedly, and without the slightest consultation with his colleagues, said that the Conservative Party would enfranchise men and women on the same terms "at the next election". Two years later this formidable gesture had to be redeemed. Never was so great a change in our electorate achieved so incontinently. For good or ill, Jix should always be remembered for that.'

When the Labour Party won the election many Tories put the blame at Jix's door. Thousands of vote-happy flappers and thousands of miserable small shopkeepers had put the Socialists in, they said. Jix went to Windsor Castle and gave King George his seal of office and the King gave Jix a viscountcy.

The Labour Government changed in an incredibly short time into a National Government, and this into a second National Government. At each shake up of names, Jix, Lord Brentford's ear was glued to Downing Street, but there wasn't a sound for him. He continued to listen so hard that he never heard the saxophones falter and the Bright Young Things putting away their toys. Quite exactly where post-war gaiety and pre-war political awareness began it is impossible to say, but it could have been on that June morning in 1932 when Jix died. He had seen the post-Armistice world as a frisky, tiresome colt which only had to be bridled and blinkered before it could be led back to a respectable stable. He had no humility and too much to say.

CHAPTER THREE

Prospero

'Be not afeard: the isle is full of noises,
Sounds and sweet airs, that give delight and hurt not.'
                                        —*The Tempest*

'A young Scotsman of your ability let loose upon the world
with £300, what could he not do? It's most appalling to think
of; especially if he went among the English.'
              J. M. BARRIE—*What Every Woman Knows*

ON St. Valentine's Day, 1922, the Postmaster General gave permission for 'vocal and gramophone selections and calibration signals
for amateurs' to be transmitted from a broadcasting station at Writtle,
Essex. There had been a good deal of intermittent broadcasting
before this, but Writtle was the first step towards a regular service.
From as early as 1919 the Marconi Company at Chelmsford, under
the direction of Captain Round and W. T. Ditcham, had been
building up a little nucleus of listeners-in whose ears had occasionally
thrilled to the imperial voice of Melba. Chelmsford had between five
and ten thousand listeners and Writtle only very few more. What
Writtle did have was Captain P. P. Eckersley, the proto-radio
personality. It was he who presented to the British Broadcasting
Company at Savoy Hill a quorum of wireless enthusiasts with some
experience of reception—even if what they received, aesthetically
speaking, was hazy in the extreme. The exciting new invention was
at first accepted by many people as an extraordinarily novel toy.
Licences to listen-in rocketed from 10,000 to 500,000 in a year. In
1924 they soared to 1,129,000 and by 1927, when the British Broadcasting Company became the British Broadcasting Corporation and
a moral force in the land, it was estimated that two and a half million
homes had a wireless set. 'Wireless' was, perhaps, something of a
misnomer, for the houses of those who possessed receivers became

festooned with aerials and local authorities came out heavily against what the blasé were beginning to call 'the babble machine' and forbade practices such as running aerials across streets and erecting masts in residential areas.

In the United States things were very different. Each nation had begun as it meant to go on. When Melba was directing her mellifluous patriotism into a funnel-like contrivance at Chelmsford in 1921 to a few thousand people, there were more than a million receiving sets in America and licences to broadcast were granted by the various states legislatures without a glimmer of restriction to challenge the gloating eyes of commerce as it surveyed the profits of the new medium. Travellers returned to Britain with tales which made the Press barons and Oxford Street shopkeepers blink, and while British broadcasting was still at the Writtle stage more than thirty applications from businessmen had been received by the Government for permission to open their own broadcasting stations. The very impetus of the wireless boom and the passionate quality of the public's interest in it made the Government cautious and with typical Anglican piety they steered the dangerous marvel into a *via media* where its delights might be balanced, diabolo-like, on a tightrope controlled at one end by the Post Office and at the other by the wireless manufacturers themselves. This is how the British Broadcasting Company was invented, though even then the Government put the whole affair on a trial and error basis, granting the Company two years' practice only and a further two years' extension if it happened to like the practices. Broadcasting, like the Church, was thus subtly attached to the Establishment.

The immediate problem which faced the broadcasters was coverage. An institution which called itself the British Broadcasting Company had its obligations and plans were at once made to construct eight main stations and to face the formidable and unprecedented task of filling these stations with sounds which wireless licence holders would like to hear. There was little anxiety about cultural standards at first; wireless was such a miracle that almost any tinkle or talk which came over it was welcome. But its potential uses were so great as to be unnerving and it was with these scrupulously in mind that the newly formed company put the following advertisement in the Press.

The British Broadcasting Company (in formation). Applications are invited for the following officers: General Manager, Director of Programmes, Chief Engineer, Secretary. Only applicants having first-class qualifications need apply. Applications to be addressed to Sir William Noble, Chairman of the Broadcasting Committee, Magnet House, Kingsway, W.C.2.

A few days before this, a tall, bitter-faced young Scot had sat in the congregation of Regent Square Church and heard a sermon preached from a text in Ezekiel: *Thus saith the Lord . . . I sought for a man among them, that should make up the hedge, and stand in the gap before me for the land, that I should not destroy it; but I found none.* The minister, Dr. Ivor Roberton, looking about him, thought that perhaps there was someone in the church that very night who might do great things for the country. On October 13th, 1922, the young Scot equated Dr. Roberton's sermon with Sir William Noble's letter by writing an application for the post of General Manager to the new company. He posted the application in the letter-box of the Cavendish Club, discovered that Sir William's family came from Aberdeen, retrieved the letter and wrote another one to include the information that his family also came from Aberdeen, posted this letter and waited. Exactly two months later, on December 14th, John Reith was appointed General Manager of the B.B.C. at a salary of £1,750. The hedge had been made up with a vengeance with an autocratic six-foot-six Presbyterian stake.

The story of the manse-born Glasgow engineer's arrival at the cot of the B.B.C. is a very celebrated one and belongs to the breathless sphere of those happy accidents which tend to make the wheel of history look uncommonly like the machinery of the roulette table. Some might call it luck; he called it Providence. The microphone was born and John Reith was there to suckle it, to guide its infant lispings, to wean it from the pap of the first years, to train it, lecture it, cherish it and protect it from the tycoons, sometimes to spank it, but finally to see it take its place authoritatively amongst the most ancient institutions in the country. And all in less than a decade.

The new Managing Director was aloof from the very start and not many months had passed before an audience of him in his office at Savoy Hill was considered to be one of the more shattering experiences to be had in London. He was thirty-five, a towering, scarred black fir of a man with a mouth made almost sensuous by the warmth with which it murmured negatives, and he loomed head and shoulders above the multitude of demobilized young officers who swarmed into the new jobs created by broadcasting, most of them knowing as much about wireless programmes as they knew about Lapland or the differential calculus. His smile was so rare as to be thought non-existent but when it did happen it was so devastatingly beautiful that it disconcerted its viewers as much as did his frowns. David Low was one of the first to notice the disparity in John Reith's eyes, how one burned violently, consuming criticism, reducing all its owner disliked to ashes, while the other contained all the apprehension suitable for a puritan young Scot forced to have truck with Babylon.

During the war a bullet had raked a shallow path across one cheek and left one of those scars which leave a man vulnerable to compassion. He had big, fine hands, the hands of his blacksmith grandfather rather than his reverend parent. He was utterly formidable and pledged—though to nothing which could actually be assessed, listed and called doctrinal. It wasn't long before his employers, the wireless manufacturers, were to learn the difference between appointing a general manager and inviting a Presbyterian prince to accept a throne. He was honest. 'I do not pretend to give the public what it wants,' he said bleakly. The public kicked against the pricks, scarcely at first believing that its enjoyment of the brilliant new entertainment was to be regulated by a benevolent tyranny, but young Mr. Reith saw these protests merely as evidence of the public's moral puniness and immature taste, and applied the goad whenever he felt it necessary, which was not infrequent.

The Press, which is often willing to concede greatness where it isn't allowed to interview it, began to decorate the legend and was at first fulsome and flattering about 'the Czar of Savoy Hill'. But when it became plain that all this meant absolutely nothing at all to Mr. Reith, the journalists stopped throwing flowers and began to search around for brickbats. If even one of these hit the mark nobody ever knew it and the newspapers soon found that they had a dour syndrome, mostly of their own invention, on their hands which they had little opportunity of checking with its onlie begetter.

'Impossible to pilfer opinions from his intimates. He has no intimates and few friends. Futile to pump his staff. They do not know him, nor he them. But by their works ye shall know them. Look then at the B.B.C. Two factors have gone into its making: experiment and discipline. The director general must often have had the profitable experience of watching others burn their fingers. His own he does not burn. He is master of the indirect rule. Discipline there is for all who work for the Corporation; discipline in long hours, in anonymity, in unrecognized and unrewarding effort. The D.G., it is said, doesn't believe in praise; blame is his chosen incentive.

'Consider some of the experiments—Broadcasting House, for example. Himself no lover of the arts, as the mixed mahogany and oak of his own room shows, he yet consents to the erection of a modern building (not too modern), to carvings (Gill not Epstein), to decorations studiously functional. Or look at his staff. Gifted amateurs, many of them, chosen autocratically. First-class ability is not encouraged and is apt to leave the Corporation. Or reflect upon the programmes. Bawdy vaudeville and bowdlerized talks. The D.G. prefers dance music, but the best classical and contemporary compositions find adequate place. The D.G. is not himself an educated man, but he believes in the medicinal effects of education—a cultural dictatorship. The B.B.C. has no politics, only as Winston Churchill said, "pontifical anonymous mugwumpery". We owe it to Sir John Reith that the B.B.C. is free from commercialism and that it has idealistic standards. For ten years he has built himself a road to travel along. No man of iron, but supreme in the art of effective compromise. For ten years he has ignored public opinion, moulded it, informed it. Has his time come to assess it and direct it?'

So asked the *New Statesman* on Armistice Day 1933 in an anonymous leader which brought to a climax a decade of Reithian criticism, none of which so much as chipped the new colossus. The root of the conflict was in the opposing conceptions of radio, conceptions which took their shape way back in the cat's whisker past and which never fundamentally altered until the early forties, when Churchill's voice and Beethoven's Fifth Symphony, plus the national devotion to the Nine o'clock News, gave the B.B.C. an almost biblical authority the world over. Until this happened the faction which saw radio as an entertaining toy with money-spinning associations, and John Reith, who saw wireless as 'potentially as important as the printing press' in terms of human enlightenment, were at daggers drawn.

John Reith soon made it quite clear that he had not entered into his airy kingdom in order to subsidize the blather of *Answers* and the *Daily Mail*, nor to endorse any of the other popular claptrap of British life. He was there—guided, he believed, by God that evening in Regent Square Church—to lead Britain through the post-war years. There was no time to argue with those who challenged his rôle, which meant that he must ignore them and their complaints. And so it began, the remarkable creation and the despotism.

The new great cham was not without his Boswells, although it is doubtful if he knew so much as their very existence. He was as near infallibility as Calvinism allows and against this the commotions of Fleet Street sounded futile and passing. The price of greatness is bound to include the cheques paid to Sunday journalists. Chief among the Reith Boswells was Garry Allighan, who filled many a column with pertinent glimpses of the never wholly seen figure of the enigmatic Glaswegian who dictated the policy of 'the wireless', the most influential and most universally absorbing development in the social life of Europe and America during the twenties.

'A queer show, that early B.B.C.,' said Gilbert Frankau. 'One remembers, for instance, a bare attic on the top of Marconi House, and three rough packing cases atop of which one sat, not without perturbation, reading a story from the *Strand Magazine* into the mouthpiece of a tin trumpet ... 1923 that must have been.'

And Ellen Wilkinson was to add, 'When broadcasting was first launched, I might almost say let loose, people thought that a mild amusement had been added to the few pastimes suitable for the home circle, and that at least there would be something cheerful to listen to when they turned the knob. But we English should have learned by now that it is unsafe to give a Scotsman any opportunity for indulging his national passion of directing other people for their own good. In six short years'—her criticism was being made in the summer of 1931—'Sir John Reith has made himself more even than the guardian of public morals. He has become the Judge of What We Ought to Want.'

The early thirties marked the zenith of anti-Reithery; they also revealed a new kind of admiration of him. 'I would like to see a dictator in this country,' said Sir Evelyn Wrench a few weeks after Hitler's emergence. 'There is a lot to be said for dictatorship. Take the B.B.C. as an example. Sir John Reith is a good illustration of the attempt to run the world that we will have in the future.'

'His real hobby-horse is the high horse,' observed Louise Morgan glacially. 'How Carlyle would have loved him!'

'If I had committed any misdemeanour I can think of few people to whom I would less like to recite the details,' confessed Ivor Nicholson.

'I have always felt that Sir John Reith would have made a very excellent Hitler for this country,' said George Lansbury. But Clement Attlee saw certain advantages. 'He puts up a splendid resistance to vested interests of all kinds,' he reminded the socialists. This was certainly true.

'He is full of prejudices and his first impressions are usually his last,' said *Punch*.

'I should not advise you to approach his house in Beaconsfield,' said the local bobby, 'as he has in the grounds two guards who are ex-Metropolitan policemen and a savage Airedale dog.'

'Every year the Prince of Wales gets more democratic and Sir John Reith more regal,' said Colonel Moore Brabazon at a dinner party at which both were present.

'Since the death of Kitchener,' wrote George Slocumbe, a few months before the Reith Age closed, 'few men have so taken hold of the imagination of thousands of people. He is the central figure of a legend. Broadcasting House is his feudal domain . . . an almost military discipline is imposed upon and observed by the staff. Sir John refuses to countenance the introduction of beer, wine or spirits into the staff restaurant. The Director General also frowns upon divorce.

'Nor are the public policy of the B.B.C. and the arbitrary regulations which control its programmes affected by parliamentary or Press criticisms. Under Sir John Reith's inspiration the Corporation continues to practise a strict sabbatarianism. A strong religious note pervades the broadcasts. The austerity of its Sunday programmes is only compensated by the characteristically English—or is it Scottish?—mixture of broad vaudeville, jokes about drink, mothers-in-law, Austin sevens and sexual abnormality broadcast on Saturdays. Its weekday entertainments are decorous, genteel, innocuous and almost epicene.

'The accents of its announcers are of impeccable correctitude.

The Napoleon of Broadcasting ... is definitely an individual—even an eccentric. He might have been a character in one of the Five Towns novels of Arnold Bennett.'

In 1931 it was believed that the B.B.C. was the most criticized institution in the country. 'D.G.', as Sir John Reith was known to his staff, was the supreme arbiter of 65,000 broadcasting hours a year and the wireless had become both an unconscious and a conscious educator as it opened up the immemorial seclusion of British village life, gate-crashed and at the same time sharply emphasized the class differences in great cities and brought to most simple people more pleasure than the sophisticated would allow was possible. The Left, many of whom had come to politics via the chapel, got abnormally worked up by Sir John Reith's sabbatarianism, possibly because it reminded them of drab Sundays at the local Bethel or Ebenezer. The intellectual Left found D.G.'s culture Georgian and refined.

Harold Laski shook his Fabian finger at Sir John, who, of course, never noticed it. 'Sunday is what the lawyers call a *dies non* on the wireless because Sir John thinks that Bloomsbury is good for us. To him, doubtless, we also owe the flawless Oxford accents of the announcers. ... He speaks with the urgency of a pontiff. ... You too rarely hear from the admirable staff he has gathered about him. He gives the impression that the B.B.C. pivots too exclusively upon his private sense of right and wrong. We have endless sermons from St. Martin-in-the-Fields, could not Sir John risk a communist? Can we have a discussion on birth control? Can we not hear about the Five Year Plan? I am agreeing that Sir John is a big man. But no man is ever big enough or wise enough to exercise what is practically unlimited power. He must learn that the wicked heresies of today are the sober commonplaces of tomorrow.'

A year after this was written, in 1932, it was thought by many people that Sir John Reith was second only to the Prime Minister in power. It had been a brief, strange journey which had brought him from Regent Square Church to a tiny office in Kingsway on December 30th, 1922, to a telephone, some circulars, three tables, some chairs—and nobody else. 'Utterly alone,' he had written. And, in its way, an equally brief strange journey which had taken him from this niche to Prospero's seat at Langham Place. No one had ever done such a thing before and no one could do such a thing again. The experience was unique, for him and for the world.

*

The task confronting the entirely unknown John Reith and his colleagues in the New Year of 1923 was formidable in the extreme. Together, they roughed-out a four-year plan. 1923 would be the 'Main Stations Year'. Following this would come 'The Relay Stations Year', 'The High Power Year' and 'The Year of Consolidation'. London, Birmingham, Manchester, Newcastle, Cardiff, Glasgow, Aberdeen and Bournemouth were chosen as centres for the eight main stations and the problem of the scattered rural areas was solved by erecting a high-power station at Daventry.

The first programme broadcast by the infant B.B.C. went over the air at half-past six on the evening of September 17th, 1922, but 1923 was the real 'wonder year', when wireless swept the western world like Ragtime, when almost any nonsensical squawking in the earphones could bring childlike pleasure, and when a relay of music from Pittsburgh and New York during the Christmas holiday brought with it a feeling of exultation for the wireless owner. This was followed, in 1924, by the event which really established broadcasting as a serious fact, broke its gimmickry and, in a sense, made it respectable. For this year the B.B.C. relayed King George V's opening speech from Wembley Exhibition and between six and seven million people heard a voice which until then had only been heard by the privileged few. A more poetic privilege was accorded the licensees when they heard the pure, untroubled notes of a nightingale's song from a Surrey wood. This became an enormous favourite.

Receiving sets were bought in vast numbers but were delicate and far from foolproof. Moreover, to the ordinary family they often possessed an ambience beyond the range of normal mechanical things which made them loth to touch them when things went wrong, with the result, as the Radio Association discovered, that thousands of sets were soon out of use simply because batteries had to be charged—or even because the owner couldn't tune in. By 1926, 40,000 people were employed in radio manufacture and the industry was showing a turnover of £10 million. The low power of the B.B.C.'s main stations was much criticized. It was found that even with very expensive receivers it was difficult to get alternative wavelengths to that supplied by the local main station, and that if one had only a cheap two-valve or crystal set, and used headphones, one had to be quite near to the local main station to get a pleasant reception. But on the whole, the grouses came from the addicts rather than the average listener-in, for whom the searching for programme and keeping it when one got it was all part of the fun.

Even at this stage the compensations of listening-in were considerable. The Women's Institute, then just beginning its Flora-Post-like invasion of the dolours of rural life, found that a wireless set in a cottage did wonders in a village. If one home had it, all the neighbours would flock round in the evenings, drink home-made wine and rejoice in the novelty. The upper classes treated it cautiously. 'Is it not a travesty that a drum comes through like the banging of a door?' asked Lord Blanesburgh. The soft *bourgeois* centre of the nation went cosy on the new invention—'On Monday evening, for instance, listeners heard, in the intervals of music, about the work of the Boys' Brigade, with clearly told narratives of gallant deeds. Sunday provides a feast of sacred music and brings the masses in touch with the best preachers. Single-room residents keep near them the magic box which admits them to the company of princes . . . who knows what surprises may follow London Calling the British Isles?' Who indeed.

The financial rewards of the new obsession, far greater than had been imagined, caused swift speculation. In early 1926 the Radio Association was all for giving them away to a national theatre, not quite comprehending the needs of the B.B.C. There were copyright fees, for example. During the first year of broadcasting they amounted to less than a thousand pounds but by 1924 there were 19,589 performances of copyright works which, at the rate of the Company's payment of 5s. per classical work for seven minutes and 4s. per dance tune for seven minutes, at once indicated that even playing gramophone records into a microphone could be expensive. The cost of collecting news was another problem. In 1935 the Press estimated that it was spending £5 million on this task, whereas the B.B.C., which always had all the plum items in its bulletins, was only spending £8,000!

Hamilton Fyffe, editor of the *Daily Herald*, thought that the wireless would soon supersede newspapers altogether. 'We shall all carry earphones about with us and be able to pick up messages. Those who regard newspapers merely as a help to passing the time would find wireless news enough for them. Journalism would become once more a serious profession. Things that were important would not be sacrificed to snappy or spicy items, reports of divorce cases and murder trials, and the mania for what the French called "*faits divers*".' O brave new world.

London theatres and concert halls showed a similar panic at what they saw as the stall-emptying tactics of Savoy Hill to that experienced by the cinematograph industry during the 1950's television boom. Walter Payne, Chairman of the West End Managers' Association, grew vituperative in his fright and declared that 'all listeners-in are potential dead-heads' and that on the night of a big wireless concert—which cost the listener-in one penny—he estimated that London's concert houses lost £5,000.

When it had been in existence for less than four years it was already becoming conspicuous that the constitution of the British Broadcasting Company was anomalous to a degree. Vaguely merchant, decidedly national, there was a classically English element in its structure reminiscent of such institutions as Lord's and the Bank of England. Even the Church of England. Patriots and culture pundits alike began to feel it wrong that so formidable a concern was still nominally in the control of wireless manufacturers, and there was a growing argument for some kind of state take-over. Broadcasting, as its general manager said, had emerged from the first flush of scientific wonder and had to be accepted as part of the permanent and essential machinery of civilization.

In March, 1926, the Crawford Committee published its recommendations. It thought that broadcasting should be conducted by a public corporation and that this corporation should hold a monopoly of the air for ten years. It should be governed by five to seven altruistic people and it should have to answer to Parliament alone. On January 1st, 1927, the British Broadcasting Company died and the British Broadcasting Corporation was born. Long live the B.B.C. The General Manager slipped away and the Director General took his place. It was a profoundly subtle elevation which misled no one. The crown had been tendered and had been graciously accepted.

It was, in many ways, a great relief. The jolly anarchism of

American broadcasting could now Never Happen Here. The *Liverpool Evening Express* gave grisly hints of what might have been, of what we had missed, thanks chiefly to Lord Crawford and Balcarres' anointed. ' "Asleep in the Deep" on a cornet, followed by "Träumerei" on an ocarina and "The Rosary" sung by a home-trained soprano.' And ads.

All through 1927, the year which ended with his knighthood, there were persistent rumours that John Reith was leaving the B.B.C. and that C. B. Cochran, then manager of the Albert Hall, would take his place—rumours which showed a feeble comprehension of both D.G. and his empire. 1927 was radio's glory year. On January 2nd it broke through the technical difficulties which had hampered so many of its dramatic productions with a brilliant wireless play by Reginald Berkeley. It was called *The White Château* and was an extremely harrowing trench-war story whose realism shook the twelve million people who listened-in to it, the more particularly as they were advised to do this while sitting in a darkened room. This was the first wireless play to be filmed.

This year, too, saw wireless installed in the Pullman cars of the 7.5 train from Victoria to Brighton. An eight-valve Marconiphone superheterodyne receiver, complete with a complicated frame aerial, stood in the corridor and was connected with a Panatrope amplifier in each carriage. It was considered *luxe* to a degree, not to mention *chic* and swish.

From Germany came particulars for bottling programmes. Speech or music could be put through a microphone, then a steel wire passing at an even speed through an electric field had the electrical fluctuations caused by the microphone impressed on it, so that the music was frozen to the wire and could be heard again when the process was reversed.

In February, 1927, the *Daily Mail* carried out a 'taste' plebiscite. None of its bottomless advice to young Mr. Reith had had the very slightest effect. Now it would present him with the considered advice of the man-in-the-street, a very holy figure in 1927, and a creature not to be mocked. The ballot was remarkable, and was conducted with real skill, the only things its promoters forgetting being the fact that a low-brow newspaper must inevitably get a low-brow result. Yet the ballot showed a broad picture of average wireless enjoyment and the result is sociologically valuable and worth quoting. Variety and Concert Parties top the list with 238,489 fans. Then came:

Light Orchestral Music	179,153
Military Bands	164,613
Dance Music	134,027
Sport and News	114,571
Symphony Concerts	78,781
Opera	60,983
Short Plays and Sketches	49,857
Sea Shanties	30,445
Chamber Music	27,059
Long Play	17,576
Recitations	2,717

This ballot was interpreted by the *Daily Mail* as a demand for more fun. Now the B.B.C. would simply have to give up pushing highbrow stuff down the throats of the licensees. The listeners wanted to be amused, not educated. D.G. was magnanimous, rather like the man who owns a chocolate factory and lets visitors feed themselves until they are sick. In April, 1927, the B.B.C. constructed a whole week's programmes in strict accordance to the humble petition of the *Daily Mail*, then reverted sharply to its own policies. As Elmer Gantry said, 'Would you like to see your own mammy indulging in mixed bathing or dancing that Hell's own fooling monkeyshine, the one-step?' D.G. had allowed Britannia to kick up her heels for seven days just to teach her sons a lesson.

Two years before this, in 1925, the *Daily Express* backed a huge organization called 'The Wireless League' to 'protect the listener-in'. The period was distinguished by the absence of cynicism shown by ordinary people for the near-continuous catch-penny schemes launched by the popular Press. The reaction to the Wireless League was rewarding, to say the least of it. By 1927 it was barracking with all its might for low-brow entertainment and under cover of its homely appeal to 'give the public what it wants' it was able to lob some really damaging Philistine rocks against the cultural autocracy of Savoy Hill. It sent the Director General programmes arranged by the man-in-the-street, naturally, but, unlike other would-be popularizers of the wireless programmes, it made it its business to howl with fury at art and intellectual achievements of all kinds. When

3

Igor Stravinsky played the piano in a concert of his own works, the programme was reviewed as 'fearsome dissonances and general uncouthness'. There were everlasting complaints about the talks, the plays and much else, which eventually caused the Cambridge Union to debate, 'Is the Listening-in habit a menace to the sanity of England?' It decided that it wasn't—by 213 to 29 votes. Rose Macaulay's 'armchair millennium' was proving itself an armchair Armageddon.

In June 1927 the B.B.C. Wireless Organizations' Joint Advisory Committee, under the chairmanship of Ian Fraser, the blind M.P., gloomily admitted that all its attempts to influence the policy of the Corporation had been so much wasted labour 'and the mandarins of Savoy Hill are simply making use of the committee as a blind'.

In August the Corporation adopted its coat of arms, consisting of a terrestrial globe on an azure shield, the crest showing a lion holding in his right paw a thunderbolt proper. The motto was 'Nation shall speak Peace unto Nation'. Beachcomber, out of loyalty, perhaps, to the Wireless League supported by his paper, was more cross than clever. 'So when you hear a dreadful din of broadcast music, or the fag-end of a lecture on varnish given by a woman in Holland, you will know that nation is speaking peace unto nation. . . .'

The Wireless Exhibition at Olympia that year, which opened in September, was notably surrealistic. Loudspeakers lurked beneath the skirts of Dresden shepherdesses, in flower vases, and were made in the shapes of celebrated works of art. The firm of Electrone exhibited an ingenious 'clock' for selecting programmes and there were also 'Cone' receivers for hanging on walls. The B.B.C.'s stand, perhaps to please D.G., who confessed to liking dance music and the tune 'Halleluja' in particular, included a small ballroom. But it was always empty, apparently because visitors to Olympia were too shy to fox-trot on an exhibition stand.

Religion and politics continued to be too controversial for wireless debates and were left severely alone, although Lord Birkenhead, among others, attempted to repeal these rules. The touchiness of the public where religion was concerned can be gauged by the outcry which greeted a travel talk by Ramsay MacDonald, which he called 'Forty Days and Forty Nights in the Sahara'. This was thought highly blasphemous. But the worst outcry of this sort came after a talk on birth control by Julian Huxley and Cecil Lewis and was caused by a well-rehearsed voice breaking into the discussion, with a dramatic, 'I protest. . . . I never. . . . It's indecent. . . . I protest!' The discussion stopped, as though shocked, then continued as before. It was all a put-up job by a realistic producer, and when this came out the B.B.C. was loudly condemned for going in for such stunts. The *Manchester Guardian* likened it to a man who blacks himself all over to play *Othello*.

Possibly nothing at this period gave such universal pleasure as the dance bands which broadcast from 2LO nightly for an hour before midnight. The Savoy Orpheans, Paul Whiteman, Jack Hylton, The Selma Four, The Romaine Four, Jack Howard, Jack Payne and, soon, Henry Hall filled front-room and drawing-room with the strains of ' 'Bye-'Bye Blackbird', 'Twilight on Missouri', 'The More We are Together', 'Valencia', 'Chinese Moon', 'Let's All Go To Mary's House', 'I Wonder Where My Baby Is Tonight', 'No Foolin' ' and 'Ukelele Dream Girl'. The wildness of the jazz age, and perhaps its sheer dedication, caused at least one eminent musician to threaten to flee his native land. Sir Thomas Beecham threatened to go to America, 'where they keep broadcasting in its place' (!). He called Britain 'the paradise of the low-brow and the bone-head. Go and blare a saxophone in a dance hall or play a one-stringed fiddle or a siren hooter in a night-club. Music has been killed by the wireless. The best of music has been reduced to a horrible, chattering, gibbering, chortling and shrieking of devils and goblins. Those who listen to it are cretins!' He was supported in his execrations by none other than Sir Oliver Lodge, who gravely inquired why, if he took out a B.B.C. licence for speeches and the addresses of notable men, should he have to pay for music? Sentimentalists, mourning for Edwardian musical evenings, with Father singing Amy Woodforde-Finden and Aunt Charlotte rendering 'Kitten on the Keys', regrettted that pianos were only now used for loudspeaker pedestals.

The year witnessed an extraordinarily determined attack by the Philistines on good music. It also heard Sir Henry Wood's first broadcast concert from 2LO on June 30th and the beginning of Sir Walford Davies's wonderful talks on musical appreciation. It was as though the enemies of music were getting in all the damaging thrusts they could before the astonishing national renaissance of the art, the

greater part of it brought about by broadcasting and the impeccable
musical standards of the B.B.C., made it impossible for there ever
to be this kind of ignorant sniping at music again.

There is no better illustration of how music stood in Britain in the
mid-twenties than the sad tale of the B.B.C.'s contemporary music
competition. This had little to do with publicity and nothing to do
with stunts. It was an attempt, in deadly earnest, by the Corporation
to discover new musical genius or, failing this, new musical gifts.
The judges included Edward Elgar, Hamilton Harty and Landon
Ronald; the prizes were respectable—£300 for a new symphony,
£150 for a short symphonic poem or overture, £150 for a short work
for voice and orchestra, £100 for a work for a military band and £50
for a song cycle. But the result was tragic. Of the 240 entries, not one
was thought worth acceptance and the prizes were withdrawn.
Later, the B.B.C. gave a quarter of the money to the Musicians'
Benevolent Fund. This competition provided a salutary shock to
the attitude adopted towards music in the twenties as well as revealing the paucity of creative musical expression in Britain. It took
years to get it into people's heads that good music was neither an
intellectual nor a class prerogative but the legitimate joy of every
sensitive human being. The struggle to destroy self-consciousness
where good music was concerned was begun. Sir John Reith said,
in 1931, 'there should be no mental unsettling which may cause a
sense of hopelessness in the minds of the listeners. . . . I raise the peg
of better music constantly, but not too fast'.

In 1926–7 there was the strangest resentment from pro- and anti-
music interests alike regarding the raising of the peg. The pro-good
music group, without intending malice, associated good music with
good everything else—with privilege, in fact. In *Howard's End*, by
E. M. Forster, published in 1910, the Schlegel sisters were amused,
intrigued and touched to find Leonard Bast, a lower-middle-class
clerk, at a Beethoven concert, and this idea that Beethoven was for
ladies and gentlemen was still deeply ingrained in the British class
structure of the twenties, causing a constant spate of letters to the
Press. Such snobbery and naïveté was making the 'raising of the
peg' tiresomely difficult and would have gone on doing so had it not
received a harsh, unflattering rap over the knuckles by Sir Richard
Terry.

'The idea that the middle classes are better educated than the masses, as far as music is concerned, is a fallacy. I generally find that these musical heretics who loudly protest against what they call "highbrow" music all belong to the middle classes. I would substitute for the term "middle classes" the classification "half educated". The half-educated person with just enough knowledge to misquote is invariably the bitterest enemy that art can have. He has just the little knowledge that is dangerous. If a man is an artist he knows enough; if he is not, whatever he knows is bad for him. It is the half-educated person who writes daily to the B.B.C. asking for "something with a tune in it". It is in the gallery that you find the perfect Wagnerites; it is among miners and cotton operatives that you find the deepest reverence for Bach and Handel. They cannot pronounce their names but they can perform their music.'

The musical re-education of Britain, the B.B.C.'s greatest single cultural achievement, had begun.

*

Not the least amusing thing about the early B.B.C. was the social prestige and indeed glamour which became attached to announcing. When little Miss Bouncer married an announcer, she did well for herself. The announcers were gentlemen—they even included a peer's brother, the Hon. David Tennant, and they always read the Nine o'clock News in a dinner jacket. Their urbane, authoritative voices were to cause a linguistic revolution. Much picturesqueness in speech wilted before them and vocal slovenliness at all levels perished from sheer shame. The malapropisms of the lower orders, so essential to the sales of *Punch*, were all to be shaken to their philological roots by 'B.B.C. English'. But the snags were soon to reveal themselves. There are certain English words, as Nancy Mitford found to her profit, which have no correct middle-class pronunciation. It is not unknown, for instance, that it takes three generations of gentle living to be able to pronounce 'girl'. And then there is 'golf', a word requiring real verbal courage whichever way one says it. In 1927 there was 'Yawksha', the 'Empah', being 'crawss', the 'Mawl' and 'Pell Mell'.

So an advisory committee was set up under the presidency of the poet laureate, Robert Bridges. Its members included Logan Pearsall Smith, George Bernard Shaw and Forbes-Robertson. Eventually they issued a list of fifty-five doubtful words and their

advice on how they should be pronounced. They said that if announcers said 'Paris', then they must also say 'Marsales', 'Reems',
'Lions', etc., though here again the whole thing broke down over
Nice, which nobody dared to rhyme with mice. The findings of the
Pronunciation Committee brought out all the English-speaking
banshees in force, for it is a notorious fact that accent differences are
not only the basis of the English class structure, but the backbone of
its comic literature. The *Observer* found it all too much, coming as it
did from 'mellifluous gentlemen who broadcast cricket scores and
appeals to missing girls to come home', and the *Manchester Guardian*
had a rollicking article entitled 'Pianoforty and Seltic Huzzifry'.
Perhaps the most destructive of the changes was the B.B.C.'s
pronunciation of the decade's sex symbol. It really would be a fate
worse than death to be hugged by a shake.

The old guard clung to their old accents more than ever after this
and the following exchange was heard at the Old Bailey. A K.C.,
Mr. David Vaisey, had used the B.B.C.'s phonetic pronunciation of
'Daventry'.

Mr. Justice Eve: 'Daintree, I think they call it.'
Mr. Vaisey: 'I was not quite sure. . . .'
Mr. Justice Eve: 'But now, since broadcasting and these vulgar
               things that come in, it may be called "Daventry".'
Mr. Vaisey: 'Sir Thomas Hughes, K.C., says "Daintry" and
               my client "Daventry".'
Mr. Justice Eve: (crushingly) ' "Daintry" is more familiar to *me*.'

Among those who were horrified at the B.B.C.'s Pronunciation
Committee was G. K. Chesterton, who accused John Reith of play-
ing Mr. Dick, and there were particularly outraged protests from
Scotland. But the English, who find an almost erotic pleasure in
their weather or the way they speak, enjoyed the uproar very much.
They were not to get such a narcissistic entertainment again until
Miss Mitford's U turn had them rolling in the aisles nearly thirty
years later.

Attitudes towards broadcasting by the performers themselves
were very varied. Great music-hall artists, accustomed to the
climatic crescendo which announced their acts, found the tran-
quillity of the tented studio disconcerting. In some cases it brought
about a kind of dramatic impotence; they simply couldn't do it.
Others, like Sir Harry Lauder, couldn't sing their songs without the

driving getting-the-words-across actions necessary for the stage and the producers would watch him prancing for all he was worth in an empty room. The comedian, John Henry, on the other hand, would sit effortlessly in a chair and reel off his jokes without the flicker of a smile on his face. Tallulah Bankhead declared that the terrors of Savoy Hill were so great that she was unable to speak for days after making her first broadcast. Nobody believed this. Jacob Epstein said he hated broadcasting worse than journalism, of which he thought it was a debased form. P. G. Wodehouse faced the new medium with characteristic urbanity and in 1926 broadcast what he called 'a series of Spasms' concerning the adventures of Bertie Wooster and Jeeves. Paderewski refused to broadcast because the microphone made him nervous and ill. But in spite of these fears and difficulties, there was no dearth of radio adventurers and by August, 1926, these were seeking auditions at the rate of 700 a week. To be on the air was the pinnacle of fame.

There were five studios at Savoy Hill, each beautifully draped for acoustic reasons. Programmes were arranged six weeks ahead and there was a staff of some 300 people. Torrential advice descended on the fascinating institution almost without ceasing. There were gaffes. When Cyril Shields explained away a few conjuring tricks on Children's Hour, he incurred the diabolical wrath of the Magicians' Circle, who accused him of taking the bread out of their mouths. Then there was Shakespeare. Sir Barry Jackson thought that the plays could not be read over the air convincingly unless the actors were costumed, and the bowdlerizing of the text to make it fit for parlour consumption brought further ribald protests. The B.B.C. was not to blame here. It was still recovering from the astonishing indignation which had followed a delightful production of Flecker's *Hassan* and was still finding it hard to understand why the British would enjoy smutty vaudeville and yet rise in outrage at the faintest sensuality in anything connected with literature and art. It could listen with glee to Nellie Wallace but when it came to Shakespeare, its moral sense proved to be so exquisite that 'wanton girl' had to be changed to 'naughty girl'. It was all very strange, very British.

One of the most significant and pleasing developments of the period was the steady growth of the outside broadcast. Sport provided a challenge to the microphone and it faced up to it with zest, ingenuity and high imagination. The technique of making a listener feel that he was, not only in touch, but emotionally involved in an event which was taking place many miles away, required all kinds of new broadcasting tricks. Sports commentators went to the St. Leger, the Grand National, the Rugby International and the Derby in 1927, with titanic success. The Derby commentary was very odd. The commentator was a journalist from *Sporting Life*, named G. F. Allison. For years it had been his duty to 'read the race' to the King and Queen and their friends in the Royal Enclosure. Such experiences had left him august. His words, as Call Boy flashed by the winning post in 1927, were Shakespeare out of the *Pink'un*. '. . . he leads, he leads. Come gallant son of Hurry On. He nears the judge. Leap then, brave heart. Look, nothing can catch him now. . . .'

Also this year, Lance Sieveking brought off an outside broadcast triumph by bringing the gaiety of May Week at Cambridge into thousands of homes. From his perch in a tree in Rectory Meadow, he described the Bumping Races and from a position on Garret Hostel Bridge he gave a heart-catching impression of an early summer evening on the river, lovers, ukeleles, plashing paddles, lanterns, gramophones and a generation of youths which was still slightly incredulous at finding itself alive after the military massacres of less than a decade ago. Lance Sieveking, himself little more than an undergraduate then, was to prove one of broadcasting's finds. He is among the small group of 'founder-inspirers' of broadcasting, a man who extended radio's frontiers in a score of directions and a great craftsman of the medium.

While all this was going on, on January 7th, 1926, the thirty-five-year-old son of another Scots Presbyterian minister was sitting in a small room in Frith Street, Soho, only a few yards from the house in which William Friese-Green showed the world's first moving picture, and watching the familiar features of his business manager, O. G. Hutchinson, materialize out of thin air. J. L. Baird had transmitted a picture by wireless. Television was born. But that, as the B.B.C. discovered, was another story.

CHAPTER FOUR

Sublimated Aladdin

'I am a sublimated Aladdin, the thousand and second knight.'
T.E.L. to Colonel Newcombe

EVERYBODY who adds to the Lawrence legend, and the accretions have been more than even he could have hoped for, feels the need to apologize. Though really there is no need for apology. Thomas Edward Lawrence is an opulent seam whichever way one digs into him. During the twenties and early thirties he was England's answer to Lindbergh, except that for all his fatal staginess he was bigger, better and richer in human complexities than Lindbergh, though his rôle was much the same. The twenties liked to think that *some* men were islands. In T. E. Lawrence they recognized the lone hero *in excelsis*. They liked his indifference to fame at a time when war honours and peerages were being snatched up like bargains. They liked his looks, which were the real McCoy after the pinchbeck sheik stuff of Valentino and the burnoused Lotharios of Miss M. E. Clamp. They also liked his amateurism, his 'modesty' and his make-your-own-kingdoms kit. He reappeared on the scene when patriotism had become rather smudgy and before empire worship had been safely channelled off into royalty worship, which left quite a lot of emotion going begging.

There was a new cult of the man who didn't fit, then called the little man and, after the Second World War, the outsider. Charlie Chaplin's films epitomized the tragi-comic bewilderment of this individual and created a climate of sympathy for the niche-less. When Colonel Lawrence returned home in 1919, having as it was popularly believed turned down the crown of Arabia, his refusal to come to terms with reality was interpreted as a refusal to come to terms with mammon. Nobody, not even his intimate friends, seems to have realized that when this acting Prince of Mecca was at last forced to strip himself of his robes he was forced to face some cruelly naked truths about himself.

Lawrence was not a liar, as Richard Aldington in particular insists; he was an arch-romantic for whom fact and fiction were intermingled, as in Mallory. His life was an invention in the same way that a novel is an invention. He used himself like a hero and when one lot of adventures had come to an end he plotted a fresh setting, a new name and began another tale. He was able to do this because when he was about ten he discovered that he wasn't 'Lawrence', and although the discovery brought with it a constant fearfulness which mounted at intervals throughout his life to near-horror, it also brought him a unique sense of freedom.

His father was an Irish baronet who had left his wife in order to live with a young Scots governess. On the face of it, the situation was unadulterated triple-decker 1880 fiction. As it was, it was scarcely more interesting than the most mundane matrimonial fact. The Lawrences were respectability exemplified. Even if Lady Chapman's religious scruples could have come to terms with commonsense, and Sir Thomas had been able to make the governess his wife, they could not have lived more conventionally than they did. Which in itself was a feat, for it was no mean accomplishment at the close of the nineteenth century for a baronet and a governess and their five sons to submerge so faultlessly in residential Oxford. Except for the actual lack of ceremony it was as whole and complete a marriage as the rigid standards of the age demanded. Thomas Edward was the second son of this prim unholy union. Among the essential qualifications for his future rôle of a Great Englishman it is worth noting that this Saxon-faced son of an Irishman and a Scotswoman was born at Tremadoc, Wales. His inheritance, from a mother who sometimes called herself Sarah Maden and sometimes Sarah Junner, and a father who was Sir Thomas Chapman and who called himself Mr. Lawrence, was a nonchalance towards names which was to border on the frivolous.

Lawrence wasn't liberated by peace; he was cornered by it. Where should he go? What should he do? And, more urgently, who should he *be*? On Sir Thomas's side he was descended from Sir Walter Raleigh, a fact he had dazzlingly acknowledged by presiding at the renaissance of Arabia. On his mother's side he sprang from artisans, a type of man for whom his affections were complex and emotional. For the betwixt and between, for all that existed outside the true gentleman and true peasant classes, he had a distaste which sometimes mounted to hatred and loathing. He had justified his Raleigh blood. Was he also not privileged to justify his humbler origins?

For the man who, as a youth, had spent all his spare time making notes of castles and cathedrals, and subduing the flesh by vast bicycle tours, there was something medievally Christian in making an act of renunciation and entering the simple monastery of a barrack-room to be nothing. Clippers all over—Lawrence enjoyed wearing his hair long—would be his tonsure. Instead of Prince Feisal's white and gold wedding clothes there would be a bundle of itching serge thrown at his feet by an unconcerned quartermaster, and always there would be the ceaseless penance of listening to Other Ranks' conversation. He had escaped once and now he would escape again.

Lawrence set about being John Hume Ross with a thoroughness which would have been a credit to any future Method actor. The only mistake he made was the choice of service. The army might have swallowed Ross as it swallowed Coleridge, and as it was re-swallowing all kinds of human odds and ends who couldn't make a go of it in civvy street in 1922. There was a certain traditional sanctuary there for misfits which even tempted demobbed officers to set aside their crowns and creep back into the secure khaki womb. Colonel Lawrence, C.B., D.S.O., Croix de Guerre, great friendships and all, might have done so too. It is just conceivable. The Prince of Mecca *might* have found the anonymity he craved at Aldershot. But of course it had to be Uxbridge.

The reasons for Lawrence's attraction to the Royal Air Force were precisely those why Lawrence did not attract the R.A.F. In 1922 the R.A.F. was a brand new military invention which was still painfully conscious of its social status in comparison with those enjoyed by the Navy and by certain regiments in the Army. It needed individualists but fought shy of eccentrics. It was novel, small and intimate, and still very much the child of its father, Trenchard. While realizing that its rôle would be something absolutely fresh in national defence, it was staffed almost entirely by officers from the older services who were touchily insistent that the ordinary airman should hold his own, bullshit-wise, with any matelot or private. The extraordinary degradation of the individual by this clean buttons-foul mouth policy is described with such vividness in A/C Ross's *The Mint* that this book might have done much to alleviate the wearisome obscenity of barrack-room life could it have been published when it was written, instead of in 1955 when the disciples of Norman Mailer had, by their asterisked persistence, almost succeeded in castrating the sturdiest word in the language. 'Darling,' as Tallulah is reputed to have said to Mailer at a party, 'aren't you the little boy who couldn't spell f*ck?' Aircraftsman Ross couldn't spell it either but he spelt out many other usually unsaid things and *The Mint*, though a damp squib as a sociological sensation, remains for the specialist a masochist's *tour de force*.

'I wrote it tightly,' said 352087 A/C Ross, 'because our clothes are so tight and our lives so tight in the service.' Screamed at on parades, harassed by total lack of privacy and total lack of comfort, Colonel Lawrence was discovering an exquisite personal pleasure in the indignities heaped upon him. It wasn't all perversity, however. He was thrilled by the potential of the R.A.F. and he was exalted by the new dimensional freedom suggested by *Per ardua ad astra*.

'The Royal Air Force is not antique and leisurely and storied like an army,' he wrote in *The Mint*. 'We can feel the impulse of a sure, urging giant behind the scurrying instructors. Squad 5 is today the junior unit of the service. There are twenty thousand airmen better than us between it and Trenchard, the pinnacle and exemplar: but the awe of him surely encompasses us. . . . Trenchard has designed the image he thinks most fitted to be an airman; and we submit our nature to his will, trustingly. . . . Trenchard invented the touchstone by which the Air Council try all their works. Will this, or will this not, promote the conquest of the air? We wish, sometimes, they would temper wisdom to their innocent sheep. For instance, they have decreed that the black parts of bayonets be henceforward burnished. . . .' The quasi-mystical language is that of Hardy, when he describes the President of the Immortals having sport with Tess.

This utterly sincere enthusiasm for the R.A.F. worried the authorities. If the Air Force could have believed that Lawrence was genuinely without ambition, that 352087 A/C Ross wanted nothing more than Hut 5, things might have become easier. Instead it remembered the brilliant Middle East adventurer who in less than three years had risen from his desk at the Arab Bureau to become the companion of princes and the maker of kings. The revolt of Arabia against the Turks was a fine amateur affair to which people had turned in relief after the bloody professionalism of Flanders. Was it not possible that Lawrence-turned-Ross might see in the infant R.A.F. another fine rich field for amateur adventure? He was, after all, only thirty-four and very famous. Except for a few saints, who had ever heard of a brilliant thirty-four-year-old giving up everything? Was Ross some kind of Trojan horse which had crept into Uxbridge and would he one day rule them all? Would he, this little A/C 2 with the big head and blue eyes, soon be writing to Trenchard as he was already writing to Air Vice-Marshal Swann— 'Dear Swann'? Would he motor-cycle to Buckingham Palace and stroll in and see the King? He had already sworn at the poor man in private audience and walked out on him. 'Luckily,' said George V to Sir Horace Rumbold, 'I have served in the Navy, where bad language did not upset me unduly. Only today I felt I had been played the Confidence Trick. . . .' If the confidence trick could be played on the King what was to stop it being played on the Air Council?

However, the Royal Air Force had no choice in the matter. 'Somebody in high authority'—nobody knows who to this day—ordered it to accept the boyish, nervous blond volunteer who turned up at the Uxbridge Depot in 1922. There was never any doubt as to his true identity. Ross they called him, Lawrence he was. The marks of the Deraa flogging made them stare at his back. His papers were forged and his health was much beneath the standard demanded, but, like a genii satisfying a royal whim, the order from the 'Somebody' forced the Uxbridge Depot to grant Colonel Lawrence, Companion of the Bath, Chevalier of the Legion of Honour, Bachelor of Arts and Prince of Mecca, his dearest wish and soon he was drawing his blankets, buying his blanco and getting to know his mates. Was he happy? Could he be?

'Our hut is a fair microcosm of unemployed England, for the strict R.A.F. standards refuse the last levels of the social structure. Yet a man's enlisting is his acknowledgement of his defeat by life. Amongst a hundred serving men you will not find one whole and happy. Each has a lesion, a hurt open or concealed, in his late history.'

His lesion or hurt was not in his late history but in his birth, a fact known to some of his friends and to most of his biographers, though not disseminated to the world at large because Mrs. Lawrence was alive, a fact which in no way inhibited Richard Aldington when he attempted, with the minimum of kindness and the maximum of fascination, to prick the Lawrence myth in 1955. T.E., a hagiographer's dream, needed cutting down to size but Aldington's method was that of the man who tries to level a table and saws it to pieces. Idolatry apart, there was something there and a very considerable something. Storrs, Bernard Shaw, Winston Churchill, E. M. Forster and Allenby were not the kind of men to be taken in by total imposture, however beguiling. And there is the fact that although Lawrence exasperated, badgered and scared all his friends throughout his life, there are few records of his ever having lost a friend. On the contrary he induced a protective affection in those who had got past his funny mixture of shyness and arrogance. The ordinary officers disliked him because of his unorthodoxy and distrusted him because they saw he wasn't Ross, a soldier-poet who was trying to forget; he was Lawrence masquerading as Ross for reasons that were faintly sinister. He swept his barrack room and then went off to dine with the great. It made them acutely uncomfortable. They wished he would go away or that he would take a commission and join them in the mess like a decent chap.

Presumably there must have been a strong sexual element in the constant posing and histrionics of his life. Only something as reckless as sex could have allowed him to indulge in his odd showing-off before such disparate audiences as Hardy and E. M. Forster and a hutful of ignorant airmen. His ambivalence was indulgent and unchecked. He flaunted his dual personality and hurt himself time and time again because of the thrill of jumping from Lawrence to Ross or Shaw, and then of jumping back to Lawrence again. He ached for privacy, yet he drew the gaze of the world on to his every action. He never hid without leaving a trail of hypotheses and rumours leading up to his very door. He longed to be lost but he couldn't bear not to be found. Churchill saw the R.A.F. immolation as a bewildered retreat by a man who could not slow down his swift genius to the jogging pace of peace. In the Allocution he gave during the unveiling of Lawrence's memorial in Oxford, he said, 'He was not in harmony with the normal. The fury of the Great War raised the pitch of life to the Lawrence standard. The multitudes were swept forward till their pace was the same as his. In this period he found himself in perfect relation both to men and events. I have often wondered what would have happened to Lawrence if the Great War had continued for several more years. . . . All the metals were molten. Everything was in motion. No one could say what was impossible. . . . But the storm ceased as suddenly as it had arisen. . . . Mankind returned with indescribable relief to its long interrupted, fondly cherished ordinary life, and Lawrence was left once more moving alone on a different plane and at a different speed.'

His legend might have been kept within reasonable limits and served up as a yarn for boys of all ages had it not been for a young American lecturer named Lowell Thomas. In 1918 Thomas was in Europe searching for film-lecture material to show the folks back home that American troops were colourfully engaged in military glory, but unfortunately he found that the drab horror of the Western Front was quite unsuitable for his purpose. With John Buchan's help he went to Palestine and was very soon face to face with what he had in mind when he set out from Princeton. With, 'I want you to meet Colonel Lawrence, the Uncrowned King of Arabia,' Ronald Storrs set the pace for what was to follow. It was a dazzling, heady pace for Lawrence, Lowell Thomas and the world at large. Soon the innocent American and the small handsome Oxonian in his Eastern costume were deep in conversation, while another American ran about the Holy City with a camera. In March, 1919, a film-lecture called 'With Lawrence in Arabia' over-packed the Century Theatre in New York and had to be transferred to Madison Square Garden. And on August 14th, 1919, before the kind of brilliant audience usually only seen at first nights, the Lawrence lectures were presented at Covent Garden Opera House by the British impresario, Percy Burton. They were a fabulous success. Eventually Covent Garden proved too small for the Lawrence legend and the entire glamorous set-up, Dance of the Seven Veils and all, was moved to that shrine of national hyperbole, the Albert Hall. The tale of how a dreamy Oxford youth had donned princeliness and led Arabia to freedom was told and re-told all over the world by Lowell Thomas and for those who could not get to his lectures there was a best-selling book to be had. This Barnum and Bailey business left Lawrence with the kind of glittering myth no man could live up to. His attitude towards it, as to everything, was of course ambivalent. He attended the lectures and let the adulation pour over him in fascinated disgust and pleasure. The Press trailed him around. Everything he did was good for a headline. He exulted in his fame and was appalled by it. Eventually fantasy and fact became richly entangled and Lawrence, in what David Garnett calls 'The years of hide and seek', tried to gate-crash ordinariness. That he should even have contemplated such a step, knowing himself with the nerve-end intimacy that he did, was either proof of great courage or of a crowning recklessness.

Lowell Thomas's eulogies were followed by more respectable but still adoring biographies by Robert Graves and Liddell Hart. Before these lives appeared Lawrence, in his tell-the-world, keep-it-dark way, had published *Seven Pillars of Wisdom*. He wrote the first draft in 1919, lost it and began again. Hints of the book's literary distinction were heard everywhere, particularly where it was unlikely to have been seen, for Lawrence made it clear from the start that *Seven Pillars* was not the usual active service memoir, neither was it for 'general publication'. Lawrence was writing to tell Doughty this on Christmas Day, 1918, before he had written a word of it. The best way to make a demand for a book is to make it practically impossible to get. Rumours of the rare and marvellous typography of *Seven Pillars* and of its heroic prose haunted the literary world. Those who had been privileged to subscribe £30 for a copy implied that a second *Odyssey*, or at least a second *Arabia Deserta*, had come into existence. Lawrence played it cool to his genuine literary friends. While knowing full well that it was mannered to an almost Old Testament degree he could describe it to Bernard Shaw as 'Daily Mailish' and to Edward Garnett as 'no good'. *Seven Pillars*, like its author, has had to suffer a grubby backwash of reaction. From being grossly over-praised it has become vulgarly belittled. Like Byron's *Childe Harold*, it hasn't the isolated integrity which allows a work of art to exist in its own right. It has to be seen as a part of Lawrence and seen thus it has a compelling interest. The Arabian-Augustan style was a literary disease to which Anglo-Arabians were prone. The elaborate, oblique and subtle vernacular of the East suited Lawrence perfectly. He enjoyed the guile and compliments, the poetry and the picturesqueness. But long before he was to crouch in the tents of the sons of the Sherif of Mecca Lawrence had learnt the value of polished words. They kept people at their distance and he had a horror of propinquity—'The difficulty is to keep oneself untouched in a crowd.' Even as a castle-exploring, brass-rubbing boy of sixteen he had learnt that he could keep his mother's natural demonstrative affection at bay by erecting a cold wall of archaeological description in his letters to her. Occasionally remorse overcame him and he would add 'Love, love, love, love, love' as he signed off yet another fat epistle about buttresses and jambs. In 1917 he had written to her from Akaba, 'Do you know I have not written a private letter to anyone but you for over a year? It is a wonderful thing to have kept so free of everything. Here I am at thirty with no label and profession—and perfectly quiet.' To stay unlabelled, to confess all and yet to give nothing away which the common herd could appreciate—how could that be done? By writing, not a mere book, but by adding to Literature itself.

In a curious way Lawrence was successful in his venture. He elevated desert raids to solemn baroque set-pieces of military adventure. He made train-wrecking sound like armour-sparkling forays during the Crusades. He lavished all his very considerable descriptive skill on the tribesmen, so that the book is encrusted with their beauty and cruelty. His references to landscape, to camels, to weather and to anything in the sphere of local colour are exalted and grandiloquent, and he spins out every name of person and place with a similar regard to the flourishing music they make as did Proust when he boosted the raddled flesh of Charlus by trumpeting the Baron's ravishing titles. Those who did not entirely succumb to the Lawrence of Arabia magic found this name-stuffed prose too much for them and likened it to the 'begat' bits of the Bible.

The glamorous Lowell Thomas publicity and the discreet fame of a literary masterpiece found Lawrence at the beginning of the twenties in an heroic vacuum which only some ethereal hero like Baldur or Lancelot could fill. All kinds of people did their level best to help him struggle out of his foggy mythology. Geoffrey Dawson, the Editor of *The Times*, secured him a fellowship at All Souls, the idea being that now the war was over Lawrence might resume those archaeological studies about which the world had heard so much. But All Souls was in Oxford and Oxford contained the Lawrence home, with its profoundly unsympathetic associations. Lawrence accepted the Fellowship, while knowing full well that no work, no new life existed for him in Oxford, nor ever could.

Winston Churchill then made him his political adviser in the Middle East and the Press hummed with prospective governorships. Publishers wrote to him and offered him jobs of all kinds. In 1927 Colonel Isham, who had bought the fascinating cache of Boswell Papers discovered at Malahide Castle, and who was saddened by the messiness of Lawrence's life, wrote and invited him to edit the rich haul, now in process of being issued in meticulous order by Professor Pottle of Yale University.

Stories about Lawrence grew and grew, capping each other in their extravagance. A generation which had been pushed around by authority took to this do-it-yourself lone adventurer. The apparent sexlessness of his life and the limbo into which he had so modestly cast himself turned him into a vessel for conjecture and dreams. His slight build and fairness allied to fables of his strength and endurance, plus the fact that he looked years younger than he was, all contributed towards an image of him as the real thing, as against the celluloid sheiks of the cinema. Nothing became impossible or improbable when it was found to be related to Lawrence of Arabia.

Lawrence complained of persecution but Bernard Shaw was sharp with him. 'You didn't keep quiet; and now Lawrence you will be to the end . . . Lawrence may be as great a nuisance to you as G.B.S. is to me . . . but you created him and must now put up with him as best you can.'

Lawrence complained again, this time, oddly enough, about the miseries of barrack-room life at Uxbridge. This forced from Bernard Shaw, 'You talk about leave as if it were a difficulty. Ask for three months' leave and they will exclaim, with a sob of relief, "For God's sake take six, take twelve, take a lifetime, take anything rather than keep up this maddening masquerade that makes us all ridiculous." I sympathize with them.'

But of course to everything which Lawrence said, did or wrote there was also its comfortingly complex reversal and, at the same time as he was complaining to Shaw, he was writing in the day-book which was to become *The Mint*, 'And me? I had shrunk into a ball and squatted, hands over face, crying babily (the first time for years) on one corner of the skudding lorry. . . . I was trying to think, if I was happy, why I was happy, and what was this overwhelming sense upon me of having got home, at last, after an interminable journey.'

Home was to be brief. In less than four months the newspapers rang with the enchantment of having discovered the secret of 352087 A/C Ross. Reporters from the *Daily Mail* and the *Daily Express* swooped down on Uxbridge. Robert Graves said that an officer at the Depot had sold Ross's secret to the Press for £30, a properly

Judas-like sum. Certainly on December 27th, 1922, the *Daily Express* had a field day, for its pages were glutted with its scoop.

UNCROWNED KING AS PRIVATE SOLDIER
LAWRENCE OF ARABIA : FAMOUS WAR HERO BECOMES
A PRIVATE SEEKING PEACE, etc.

The publicity was all the excuse the Royal Air Force needed to rid itself of its distinguished rooky and to his very real distress Lawrence was discharged from the service. A few weeks later he turned up in the Tank Corps—another recent creation—under the name of T. E. Shaw. He was terribly unhappy and shortly after this enlistment he wrote to Edward Garnett threatening suicide if he was not soon reinstated in the Air Force.

'Trenchard withdrew his objection to my rejoining the Air Force. I got seventh heaven for two weeks; but then Sam Hoare came back from Mespot and refused to entertain the idea. . . . I'm no bloody good on earth. So now I'm going to quit, but in my usual comic pattern I'm going to square with Cape before I hop it! . . . I shall bequeath you my notes on life in the recruits camp of the R.A.F. They will disappoint you.'

Garnett was so alarmed when he got this letter that he immediately wrote to Bernard Shaw, who in turn got in touch with Stanley Baldwin in Downing Street. The suicide threat was made on June 13th, 1925. On July 16th, Lawrence's transfer from the hated Tank Corps to the beloved Air Force was signed by the Chief of Air Staff. Lawrence was ecstatic. 'My sense is of something ineffable,' he wrote to Garnett, 'like ship *Argo* when Jason at last drew her up upon the beach; surely nothing but time and physical decay will uproot me now.'

He was posted to Bovington Camp in Dorset and shortly afterwards he bought Clouds Hill, a remote cottage not far from the camp, where he could keep his books and write in his spare time. He was now vaguely and subconsciously 'adopting' the Shaws. Charlotte Shaw, a charming and interesting woman who seems to have possessed a built-in genius for comprehending the connection between aggressive behaviour and low sexual feeling in men, had a very great appeal for Lawrence. He leaned on her a little, finding her stable and docile and quietly loyal. Their relationship was a remote mother-son affair and his assumption of the name Shaw, plus the fog of romance which by this time was beginning to hide any reality he possessed, led many people to believe that he was literally Bernard Shaw's son, a notion which flattered both of them. His father had died in 1919, a necessarily vague shade, and by letting such rumours settle he did no great harm and helped to keep facts cloudy. Although Bernard Shaw himself and nearly all Lawrence's friends were certain that he had taken the name Shaw because of the close relationship which had sprung up between these two Irish outsiders, Lawrence was to write to Ralph Isham in November, 1927, with a very different tale. 'I chose Shaw at random. The recruiting Staff Officer in the War Office said I must take a fresh name. I said, "What's yours?" He said, "No you don't." So I seized the Army List and snapped it open at the index and said, 'It'll be the first one-syllable name in this."

The getting rid of his rank and decorations had been a very different matter. Lawrence threw them away, certainly, but with the fine carelessness of one who would want to know where to look for them when he needed them. It was the Rossetti gesture. Aircraftsman Ross and Shaw never hesitated to exhume the unquiet corpse of Lawrence of Arabia, to strip from it some influential ornament when an ordinary cap-badge wouldn't do. A prince turned monk turns his back on privilege. He doesn't correspond with the hierarchy behind his abbot's back. It is the frequent invocation of the powerful, all-doors-opening Lawrence which makes any close study of A/C Shaw's progress such an unattractive business. His dead past was the breath of life to Lawrence. He knew when they ordered him to clean out grates in the mess or sweep floors they were ordering a very distinguished man to do these humble chores. Every such request, meaningless in ordinary circumstances, carried with it a strange emotion for Lawrence the masochist and could, if he had it in his nature, awaken a desire to humiliate in the person giving the order. All through his twelve years of ranker's life he never ceased to enjoy the practical joke aspects of his position. David Garnett says that 'Being in the ranks gave Lawrence unbounded opportunities for indulgence in his special brand of humour. Though he might be driven by conscience, or by an abnormal readiness to make himself suffer, he never lost his sense of humour. Life in the ranks was for a large part of the time a secret joke, by which he kept himself in a rich state of amusement at the expense of his officers and sergeants.'

This was inverted snobbery and the fact that he could revel in the changes to be rung on such a situation for so long is one of the clearest indications of his immaturity.

The officers, for their part, were nervous of him and tended to keep out of his way. Writing to one of his brothers from Karachi, Lawrence describes the isolation of his life. '. . . I never go out. So only the airmen know of my existence, and they are too used to me, as a daily object, to be interested in a reputation which comes to them as a faint echo from the London papers. . . . I am not bothered by anybody at all. The officers steer clear of me because I make them feel uncomfortable.'

The Press played up this loneliness, this stoic withdrawal from the world, this abnegation of the world's rewards and tributes, with the result that the Karachi Post Office became inundated with parcels and letters. Lawrence refused to accept mail from anyone except friends and no parcels or registered letters addressed to him were even brought up to the camp. During this period, 1927, there are indications in his writing that Shaw was sincerely craving the solitude that Lawrence denied him. But while one side of him could truthfully say, 'I am afraid of causing more talk,' his exhibitionism refused to submit to conditions which could have made 'more talk' less inevitable. As the twenties drew to their close he began to fret about what would happen to him when his enlistment period was over and in a letter to E. M. Forster he said that he had the promise of a night watchman's job in a City bank.

Early in 1929 the Press exploded into one of those orgasms of conjecture which can afflict it when the object of its attentions teases it beyond endurance. Lawrence was translating Homer at Miranshaw and was relatively at peace. So at peace was he that he could afford to break the taboo of his birth by telling a friend that his translation might quite truthfully be called 'Chapman's Homer'. But ever since the July of 1928, when the New York *World* accepted a story headed,

Colonel Lawrence's Mysterious Mission
New Air Force Corporal's Long Trek Through the Far East

a great cumuli of rumours had been building up and when, in December, the *Daily News* reported that Lawrence was learning Pushtu and that 'It is inferred that he intends to move into Afghanistan', the storm burst. Was Lawrence going to organize Right-wing elements in Afghanistan and fight King Amanullah's social reforms? the *Daily Herald* wanted to know. Calling Lawrence 'the arch-spy of the world', the *Daily Herald* went from strength to strength. All this was too much for the Government of India and on January 8th the indignant Homeric scholar was hustled out of Miranshaw and flown to Lahore. Four days later he was sailing to Tilbury on the S.S. *Rajputana* with orders not to speak to anybody. He arrived home to uproar in the papers and to questions in Parliament about his identity. The *Daily News* was fed-up with the whole elaborate business.

GREAT MYSTERY OF COLONEL LAWRENCE
SIMPLE AIRCRAFTSMAN OR WHAT?
TIME THE TRUTH WAS KNOWN
THE ARCH-SPY, etc.

The noisy homecoming was to have an unexpectedly quiet and peaceful sequel. Lawrence was smuggled ashore from the *Rajputana* at Plymouth and hurried off to a flying-boat squadron at Cattewater, where, as clerk to Wing Commander Sydney Smith, he was to find something approaching contentment. Ernest Thurtle, the M.P. who had asked all the frightening questions in the House about Lawrence's name-changes, succumbed to the spell of the enchanter when they met and became Lawrence's friend. Five years remained of the enlistment period, five years in which he could safely go on tangling the double threads of his existence, enjoy deepening friendships in the Bloomsbury of Keynes, Garnett and Forster, speed along the Dorset lanes on the Brough motor cycle the Shaws had given him and entertain simple R.A.F. companions to cocoa and Beethoven at Clouds Hill.

And then? A second abyss, such as that which cut the ground from beneath his feet after Arabia? Apparently not, merely the classic withdrawal to the cottage of the middle-aged literary bachelor. A Georgian solution to the puzzle of life. For Lawrence the situation was one of full-circle. At sixteen he had cut himself off from much of the activities of 2 Polstead Road, Oxford, by retreating to a garden-shed den papered with brass-rubbings of knights and ladies, or by bicycling off for weeks at a time with just enough money to exist on. At forty-seven the retreat equipment was almost identical, a den (Clouds Hill was spectacularly uncomfortable in the conventional sense, a kind of boy's hide-out with makeshift sleeping and cooking arrangements; a cottage imitating a tent) a motor cycle and £2 a week.

On April 5th, 1935, Lawrence wrote to H. S. Ede, 'I have no dependants, no sense of public spirit, or of duty to my neighbour. I like to live alone for 80% of my days, and to be let alone by 80% of my fellow-men and all my fellow-women below 60 years of age. The golden rule seems to direct me to live peacefully in my cottage.'

And so perhaps he would have done, for the tenuous, abnormally protracted youthfulness had slipped away at last and with it much of the glitter and poise. Lawrence was one of those men who think and look and feel like twenty-five until they are almost fifty. His end was timely, if only because his was the type to whom maturity is never granted. Had he lived it would have been a kind of agony for him to see the R.A.F. during the Battle of Britain claim the poetic greatness he had prophesied, and not be part of it. He would have been fifty-two and the Spitfire pilots 'putting out their hands to touch the face of God' would have been more like twenty-two. It would have been galling for him. Professional heroes are not charitable. They leave the stage as reluctantly as ageing divas. Saki's Reginald said, 'To have reached thirty is to have failed in life' and in a sense it was true of Lawrence. He had made his way by charm, derring-do, physical courage, narcissism and romantic cheek—the whole armoury of youth. Those who fall for these things fall for them unconditionally. His plunge into the R.A.F. at thirty-four was partly an Ayesha-like gesture to recapture youth by submitting to the flames of this most youthful of services. At forty he could tell E. M. Forster, 'Do not take my illnesses seriously. They are only dispositions: and may be partly due to my refusal to see that I am too old to lead a boy's life much longer. They do not allow, in the Services, for grown-ups. . . .'

His looks were subtly changing. The first full description of him was made by M. O. Williams in 1913 when he was digging at Carchemish. '. . . a clean-cut blond with peaches and cream complexion, which the dry heat of the Euphrates seems powerless to spoil . . . wearing a wide-brimmed panama, a soft white shirt open at the throat, an Oxford blazer bearing the Magdalen emblem on the pocket, short white flannel knickers partly obscured by a decoration hanging from the belt, which did not, however obscure bare knees, below which he wore heavy grey hose and red slippers.'

The only reason why this exact description should be recalled is that it was written when Lawrence was a nobody and is indicative of how people were already compelled into extravagance when they met him. Another visitor to Carchemish, an American called L. R. Fowle, also felt it his duty to leave something for the record.

'Lawrence, also fresh from the works, was stepping lightly across mounds of earth, clad in what we Americans would call a running suit, and wearing at his belt an oranted Arab girdle with its bunch of tassels in front to denote an unmarried man. He was out of sight in a moment, and when we gathered for supper a freshly tubbed young man in his Oxford tennis suit of white flannel, but still wearing his Arab girdle, launched into a fascinating study of the excavations.'

Lawrence preserved and managed to project this mint, virginal image of himself for an astonishingly long time. He had the total self-absorption of the dandy. He was as jealous of his person as most people are of the person they love. When his most private and fastidious body was flogged and raped at Deraa, he experienced the kind of agony another man might feel if he had been forced to witness the outrage of his wife. Yet Deraa was also a moment of enlightenment. Pain, which had been 'my obsession and secret terror, from a boy', had proved to be a terrible joy. He was defiled, disfigured and he was to 'carry the burden, whose certainty the passing days confirmed': how in Deraa 'that night the citadel of my integrity had been irrevocably lost', but he had found a very important part of himself—his masochism. 'If that Deraa incident had happened to you,' he told Edward Garnett, 'you would not have recorded it . . . the sort of man I mix with doesn't so give himself away.'

As he grew older he made a virtue of the warts-and-all kind of candour and told James Hanley, 'People with dirty patches in them skirt round and round them, alluding but never speaking out. They are afraid of giving their spots away.' Lawrence seems to have realized how greatly he lacked normal reticence and his habit of neither confirming nor denying so many of the wild tales which floated around him like an outsize banner was probably deliberate. He not only confused the world, he confused himself, and that, he found, was a comfort. Although he was far from innocent about the conjectures of Freud and moved in literary circles in which Freudian ethics were used as the basis for poetry and novels, he wrote with the rather alarming pre-Freud freedom of a Francis Kilvert.

The 'spot' which he so recklessly gave away, and which always brings his biographers up with a jolt of yea or nay, was quite obviously to do with his feelings for men. Was he or wasn't he, that is the question. The one thing he certainly wasn't was heterosexual. Women scared him. A bawdy tumble by a well when some Arab women tried to strip him to see if he was white all over left him frightened in a way the Deraa incident could never have done. Except for the beloved Dahoum, an Arab youth he brought back to Oxford and to whom he possibly dedicated *Seven Pillars of Wisdom*, and the outrage at Deraa, he was probably chaste, though not so much because of any moral reason but because he was selfish. He was too obsessively engrossed in himself to give himself in love and too remindful of what the 'filthy business' of sex could lead to—the traumatic distress of his own origins—to have any taste for promiscuity.

'I am a very normal sort of Anglo-Irishman,' he told Ernest Thurtle. 'Women? I like some women. I don't like their sex; any more than I like the monstrous regiment of men. Some men. There is no difference that I can feel between a woman and a man. . . . I can't understand all the fuss about sex. . . .'

What did this mean exactly? That men and women are the same? Obviously not. That he feels nothing abnormal if what attracts his feelings should happen to be male—that it is 'all the same', mere sexual attraction and something not to be pursued? Possibly. But the rich ambivalence, as usual, provides two answers to every question. He was far from ambivalent towards the mysterious S.A. of *Seven Pillars* dedication. Dahoum means darkness and was the nickname of a very handsome youth called Sheik Achmed. The boy died of typhus in Syria in 1918. There is little hedging in Lawrence's many references to him and there is little doubt that he loved him. The dedicatory prose-poem which prefaces *Seven Pillars* has all the convincing badness, literarily speaking, of a genuine love-letter.

> *I loved you, so I drew these tides of men into my hands*
> *and wrote my will across the sky in stars*
> *To earn your freedom, the seven pillared worthy house,*
> *that your eyes might be shining for me*
> *When we came.*

Death seemed my servant on the road, till we were near
   and saw you waiting;
When you smiled, and in sorrowful envy he outran me
   and took you apart:
      Into his quietness.

Love, the way-weary, groped to your body, our brief wage
   ours for the moment
Before earth's soft hand explored your shape, and the blind
   worms grew fat upon
      Your substance.

Men prayed me that I set our work, the inviolate house,
   as a memory of you.
But for fit monument I shattered it, unfinished: and now
The little things creep out to patch themselves hovels
   in the marred shadow
      Of your gift.

Lawrence's dandyism was not necessarily an aspect of his homo-sexuality, as some of his critics maintain. Lawrence lived when to be a gentleman was to be meticulously drab. The short-back-and-sides brigade used this drabness as a virility symbol and 'suspected' any man who departed from it. Lawrence's long fair hair and sumptuous robes were used as a protection from this kind of man. They put him beyond the pale, which is where he liked to be. He had something in common with the young Arab warriors with whom he surrounded himself who spent hours dressing their hair and scenting their bodies but who fought with tenacious brilliance. The Persians had mocked when the Theban Band had beautified itself for battle. Lawrence's behaviour in Arabia is filled with examples of how to put a late-Victorian classical education into practice.

The obsession with clothes continued when he joined the Royal Air Force. But now it had descended to something less innocent than gallantry.

'These boys, in fancy dress for the first time, went stroking and smoothing their thighs, to make the wings of the breeches stand out richly. The tailors had taken them in at the knees, by our secret request, so tightly that they gripped the flesh and had a riding cut.

Dandies put a wire in the outer seams to spread them more tautly sideways. . . . These clothes are too tight. At every pace they catch us in a dozen joints of the body, and remind us of it. The harsh friction of the cloth polishes our skins and signals to our carnality the flexure of each developing muscle and sinew. . . .'

The first half of the thirties decade passed with rumours massing, cracking and coming to nothing. A new chill was in the air, which some people welcomed as a break-through to the brave new world and others slowly recognized as political obscenity. In Europe it was 'follow my leader'. The British Union of Fascists saw in the recluse of Clouds Hill a leader waiting his hour, such as pre-war Churchill at Chartwell and post-war de Gaulle at Colombey-les-deux-églises. They saw his enormous emotional value to the movement and in a sense his respectability. If they won him they would have a first-rate popular hero. In May 1935 there was speculative talk about a meeting between Lawrence and Hitler. On May 13th Lawrence went off on his motor cycle to send a telegram to Henry Williamson asking him to lunch—'Lunch Tuesday wet fine cottage one mile north Bovington Camp—SHAW.' He rode back very fast and coming over the crest of the hill he had to swerve violently in order to miss hitting two errand boys on bicycles. He was thrown over his handlebars and terribly injured. He died five days later.

Immediately, a great cry went up. Was it an accident? A Corporal Catchpole, who was near, heard the crash and insisted that he had seen a black private car going towards the speeding Lawrence just before the accident happened. The errand boys did not see the car. Was it suicide? Most unlikely. A man with Lawrence's knowledge of wounds and death would not have sought oblivion so haphazardly. It was a youthful, even a boyish way to die. Would he have died very differently, in a moral desert and as an internee detained under M.I.5? It is hardly likely. For one thing there was still the friendship of Forster, Garnett, Storrs, Churchill. Besides, as he wrote to Lady Astor at Cliveden,

'No: wild mares would not at present take me from Clouds Hill. It is an earthly paradise and I am staying here until I feel qualified for it. Also there is something broken in the works, as I told you: my will, I think. In this mood I would not take on any job at all. So do not commit yourself to advocating me, lest I prove a non-starter.

'Am well, well-fed, full of company, laborious and innocent-customed. . . . TES.'

That was the key to it, perhaps—'innocent-customed'. He was pushing fifty and contact with Fascism would be another Deraa, with dirty hands all over him. 'The difficulty is to keep oneself untouched in a crowd: so many people try to speak to you or touch you: and you're like electricity, in that one touch discharges all the virtue you have stored up.' And so it was the act of avoidance until the very end, when the Dorset lane crushed him. *Requiescat*, concludes Aldington. To which now may be surely added for the benefit of yet further prospective biogaphers, his own plaintive *Noli me tangere*.

CHAPTER FIVE

Miss Amy Johnson

'And a handsome old lady, dressed from head to foot in the
smartest flying kit of black leather, advanced to meet the
astounded party. Her hands were stretched out in welcome.
" 'Tes Aunt Ada! 'Tes Aunt Ada Doom!"
"Goodness . . . It's nothing but people going off in aeroplanes," said Flora, rather crossly.
. . . She smiled up at Elfine's lovely little face framed by the
black flying-cap, and Elfine blew her a tender kiss. The roar
of the engines swelled to a triumphant thunder. They were
gone!'

Cold Comfort Farm, BY STELLA GIBBONS, 1932

HER name tunes in her era. She scrawled it brashly and bravely
across the thirties sky—her blue heaven—Amy Johnson. The dole
queues lifting up their eyes unto the hills, since they had given up
all hope of lifting them in any other direction, saw her just missing
them. She crackled over continents like a rather chic seraphim in her
soft leather helmet, enormous astrakhan collar, khaki shorts, puttees
and gauntlet gloves. She was true-blue and 'a brick'. She had a
pretty, heart-shaped face with a fresh clear skin, eyes stretched wide
by tremendous horizons, dreamily plucked eyebrows, a slightly hard,
gamin little mouth, neat useful hands like a mechanic and an accent
which Beverley Nichols described as 'pure Wapping' but which was
in fact impure Yorkshire. Her entrance and her exit were as perfectly timed as anything invented by Ethel M. Dell. On May 5th,
1930, she put the cover on her typewriter in a solicitor's office,
locked up her bed-sitter in Maida Vale and went to Croydon Aerodrome. There were no crowds, only her father and a few chaps from
the London Aeroplane Club, where she had learned to fly. Her father
called her Amy and the chaps called her Johnnie, which is what she
preferred. The aeroplane was called *Jason* after the trademark of her
father's fish business at Hull. At 7.45 that morning she left the

ground and for the remainder of her brief story-book life she never quite managed to return to it.

It took 1940 to bring her to earth. 'A brave, naïve, *déracinée*,' said Lord Vansittart, 'she came to my room in the Foreign Office eager for some dangerous mission in Secret Service, eager above all to die for Britain. . . . She found the means but not the end. I wished that I could have helped her. . . .'

Eventually Amy joined the Air Transport Auxiliary as a ferry pilot. For a few months it looked as if the *Girls' Own Paper* heroine was lined up for another decade of dazzling adventures in which she would beat the Luftwaffe single-handed. After all, she had faced great hazards before—the Timor Sea, the *Daily Mail*'s patronage, the Arabian Desert and her marriage to Jim Mollison, so why should she hesitate now? She did her bit, though in a silence and anonymity which was frightening after ten years of jolly noises winging up to her from a hundred asphalt aerodromes from Heston to Calcutta. And the silence was scarcely broken when she crashed on a bitter January day in 1941. In December, 1943, her death was presumed by the Probate Court and when her name appeared in the flimsy wartime papers it seemed to possess little more substance than an evocative number from a Jack Buchanan musical. It was the price she paid for being the sublimation symbol of a nation's light romance. It wasn't brightness which fell from the air; it was only poor old Johnnie, the girl next door.

Amy was born in Hull in 1903. Her grandfather was a Dane who at the age of sixteen had sailed away from Denmark all on his own to seek his fortune in England. His name was Anders Jorgensen and when he settled in Yorkshire he anglicized it to Anders Johnson. The sixteen-year-old Danish adventurer and her grandfather Johnson were never fully integrated in Amy's mind. They both undoubtedly belonged to her but they didn't seem to belong to each other. The boy Jorgensen was continually urging her to run away and find a fairy kingdom, while grandfather Johnson insisted that she should settle down in the ugly house in the ugly Hull side-road and tot up the fish profits. These conflicting influences converged on the teenage Amy as the war ended and the twenties began their frenetic progress. But like nearly all young people of the period she could only express her spirit and rebelliousness in surface antics round the gramophone. If she jumped further than this she would land in the dreaded economic mess of the times. The meanest office or shop job was scarce and it was nothing to write twenty applications before one succeeded. Lower middle-class people—the class to which Amy belonged—were particularly canny when it came to taking an action which might jeopardize or dislodge even a fragment of their precious 'security' and any individual in a family who showed signs of instability where an honest job was concerned could cause quite a disproportionate amount of neurotic bickering and worry.

Presumably Amy began to not fit in as soon as she could walk and talk, for at the age of three she trotted up the dreary Hull street announcing to the neighbours, 'I'se run away to be a queen.' It was her first memory. It was not surprising that it should have been connected with running away for this was to be, curiously, the recurring motif of her whole life. She had almost no need for courage in the sense in which it was popularly attributed to her. It was always easier for her to go off into the unknown, be it jobs, digs or deserts, than to face the uncongenial certainties of life. Her intense conviction that these were not for her, that she was an exception to the rule and in a sense 'privileged' began to make itself felt in earliest childhood. She had the same driving egotism of the writer, painter or actress but none of their outlets for it. Her actions and her attitude seemed inexcusably conceited to others, though not to herself, for from the very first time she began to notice them she successfully coated the ordinary irritants of life with solid romance, so that what the world saw and what *she* saw rarely had the vaguest connection. Before she became a flyer the chief reason for the trail of fractured friendships and false starts which followed her everywhere was that she was already absorbed and even dazzled by something very special in her nature which nobody else had the least reason to believe existed. Given the gift to see herself as others saw her, Amy would have been blankly incredulous, and had some early psychologist managed to divest her of her emotional finery it is doubtful if she would ever have got off the ground, so to speak.

She was taken to and then abruptly taken away from a number of little private schools. The schoolma'ams and the fish merchant's pretty daughter faced each other in mutual incomprehension which quickly developed into mutual disgust. When it became obvious that the teacher and the class were not going to acknowledge her royalty Amy would do things to draw attention to it. 'Headstrong, and

probably spoilt, with an insatiable desire to know everything, I seem
to have pushed my way through each school in turn, enlivening the
hours spent amongst girls twice and three times my age by pranks of
incredible foolishness. It was, perhaps, my tomboy spirit which
saved me from the danger of becoming a blue-stocking. I brought
homework home with me for the sheer love of doing it. I learned a
queer mixture of elementary and advanced subjects. . . .' The
cleverness and the bossiness combined were not appealing. The truth
would dawn on Amy, there would be ructions and then a clean
break and a fresh start somewhere else.

When she was eleven she was sent to the Boulevard Secondary
School, Hull, a co-educational place where for a while she was
startlingly happy. She associated more with the boys than with the
girls and was the only girl in the school who could bowl over-arm.
She spent hours and hours in the gymnasium, where the trapeze
fascinated her. In the evenings there was more trapezing at the
Young People's Institute. She led rebellions against what she believed to be injustices which in turn led to, what was for Amy, a
particularly terrifying form of revenge.

'Punishments at our school were meted out on a most peculiar
system, reminiscent to some slight extent of the methods of the
police in modern Russia when dealing with political prisoners. . . .
To prevent them appearing as heroes, or even being allowed to face
death with any semblance of heroic dignity, they are shot in their
underclothes. Nothing of this kind exactly happened at school, but
the method of punishment seemed specially calculated to strip one
of all the trappings of a heroine. . . .'

She now began to take great care to preserve these 'trappings',
and for the only time in her life. Later, she was simply to walk away
from any situation which refused to allow for her natural superiority
without her doing anything to force people to realize that she
possessed it. But at the Boulevard Secondary she went out of her
way to impress the boys and she might have continued to do so had
it not been for one of those trivial mishaps which in retrospect are
seen to have so much to do with destiny. A cricket ball broke one of
Amy's front teeth, establishing a lisp. When the boys heard this lisp
their eyes were opened and Amy was dropped. To make up for the
way in which she had almost convinced them that she was one of
themselves, they mocked her. And, of course, Amy ran away.

Photo: Radio Times Hulton Picture Library

Sir John Reith—the Judge of What We Ought to Want—at the National
Conference of Wireless Group Leaders, January 2nd, 1932.

Amy—'Call me Johnnie'—sets off for South Africa,
November 8th, 1932.

Jim Mollison after his record Atlantic flight, October 30th,
1936.

Sometimes she ran away from home and had to be brought back to the Johnsons, who were becoming increasingly bewildered by her. Sometimes she escaped on a bicycle, pedalling long distances through the Yorkshire countryside and hugging her dreams to herself in a delicious orgy of self-pity. She was already beginning to realize that it was better to travel than to arrive. A journey was always the most exquisite form of unreality and while it was taking place the absurd romantic platitudes which served Amy as a philosophy even during very real dangers could not be challenged. If her talents had been literary and her convictions plotted she could have made a fortune in the Ruby M. Ayres market. She could tell Lady Oxford, 'I tend to look at life through rose-coloured glasses. I always see the light before the shade, the good before the bad and I expect a happy ending. Disillusionment has been hard and bitter, but it has never been complete, for the habit formed in childhood always in the end transforms the toad . . . into a prince.'

There was an aeroplane factory on the outskirts of Hull and Amy often bicycled to it in the part-hope, part-dread that she might see an aeroplane close to. At this period she began to half live in the local cinema where the unique *Schwärmerei* of the early silent films suited her mood exactly and if, on the mildly coruscating screen, an aeroplane should pass, she would sit the entire programme round a second time. Her emotions were now those of Wendy who was compelled to soar out of the window and leave the dinginess below, and to leave Mummy and Daddy, too, in spite of the fact that they were Darlings. Only soar where? Amy didn't know. All she knew now was that Jorgensen was in full control.

It was the hey-day of the five-bob flip. The armistice had unloaded a great many ramshackle flying machines and a lot of experienced flyers on to the market. Nobody wanted either. Quite a few young pilots sank their gratuities into war surplus de Havillands and Faireys and entered this extension of the circus business, and thousands of customers had an unforgettable glimpse of the gasworks from a few hundred feet up. Such a plane came to Hull and established itself in a big field outside the town. Amy, aged just seventeen and clutching her birthday money, approached it in a mood of mystical fatalism. She and her sister took off together, she waiting for, and tremblingly prepared for, the supreme experience.

'There was no sensation. Just a lot of noise and wind, smell of

4

burnt oil and escaping petrol. My hair was blown into a tangled mess which could not be combed out for days and I was almost cured of flying for ever.'

The only thing that happened after this anti-climax was that Amy cut off her masses of long, curled hair. It was the most obvious declaration of independence she had so far made and her father met it with suitable harshness. She would stay on at the secondary school, he said, until it had all grown again. This meant that she was at a secondary school until she was nineteen, enjoying a position of false privilege in the upper sixth and becoming such a big fish in her little pond that the disasters she met with at Sheffield University were inevitable.

In the first place, in spite of all this extra schooling, she fluffed the ordinary entrance and was only allowed a place through the kindness of the dean, who said she could take Economics or Logic. She chose Economics. The second shock was to discover that nobody liked her. She tried to make friends but barely succeeded in making acquaintances. She shared her rooms with other girls and was nonplussed when they ignored her 'specialness' and furious when they swept aside her natural leadership. 'Within a few short weeks I had decided to run a lone course, so I gave in my notice and chose other lodgings. . . . I changed again and again and again. In my three years at Sheffield I changed probably thirty times.' Eventually, of course, she ran away. She rented a remote and beetle-ridden cottage in the Peak District and she only came to Sheffield when she absolutely had to. She got into debt—£50, a huge sum for her—and she had to forego her fourth year at the university in order to get a job and repay it. She worked in a Hull advertising agency, where the other typists laughed at her B.A. degree and her pretensions. She was so unhappy in this job that she left it the very same day as she paid back the last pound of her debt. Her egotism and all the normal pleasant poise of youth were now severely lacerated and her father made a great effort to interpret her problem. The restlessness was strange but not so strange as all that—after all, *his* father had been Jorgensen and he had a brother who had gone off to Klondyke. So he offered to pay Amy's fare to Canada, that Siberia or Shangri-la of all English misfits at the time. The offer tempted Amy but something told her that running away and being paid to go away were two very different things, so she refused it. Instead, she fled to London.

It was the first time she had been away from the North and she was bewildered. She was quite alone. Work was almost non-existent. She wandered in and out of bed-sitters and 25s.-a-week jobs, as well as in and out of a whole series of forced little friendships. She worked in a West End draper's which cashed in smartly on the slump by advertising that it only employed shop assistants who held degrees or who were gentlefolk. Amy as a B.A. was allowed to pack up the ribbon boxes when the customer had left. She stuck the vulgar dreariness of this for a month and then she became ill. Then came what she would have called—for she never used an original phrase where a cliché would do—the first glimpse of a silver lining. A distant cousin introduced her to a solicitor, who gave her a job at £3 a week. Immediately after this she met an ex-Sheffield University girl who accepted Amy's conditions for friendship and who trailed after her from digs to digs quite uncomplainingly, like a dog.

One day Amy found a garden room in a huge dull house in Maida Vale and once more they moved. Above the garden, crackling and throbbing all day long, and loathed by the rest of Maida Vale, were aeroplanes. They came from Stag Lane Aerodrome, which was nearby. Amy was transfixed, transported. To her it was as good as living on the direct route to Elysium. 'I longed for the freedom and detachment it seemed they must enjoy. . . . I became more and more absorbed. In some intuitive way I felt that there was a link, as yet to be forged, between the planes flying over that Maida Vale house and myself.'

She wrote, half in fun, to the de Havilland Company asking how much they charged for tuition and was told £5 an hour. As she earned £3 a week and had to live on it this was hopeless. Then, 'One fine Saturday afternoon, drawn irresistibly by those tiny darting planes, I climbed on top of a bus going to Stag Lane. As I drew near the planes came lower and lower until they seemed to be landing almost on my head. . . . Wild with excitement, I jumped off the bus and ran up Stag Lane, to find at the end a notice "London Aeroplane Club, Private". My keenness to explore outweighed my natural shyness and, disregarding the notice, I walked on until the green of the aerodrome itself came into view. Two yellow aeroplanes were lined up ready to fly and caught my interest. There was a small club-house, in front of which people were seated on deck-chairs. No one took the slightest notice of me as I nervously approached an unoccupied chair and sat down. Every minute I expected to be challenged. Nothing happened. For half an hour or so I sat enthralled. . . .' The yellow planes flew away and Amy walked in a trance towards the instructor. 'How much?' she asked. 'Two pounds an hour,' said the instructor. It was thirty shillings an hour solo, three guineas entrance fee, three guineas subscription and it took from between eight to twelve hours to learn. Amy was twenty-five and had a pound in her purse. These figures were the first small investment of the slight sum which was to bring her a tidy fortune and a kind of immortality.

In September, 1928, Amy began her lessons at the London Aeroplane Club. Every minute of her spare time, every ounce of her energy went into them. She had the rapt serenity of all totally committed novitiates. It soon became obvious that she was a natural so far as aeronautics were concerned and that she couldn't have used her wings more easily if she had grown them. She learnt to fly in record time and followed up her aviator's certificate with a ground engineer's licence. But the real triumph of Stag Lane was her unquestioned re-entrance into the acceptance masculine world. The brash, cheerful and informal atmosphere suited her exactly. The mateyness purged away the insolence of offices. She was openly admired, not because she was a pretty girl but because she was a jolly good mechanic. Her hands were oily and her short hair flopped across her brow. As in all communities where there is overdedication and not much sense of proportion, at Stag Lane there was more fun than feeling. Amy was 'Johnnie', a dab hand at maintenance, a wizard with a joystick and a sister where she wasn't an actual chum. She flew the little yellow planes over London, pleased to be where she was, though now faintly and uncomfortably aware that if she stayed there she would be just a fragment of the looping-the-loop individualism of her epoch. If this was all she might as well have crossed the Thames on a tightrope or walked from Land's End to John o' Groats. It had all been too easy and having got so far she was again thrust against the dreaded line of limitation which so far had halted all her ventures. In the past she relied on her over-developed dream equipment to get her past such barriers but now she had to turn fantasies into facts. The trouble here was that countless other people were doing the same thing.

In 1929 the air was full of noises. Aviation was at its amateur zenith. The fashionable and somewhat deliberately non-professional flying of young Edwardians like Moore-Brabazon, the Hon. C. S. Rolls and S. F. Cody had naturally lapsed during the war when it was disciplined by the service conditions of the R.F.C. but no sooner was the armistice signed than it broke out again with an intensity which was spectacular, and which the Press took every care to keep spectacular. On the circus side there were air weddings and air christenings, aerobatics and songs like 'Airman, Airman, don't put the wind up me', and on what might be called the get-there-first side there were long queues of prospective leather-wrapped heroes and heroines, each with a route and a time schedule to which they intended to pin their names for ever.

On May 1st, 1919, civil flying was authorized in Britain and it was in effect the starter's pistol. The first to get off was a flying-boat which crossed from Newfoundland to Devonshire. A month later John Alcock and Arthur Brown flew non-stop across the Atlantic for the very first time, taking just over sixteen hours, and were, to their very slight embarrassment, knighted for doing so. In November of the same year two brothers named Ross and Keith Smith flew a Vickers Vimy from Hounslow to Darwin, taking about a month to do it and weren't knighted. In September, 1922, James Doolittle flew across the United States in a single day and the same year the first King's Cup Air Race was held between Croydon and Glasgow.

From this point the development of flying rushed ahead in a romantic whirl of competitive anarchy. The great thing was to be first. Alan Cobham was the first man to fly to Australia *and back*, so he, too, was knighted. There were first airships over the North Pole, first flights to Cape Town, first wings over Hawaii, over Karachi, Tokyo. The world was so crowded with places that it looked as though it would take ages to use them all up in aeroplane records and that the *Daily Mail*'s £10,000 and King George V's accolade would continue to rustle and fall respectively for many years. But after a while the public itself became bored with the automatic nature of many flying achievements. It was becoming obvious that anyone who could fly, could fly to Timbuctoo, given a certain amount of time and petrol, and although it was brave or even good to do so, it wasn't miraculous. So interest grew in the personalities of the flyers themselves.

The Press were quick to sense this change in public taste and began to blow up the hitherto conventionally bashful airmen to film-star proportions. The personality cult amongst flyers rose suddenly and brilliantly to its glittering climax on May 20th, 1927, when a handsome, humourless American youth called Charles Lindbergh flew solo from Long Island to Paris in a monoplane. Lindbergh's flight and achievement were extraordinary, though scarcely less extraordinary than the behaviour of his country in its greed for a hero. When he returned he was met with a kind of hyperbole with which the Romans kept their emperors sweet. Some people weren't at all certain that he hadn't been deified and there were later indications to show that Lindbergh wasn't absolutely sure on the point himself. Chilly as dead mutton though he was, he loped neatly into the niche made for the All-American Boy and shared with Valentino's ghost and Babe Ruth the patriotic ululation of his native land. It is doubtful if any man in history was ever rewarded as Lindbergh was rewarded for a career which lasted precisely thirty-three hours and twenty-nine minutes.

The effect of Lindbergh on what might be termed 'personal flying' was profound, though unintentionally so. Aviation up to the moment when this lanky young man extricated himself from the cockpit of 'The Spirit of St. Louis' on Le Bourget airfield had been a pleasant, somewhat bumbling business indulged in by noticeably diffident people. Now it became mannered and tense. There was a rush by the newspapers, the *Daily Mail* in particular, to put back all the heroic stuff shrugged off by men like Alcock and Brown, and to keep the 'marvellous' element intact. The results were bathetic. People who very often were performing miracles of courage had their unique deeds vulgarized by the full razzle-dazzle treatment and were pushed into the ranks of silly-season entertainers by reporters and ad men. Presumably Jim Mollison, a temperamental young Scot, was suffering from this when he tried to stem the broohaha surrounding his overwrought person with an autobiography called *Death Cometh Sooner or Late*. As the title suggests, it was Hamlet in goggles but the author, not being a Saint-Exupéry, failed to convince the reviewers, who seemed to have gone out of their way to misunderstand it. 'Mr. Mollison tacitly announces the arrival of a new type of public figure, presumed to have a personal following similar to that which fame has assembled at the skirts of other performers . . .' remarked *The Times* sardonically.

As the twenties drew to a close flying became more and more the preserve of smart rich women who, had they lived a bit earlier, would have been called 'indomitable' from having crossed China in a crinoline, broken windows for Mrs. Pankhurst or raced four-in-hands like Lady Warwick. On May 17th, 1928, Lady Heath made the first female solo flight from the Cape to Croydon and a month later Lady Bailey, the wife of the South African millionaire Sir Abe Bailey, established another 'first' by flying alone to the Cape and back again. Aviation was stylish and had been ever since Vera Butler took off in a balloon called 'The City of York' from the Crystal Palace in 1901, though the first woman to venture into an actual aeroplane was a Mrs. Hart O. Berg, who went up with Wilbur Wright at Le Mans in 1908. The first woman pilot, disconcertingly enough, was the wife of Maurice Hewlett, an inventor of exquisite Arcadian romances which were like jewelled footnotes to *Greensleeves*. Mrs. Hewlett learned to fly at Brooklands in 1911. After the war, thrown dizzily aloft by the same great wave of emancipation which did away with their skirts and breasts and hair, the sky became so full of ladies that their names read like an astral presentation party. Mrs. Dulcibella Atkey, the Hon. Elsie Mackay, Lady Anne Saville, Mrs. Elliot Lynn, Miss O'Brian, the Hon. Mrs. Victor Bruce and the redoubtable old Duchess of Bedford who was sixty—some said seventy—before she ever set foot in an aeroplane. For ten years her Moth raced up through the trees of Woburn while the world and the Russells held their breath. She possessed a rare brand of fatalism which was the combined result of being a country clergyman's daughter, a duke's wife and, for most of her life, a surgeon's assistant in an operating theatre. On a fine March day in 1937 when she was seventy-one—some said eighty-one—she took off in her Moth from Woburn park as usual, zoomed out over the Wash and was never seen again. Evelyn Waugh never succeeded in inventing a character more bizarre or more gallant.

Although flying clubs and aerodromes were springing up everywhere and the Royal Air Force had been created, to the ordinary person aeroplanes and airships still retained an extraordinary glamour. Flyers, looking down over the edge of their machines when they passed over markets or playgrounds, would be met with the massed, faintly rapturous stare of hundreds of uptilted faces, while the whole nation would follow each new record attempt with the same bated interest that it later followed the four-minute mile. It was the grand epoch of 'trophy' flying. There was the Schneider Trophy, the Gordon Bennett Aviation Cup, the Aerial Derby, the Britannia and Segrave Trophies, the King's Cup Race and any number of lesser inter-club events which gave to flying a sporting ethic which was as strong and individual during the thirties as anything emanating from the Turf or the wicket, but which seemed to fade round about the time of Munich, never to flower again.

Such was the scene when Amy, now a fully fledged pilot and mechanic, though still a solicitor's typist, flew into it and seized the astral crown. She had no money, no real leisure—only evenings and week-ends—and, except for a few flips over London and one long ride to Hull and back, no flying experiences to speak of. What she did have, however, were her dreams and her unquestionable belief that the sky was her right, as it were. These assets tended to make her ten-year monopoly of air fame natural and acceptable both to herself and to others. When she was famous her favourite fan communication was a photograph of a huge negro with a cobra round his waist on which was written, 'From Johannes, King of the Snakes to Amy, Queen of the Skies'. It stood on her dressing-table and when she saw it Amy would smile to herself and say, 'Well, I always said I would be a queen.'

In 1930, although air activity was intense, it might almost have not existed so far as she was concerned. She had learned to fly and now all she had to do was to go on and on for ever in the blissful barrierless blue of her kingdom. Below her would float the wonderful red bits of the British Empire, where sometimes she would have to come down and chaps would rush out of the sugar and rubber plantations in neat drill shorts shouting: 'Hurrah! It's Johnnie! Put the kettle on!' Her petrol tank would be like the widow's cruse and when she passed over countries which hadn't the good fortune to be painted red in atlases, sheiks and Indians and cannibals would have second thoughts about their conduct. There would be no more offices, no more bed-sitters. She would run away and run away, and one day she would simply fly through the blue into the Great Unknown where Grace Darling, Nurse Cavell, Boadicea and a whole heaven of heroines would meet her.

Not the least curious thing about Amy was the practical way in which she always set about realizing her fantasies. She treated the attainment of dreams as other people treated applications for jobs. She saw to it that she was fully qualified for the appointment before she put in for it. She pored over maps. Her Yorkshire common-sense told her that she must convince everybody at the very first go if she was to gain her freedom, and this was all she really wanted to gain, not cups, not fame. The shorter routes were by now all bespoke and to try and shorten Amelia Earhart's Atlantic record or Bert Hinkler's African time would not do her any lasting good. The most she could do would be to cross the world. 'I expect,' remarked a guest to the hero of a record flight at the inevitable newspaper luncheon which followed it, 'that you find the world a very small place.' 'On the contrary,' said the airman, 'I am constantly surprised by how enormous it is.' Amy thought hard about the world and finally decided the best thing to do would be to fly right over it. As a pal said to her, 'Well, you've always been a woman of extremes—Australia and all that!' But to Amy 'the sequence of events seemed natural and inevitable' and all she really had to do was to find the means to set them in motion.

She wrote to the Director of Civil Aviation, Sir Sefton Brancker, himself a record-breaker. The letter, oddly enough, wasn't signed but Amy's mountain-moving artlessness impregnated every line of it and Sir Sefton, after tracking her down, introduced her to Lord Wakefield, with the result that he promised to back her. With heaven almost literally in her grasp Amy went off to shop for a second-hand aeroplane. She bought an old green Gipsy Moth from a firm called Air Taxis Ltd. Before it had become a taxi it had belonged to a Captain Wally Hope, who had used it to follow the Prince of Wales during his African tour. Altogether it had done something in the region of 35,000 miles. It was a two-seater but the back seat had been taken out and tanks put in its place, which meant that it could carry seventy-nine gallons of petrol—Lord Wakefield's never-ending supply of petrol. Amy took her aeroplane to Stag Lane and then took it to bits. When she had overhauled every nut and bolt of it with her own useful hands she had a friend paint the word *Jason* on its nose.

All through the winter and spring of 1930 she prepared herself. She studied map-reading and meteorology. She learned ju-jitsu just in case she was forced to come down in some place where men were swine. Her body was spare, lithe and well muscled like a boy's

4*

and now that the great adventure was so near her face had the faintly polished sexless good looks of all true-blue heroines. Her blissful serenity became infectious. Her father came up from Hull and stood about in the May sunshine with the small groups of waiting airmen on the Stag Lane grass while in the distance the Edgware buses rumbled by. On Sunday May 4th she flew *Jason* from Stag Lane to Croydon Aerodrome, solemnly escorted on this little journey by five of the planes she had so recently stared up at from her Maida Vale garden. At a quarter to eight on the Monday morning, with the minimum of fuss and farewells, she took *Jason* up over the Surrey hills and headed for Vienna, where she arrived, looking very neat and tidy, just in time for tea. The clean, confident freshness of this 800-mile flight settled any faint remaining doubts her friends and backers had, while her 'ordinariness' after the surfeit of airborne ladies was immediately recognized by the popular Press, which lost no time in exploiting it.

Amy knew nothing of this at first. She woke up at the Aspern aerodrome on the outskirts of Vienna with a full heart and brimming tanks, and flew off in *Jason* to Constantinople, again arriving on the dot of 5.15. She travelled at a height somewhere between 3,000 and 5,000 feet and for twelve hours at a stretch. Her entire food consisted of a packet of sandwiches and a thermos of tea. As at Vienna, she spent from three to four hours overhauling *Jason* before turning in for the night. Between Aleppo and Baghdad she ran into a sandstorm and had to come down in the desert for two hours, where she braced herself for the unpleasant possibility of passing sheiks. The next 1,600 miles to Karachi were lapped up with superb self-confidence and when Amy landed in India it was to find that she had beaten Bert Hinkler's record by two whole days and that she was famous. She was garlanded and received by the Chief Officer of the Karachi Municipality and the next morning she was escorted for some miles by an R.A.F. plane and by a Moth flown by the local de Havilland agent.

Amy was neither overwhelmed nor surprised by these favours; they were all part of the dream. It seemed quite natural that a certain amount of protocol should surround her arrivals and departures, for she had never doubted, not even during her dog days in the mean bed-sitters, that she was a very special person. She had flown 4,140 miles in six days by herself in a little second-hand machine. It was brave, epic, glorious—all the things the world was busy saying it was—yet in what way was it unique among all the record-breaking which had been going on for the past ten years? At the very moment when Amy was leaving Baghdad an Indian pilot was taking off from Karachi for London with the Aga Khan's prize carrot of £500 to spur him on. So why should her flight in particular have caught the imagination of mankind, pushed all the rest of the news into small type, monopolized conversation and set reception committees in action wherever she touched down? The answer must remain hypothetical.

In the first place she was not so much an amateur flyer as a professional heroine. She had a brilliant and intuitive understanding of her rôle and played it, for as long as the world allowed her to play it, faultlessly. In the second place, aviation during the whole of the twenties had necessarily been a rich man's sport and was associated in the depressed proletarian mind with 'them'. Being somewhat dim about the comfortably solid backing Amy had been given by 'them', the great British public saw her as a plucky working girl who had reached the heights without any of the usual advantages. Amy never liked this humble picture of herself. Humility in this sense was unknown to her. She treated those who pressed the point with a decided hauteur. Her efforts to change her Yorkshire accent were entirely unsuccessful and caused a lot of malicious amusement among the middle and upper classes which still lapped up *Punch*'s jokes about h-less, malaproprian charwomen with insatiable enjoyment. One of the many enigmas of Amy's career was the strong dislike she engendered in certain sophisticated quarters.

Amy was vague about money. The Lord would provide—she meant Lord Northcliffe or Lord Wakefield—and the Lord would take his cut. Flying stunts had contributed much to the circulation figures of the *Daily Mail*, and no sooner had Amy reached Karachi than huge ads appeared declaring, 'Am delighted with the Wakefield Organization and Castrol XXL Motor Oil gave magnificent and faultless lubrication—Amy Johnson.' So nobody could call it altruism, and nobody ever did.

Amy came into her kingdom at Karachi. At Calcutta she reached an unreal pinnacle of exhilaration where any lessening of the heady pace she was making, romantically as well as geographically, became unimaginable. She told everybody that she was not only going

to fly to Australia, but back again and all in a month. Now that she
was half-way there the Australians began to worry about how they
should receive her and gala-like plans were set in motion. The
Secretary of State for Air, Lord Thompson, who was to perish on a
French hillside six months later when the airship R101 crashed on
its maiden flight, had sent Amy a congratulatory telegram which was
in effect the official recognition of her feat, and this was interpreted
as a sign that she was to be given the full celebrity treatment. The
quick stepping-up of publicity bothered Amy for a moment or two
and she insisted that she was making just an ordinary flight, except
that it was *longer*. 'Every woman will be doing this in five years'
time,' she added, a prophecy which made a lot of people extremely
gloomy.

On and on she pressed, drinking tea from her thermos, dreaming
her dream and sleeping an average of three hours a night. In
Sydney the *Evening News* opened a subscription fund for her and at
home the *Daily Mail* began to behave as though it had invented her,
which some critics later declared that it had, though this was
untrue. If anyone had invented Amy it was Angela Brazil. She made
a perfect landing at Rangoon but taxied into a ditch and did some
damage to her wings, wheels and propeller. 'Here's luck to Miss
Amy Johnson!' shouted ten thousand posters. 'We are proud that
she relies upon Summer Shell.'

Meanwhile, Amy had lost so much time through minor accidents
and a bad weather patch that there was no hope at all of beating
Bert Hinkler's Australia record, though strangely enough this no
longer mattered. In fact the elimination of the time factor was a
great help to her because it let the public see her journey in noble
non-competitive terms of unrelenting distances and girlish endurance. At Singapore, where she was received like a princess by
Flight-Commander Cave-Brown-Cave, there were hundreds of
telegrams waiting for her. This was on May 18th, when the aero-
nautical obsession of the period was felt to be reaching its climax.
In Australia six lady pilots were waiting to escort Amy to Melbourne
in a kind of helmeted maiden homage. Feminist feeling was running dangerously high in this man's own country. Letters and telegrams were accumulating in such vast piles that the Minister for
Home and Territories ordered the Government Resident to order
a private secretary to look after them, and three thousand women

and girls who worked at Myer's Emporium in Melbourne made a joint statement which said, 'We thrill with pride at your glorious achievement. Welcome to Australia.' The Shell Company was now billing Amy on the hoardings as 'the 22-year-old Lady Pilot', though in fact she was twenty-seven.

While all this was going on Amy was making an emergency landing on a sugar estate in Java, where bamboo made holes in her wings, though these were soon patched up with sticking plaster. On May 22nd she flew to Atamba, which is on the coast of the shark-filled Timor Sea. Two days later she landed at Darwin, gracefully and efficiently. The huge Australian crowd watched as she extricated her stiff body from the cockpit. She was wearing khaki shorts, puttees and a green sun helmet and looked the part so perfectly that everybody was slightly nonplussed. Then somebody called out, 'Three cheers for Amy!' and the immense applause began. At the Town Hall she told them, 'Don't call me Miss Johnson, just plain Johnnie will do, that's what my English friends call me.' The Australians were enchanted by this. A song called 'Johnnie's in Town' was instantly composed and sung in the streets. A telegram came from the King and Queen to let her know how thankful they were that she had arrived safely and in Hull all the ships flew their flags in her honour and the Lord Mayor opened a fund to buy her a present. A quite extraordinary number of people who had made fleeting and on the whole highly unsatisfactory contacts with Amy during her wilderness days of tin-pot jobs and ephemeral digs cashed in by giving the newspapers details about her private life, though they proved highly disappointing since all they were plumbing was a quite prodigious innocence.

She was the first woman to fly solo to Australia and although she was four days short of Bert Hinkler's record in 1928 and was in danger of being, like her namesake Doctor Johnson, encumbered with patronage, her deed had been one of unquestionable valour and audacity. None knew of the other, greater triumph, the breakthrough into dreamland. She did it from a real love of flying, said *The Times*. Nobody said, flying from what?

She sent a telegram to Lord Wakefield: 'Hurrah! Hurrah! Arrived Darwin and feel proud that my flight is all-British achievement. I realize that it was only possible through your generous support, paying for my petrol and contributing the required amount to complete purchase of *Jason's Quest*—A.J.' She followed this up with another message which trusted that 'I will be able to emulate your true British sportsmanship'.

She made lots of impromptu speeches which enraptured the Australians. 'When I saw the shores of Australia I shouted with joy . . . you met me with love and friendship in your hearts.' Mounted police protected her wherever she went; governors and mayors received her. Her doughtiness, linked as it was with the authentic accent of Wilhelmina Stitch, touched woolly Australian hearts. She told the Brisbane Women's Christian Temperance conference that each day she had prayed for guidance and once, when she thought all was lost, a double rainbow appeared round *Jason* and an opening was seen through the clouds. At a mayoral reception she was drawn to defend her long frock as against the familiar public image of a brown-faced lass in tan top-boots, shorts and stiletto down her sock, with, 'I am just as feminine as anyone here. It is lovely to wear beautiful clothes again. I feel like Cinderella and wonder whether I shall wake up and find black people round me. . . .'

On June 3rd there were photographs in all the papers of Amy and Annie S. Swan. They had both been awarded the C.B.E., though neither could have possibly understood how much they had in common.

The Australian triumph ended in a torrent of publicity and then Amy sailed home, quietly and comfortably, in a liner—her ticket a present from the steamship company, for now it was being made impossible for her to pay for anything. Lord Thompson received her when she arrived and then Lord Northcliffe sent her along the Strand and up Fleet Street in an open motor-car. It wasn't the papery apotheosis of Fifth Avenue but it was something. The procession was followed by a banquet and the banquet by a cheque for £10,000.

The pace was set, the pattern fixed. The uproar around Amy grew and grew, and soon it was as necessary to take to the air to escape the din of recognition as it had once been to fly away and find fame. Amy flew a lot during 1931. So did Amelia Earhart but the personalities of the two girls were so different that it seemed as if they had some tacit arrangement with regard to the competitive side of their adventures.

While Amy was being ferried from Brisbane in a National Airways plane during her triumphal tour of Australia, its good-looking but highly strung young pilot had suggested that she might care to take over the controls for a bit. Amy had—for about two hours. The pilot was the son of a Glasgow engineer. His name was James Alan Mollison and two years later he and Amy were married. It was all a terrible mistake. The public, however, thought otherwise and was so entranced by a romance at this altitude that it steadfastly refused to believe anything against it. The Mollisons, as they were called—rather as though they were a music-hall act—were the very latest line in lovers. Their connubiality was stressed and emphasized in every paragraph written about them and in thousands of photographs. The fact that they were each quite idiosyncratically 'solo', as it were, was dismissed by the gossip writers and by those who should have known better. When Amy and Jim landed anywhere it was now, not only *de rigueur* that they emerged from their twin cockpits like heroes, but with blissful grins like the winners of the Dunmow Flitch. They were the Mollisons!

Amy was a better flyer than Jim, which meant that she was expected to be generous and share triumphs which were hers by rights. She *was* generous, fortunately. Her code made every provision for slapping the back of the chap who had done his best. Jim shrank from this—even when recognizing its decency. He was intellectually superior to Amy and far more sensitive. Both had taken to the air for complex personal reasons which had scarcely anything in common. And each, like the late Gilbert Harding in a future entertainment medium, had become trapped unwittingly in a bogus situation which they were forced to go on pretending had real values.

Amy made several flights on her own immediately after her marriage. On November 14th, 1932, she flew solo to the Cape in a Puss Moth, taking four days and seven hours, and about a month later she flew home again. In July 1933 Colonel and Mrs. Lindbergh flew from New York to Copenhagen and when Mr. and Mrs. James Mollison flew from Wales to Connecticut a fortnight later, everybody was delighted by the propriety which had entered aviation. The Lindberghs continued to fly about together and so did Jim and Amy, while Jean Batten, who was still single and solo, was thought brave but rather old hat. Some newspapers went so far as to hope that soon there would be a proper air family of mother, father and little ones looping-the-loop and setting up a whole new set of records.

Jim and Amy continued to play the 'first there' game. They were the first husband and wife to fly the Atlantic together. Grounded, however, their lives immediately soared off in opposite directions. Jim, when he wasn't flying, enjoyed the social round and was made much of by society. Amy, when she wasn't flying, tended to be gauche and rather at a loss. Her transparent nature with its mixture of girlish eagerness and mechanic's practicality irritated sophisticated people and made them vaguely uncomfortable, and eventually the qualities which entranced Australia in 1930 were the very ones which bored London in 1935. She was patronized and even snubbed in some quarters. Her answer was the old one—she ran away. She went on flying and flying without her husband and in 1938 they were divorced. The popular Press was really very angry about this as it had spent a lot of time and a small fortune boosting the marriage. Those whom Fleet Street has put together oughtn't to have the face to come asunder.

Something else was also breaking up—the brief and adventurous extravaganza of the lone aviator. The rickety, amateur, exciting carelessness of the open cockpit, the creaking, swaying struts and all the charm of the string-and-sticks light aeroplane had had its day —a mayfly's day. So had Amy, whose private fantasy of 'Johnnie the Wonder Girl' fitted so exactly into it. Her serial ran out with her decade and she was killed off as neatly as both herself and her great reading public could have wished. They put *Jason* in the South Kensington Science Museum, where it rests like an old toy. But as Amy said, 'the sequence of events is natural and inevitable'.

CHAPTER SIX

Comrades O Comrades!

Now the day is over
Night is drawing nigh
Shadows of the evening
Steal across the sky.
S. BARING-GOULD

In the red theatre of the flesh I stage
The anatomical tragedy of this sad age . . .
GEORGE BARKER, *Holy Poems II*

THE drift towards the second holocaust had more to do with inertia than Nemesis. Hitler not only need not have happened but actually could not have happened had not the ground been marvellously well-dunged for him. History, Ernst Toller said, is the propaganda of the victors. That was bitter. More likely is the unintentional injustice brought about by action taken from looking at events in close-up. It would have been better for mankind if the Treaty of Versailles hadn't been signed until 1925; it would have given the self-righteous time to repent, the professional haters time to see their doctors or their priests and the merciless time to realize that the cries of starving children would be almost certain to drown the satisfying sound of pips squeaking. However, the deed was done and God was held witness to its lawfulness. The natural pride, energy and dangerous mysticism of the German nation were discounted as if they had no existence, then the victors returned home and Germany was forgotten, except when reparations became due. The fashion for torpor in high places grew. Writers contented themselves with letting off an occasional squib behind the frock-coated backs of politicians, tweaking bishops' aprons and by virtually ignoring the militarists, since Sassoon and Wilfred Owen had had the last word in obloquy where they were concerned.

There were three main escape routes for writers after the war, Bloomsbury, Mayfair and leafy Blankshire. Bloomsbury was withdrawn and aristocratic, Mayfair was witty and iconoclastic, and Blankshire was the glade in the forest to which British poets have always fled when they find the world too much for them. Bloomsbury had its own code. It believed that what people did in bed together was their own affair, but that how they treated their friends was of paramount importance to civilization. E. M. Forster provided the exact synthesis of what Bloomsbury held dear when he wrote, 'If I had to choose between betraying my friend and betraying my country, I hope I would have the courage to betray my country.' Bloomsbury was practical. It never underestimated a writer's need for leisure and economic freedom, which Virginia Woolf assessed at £500 a year and a room of one's own. The club was not exclusive but the terms for belonging to it were so ethically and culturally high that a comfortably small membership was guaranteed. Bloomsbury was never the ivory tower of its enemies' imagination. It was more of a private power-house and just as, in Wyndham Lewis's phrase, Eliot's early poetry had the effect of a little musk that scents a whole room, so did the quintessential humanism and literary dedication of Bloomsbury provide their own pungent standards. The morality of Bloomsbury, rooted as it was in endless concern for the private individual and in a persistent questioning of political expediency, was to be extremely important later on when neighbours in German streets failed to notice that the family next door was being collected for incineration, or when every new art venture was confronted with the automatic derision of the yellow Press, and Philistinism as a policy for catching pennies was openly resorted to by owners and editors. Bloomsbury was chiefly the Woolfs, Clive and Vanessa Bell, J. M. Keynes, Lytton Strachey, Duncan Grant and, almost but not quite, E. M. Forster.

Mayfair in 1929 represented the higher irreverence in literature. The novels of Evelyn Waugh and Aldous Huxley weren't nice but they were fabulously funny and anti-cant. As for Blankshire the poetry traditionalists at this time were very busy keeping their fingers green and went on expressing themselves in what they mistakenly believed to be a timeless lyricism. Georgian Poetry was slain by a little volume called *Poems* by W. H. Auden in 1930 and nothing either Sir Edward Marsh or Harold Monro could do could bring it back to life. *Poems* was dedicated to Auden's friend Christopher Isherwood and the four lines of the dedicatory verse became the epitome of the decade's anger and protest.

> *Let us honour if we can*
> *The vertical man*
> *Though we value none*
> *But the horizontal one.*

Or, in other words, by all means let us lay poppies at the war memorials but let us remember, too, the living.

This was the clarion call which rang through the Waste Land of post-war fecklessness, doubt, ruined landscapes, desecrated lives, shameful apathy, degraded standards, greed and stagnation. When *The Waste Land* was published in 1922 it had an immediate response from young poets, who swiftly recognized a new master. They at once jettisoned all the old imagery and sought tragic symbols of a shocking nature in the refuse which still insisted that it should be addressed as civilization. '. . . they for a time took to inhabiting exclusively barren beaches,' wrote Edmund Wilson, 'cactus-grown deserts and dusty attics overrun with rats—the only properties they allowed themselves to work with were the few fragments of shattered glass or a sparse sprinkling of broken bones. They had purged themselves of Masefield as of Shelley for dry tongues and rheumatic joints. The dry breath of the Waste Land now blighted the most amiable country landscapes; and the sound of jazz, which had formerly seemed jolly, now only inspired horror and despair. . . .'

So busy were the young poets of the twenties finding their way about in this charnel wilderness that it took them the whole of the decade to realize that Eliot himself was not with them. He had opened up a terrible frontier and had then retreated to a peace which passed all comprehension—the higher reaches of Anglicanism. In *The Sacred Wood* Eliot murmured, 'Poetry is now perceived to have something to do with morals, and with religion, and even with politics, perhaps, though we cannot say what.'

The new poets, Stephen Spender, Louis MacNeice, Cecil Day Lewis and, above all, W. H. Auden soon made it plain that not only could they say *what* poetry had to do with morals, religion and politics, but that they intended to prove the relationship at the tops of their voices. The literary political consciousness of the thirties broke like daylight—some thought, like a boil—with Auden's *Poems* and his *The Orators*, and with Hugh MacDiarmid's *First Hymn to Lenin*. The Pink Decade opened with scarlet fanfares and a flat kind of wit which smacked the hysteria out of those still gaily twitching to the echoes from the twenties. Now, most certainly, all the literate youth of England was on fire and determined to blast the truth at the burnt-out old men who had dared to see in *The Waste Land* nothing more than a perverseness which invited anger and an obscurity that was risible. It was the poets and not the politicians who were first to sense a new climate of violence as reactionary elements the world over, but especially in Germany, saluted each other and fascism emerged. The poets had travelled and, on the whole, the politicians had stayed at home. 'Wake me up when that's finished,' Baldwin used to say when foreign affairs were discussed. But John Lehmann, Christopher Isherwood, Wystan Auden and Naomi Mitchison were eye-witnesses of Nazism. They had been present at the birth of the beast. Spender and Isherwood in particular had identified themselves with the victims of Versailles, the fragile children, emaciated men and the young people who were so spiritually crippled that when the time came, in 1933, they could actually *welcome* Adolf Hitler and Hermann Goering. Julian Bell, Clive and Vanessa's son; William Empson and William Plomer had all been to the Far East and knew what was happening there. George Orwell had submerged himself in the grey ocean of the unemployed. The poet's tongue wagged from the horse's mouth; all declaimed their protest from positions of unique authority.

Simultaneously and apparently unrelatedly, other voices joined in. The most influential at the beginning of the movement was the Scottish poet, Hugh MacDiarmid. John Lehmann's genuine anxiety that MacDiarmid's Scots vernacular would limit the influence of his work was to bring about a comic quarrel. MacDiarmid soon proved himself a Scotsman first and a comrade second and advanced on the clever Sassenachs with accusations of effeteness. He called their combined efforts the 'Yellow Book of the thirties' and Auden called MacDiarmid's stories 'lots of things lying on the ground', and there was schism. George Orwell became really angry with what he called 'bourgeois baiting' and reminded the comrades that it could end in many members of the middle classes being lost to the movement. Harry Pollitt's give was the kind which may well have lodged itself firmly in the author of *Animal Farm*'s mind, with frighteningly bitter results. 'Orwell was a disillusioned little middle-class boy,' said Pollitt.

The poets of the thirties, as it happened, were extremely bothered and embarrassed by their middle-class backgrounds. It seemed ungrateful and even vulgar to denounce a system which had provided them with a public school and a university, with a fascinating cat's cradle of blood and artistic relationships, and with the very poise they needed to make their work influential. They were also, Stephen Spender particularly, perturbed by a new self-knowledge which forced them to realize that public gestures were often motivated by emotional desires which were deeply personal. Orwell was, perhaps, the only true altruist among them and, saintly though he was, even he found it impossible to turn himself into a proletarian by a kind of moral deed-poll.

The new Soviet Union, mysterious, vast and seemingly unsullied, became the land of hope. An acceptance of Marxism appeared not only ideal but plain common sense. The tremulous revolutionary excitement showed itself in the most unexpected places; even clubmen, looking at David Low's Colonel Blimp in the *Evening Standard*, were beginning to see the Red light. Blimp was the wuffling old guard stripped down to the flaccid buff, pappy, mindless but still dangerous. Even the Prince of Wales revealed a dislike of the Establishment. The intelligentsia's 'democratic communism' did not seem particularly extreme in such a swiftly changing climate; rather the reverse, it had a remarkable logical force when seen in the context of its time. The Communist Party of Great Britain has always been a very small affair in proportion to both population and the world status of the country. Like all minorities, it was both flattered and disdainful when it was sought out and made much of. It had begun with two and a half thousand members, which had soared to a thrilling 10,730 members in 1926 and then had slumped to a mere 1,376 in 1930. It was to pass the fifteen and a half thousand mark by the close of the thirties, but its real power and success was not to lie in the paid-up party card man, but in the enormous pink and fertile multitudes of all classes and conditions which were willing to ignore certain of its dogmas for the sake of a roseate broad view. On the whole the comrades hid their dissatisfaction with a state of affairs which robbed them of the useful fury and indignation of the social outcast, though there were eruptions, particularly when at the height of the Spanish Civil War and during the rapid growth of the Left Book Club it seemed that the C.P.G.B. was being taken over by an intelligentsia which remained obdurately British and moderate even when it died by fascist bullets in Catalonia. Hatred in Britain, as Neal Wood observed, has not been as significant as elsewhere. . . .

And so, as the decade advanced towards its horrible conclusion, two strongly emotional quasi-political masses, each of which was a typical British compromise of the brutal philosophies which were to ruin Europe, and which might be called democratic-communism and conservative-fascism, lined up for the fray. A Popular Front became discernible. There was a huge outburst of oratorical poetry and a flood of pamphlets. There were tales out of Germany of the like that had never been heard since the world began. But nothing happened. The country was divided into the eloquent and the deaf. It was jug-jug to dirty ears.

The resurgence wasn't palatable to every young writer of Auden's age and class. In 1932 Peter Quennell returned home from teaching in a Japanese university and found a transformation which he viewed both then and in retrospect with the greatest distrust. '*Georgian Poetry* was dead, its contributors had vanished or scattered. The new poets were partisans of the Left; and their sympathies, heightened by a sense of impending conflict, coloured or clouded much of the verse they wrote. This is not the place to discuss the political efforts of English and American intellectuals during the third decade of the twentieth century, or that long, sad courtship of the Russian Communist Party by Western Men of Good Will, which exposed the wooers to so many rebuffs, provoked such bitter searchings and plunged some of them into a state of moral perturbation from which they have not yet recovered. But it is clear that the "Fight against Fascism", notwithstanding the valour that a number of young poets displayed in the Spanish Civil War, and the eloquence displayed by an even larger number in support of democratic principles, was directly productive of no more genuine poetry than the struggle against Napoleon Bonaparte . . . the artist who aspires to be a political force seems to completely misunderstand the nature of the art he practises. . . . Between writers who have helped to change the world and writers who have set out to change it, there exists a very sharp distinction.'

By mid-decade art talk and sex talk were out and political talk
was in. It absorbed every stratum of society and the mass entertainers were obliged to note the trend and cater for it. Auden and
Louis MacNeice, in *Letters from Iceland*, published in 1937, summed
it up.

> *More, it's a job* [teaching], *and jobs today are rare:*
> *All the ideals in the world won't feed us*
> *Although they give our crimes a certain air.*
> *So barons of the press who know their readers*
> *Employ to write their more appalling leaders,*
> *Instead of Satan's horned and hideous minions*
> *Clever young men of liberal opinions.*

Bloomsbury added its support. 'There is no one in politics today
worth sixpence outside the ranks of liberals except the post-war
generation of intellectual Communists under thirty-five,' declared
J. M. Keynes to Kingsley Martin. 'Perhaps in their feelings and
instincts they are the nearest thing we have to the typical nervous
nonconformist English gentleman who went to the Crusades, made
the Reformation, fought the Great Rebellion, won us our civil and
religious liberties and humanized the working classes during the
last century.'

Two poetry anthologies, *New Signatures* and *New Country*,
followed up Auden's *Poems*, the first in 1932, the second in 1933.
They contained work by Auden, Plomer, Empson, Day Lewis,
Spender and Lehmann. In *New Country* Michael Roberts assumed
the rôle of Baptist and demanded that the poets should make ready
for an Anglican Lenin. Working-class people took on a new fascination. For some of the upper-class Marxists, who had never seen the
proletariat except as 'hands' or servants, the new awakening had the
temporary paradisal quality of a dose of mescalin. The proles were
beautiful, they discerned, like the Fulani or the Dinka. There was
a *chic* in having one for a friend or a lover, and it was noble to adopt
certain working-class standards, most of which in 1935 remained
fairly untouched by admass influences in spite of intensive cinema-
going. The working class took on the same sacred status as children
in Christian ethics and many a careless columnist, slipping back into
old class-conscious attitudes, found a millstone round his neck. The
little child who could lead the English *bourgeoisie* to the Russian

heaven, which as yet had no unemployment, no known injustice and no Five Year Plan, wore a cloth cap and muffler. People now began to make pilgrimages to the Soviet Union and the analogy to religion was strengthened. George Bernard Shaw went; so did Gide and Lady Astor. Anglo-Soviet friendly societies sprang up and there were film clubs which showed Russian films, like *The General Line*, *Earth* and *Mother*. The atmosphere during the showing of such films was tense, non-critical and reverent, and was sometimes accompanied by handouts of Soviet literature whose typographical naïveté added to the impression that it derived from a purer land.

The tiny Communist Party of Great Britain was pleased, embarrassed and bewildered by the infatuated *bourgeoisie* intellectual, a bewilderment which soon turned to disgust when the good old British genius for the *via media* brought Red politics into the open in the most casual way and robbed cell meetings of their drama and revolutionary mystique. 'When England goes Communist,' said Douglas Goldring sceptically, 'no doubt the party in power will call itself the "Conservative Co-operative Party" and, as usual, half the Government will be Old Etonian.'

The fact remained that Great Britain had at last what most Continental countries had had for upwards of a century—a radical intelligentsia. In more normal times it would have identified itself with Christian liberalism, although in more normal times, of course, it would never have happened. The Labour Party needed such moral support badly but after 1931, when Ramsay MacDonald had defected, the Labour Party to a Left-wing poet was like a man who had 'lost his character' and who might be thrown a little charity now and then but could not be trusted any more. On the other hand, Russia, which had been snubbed by the West and left to its own devices ever since the Revolution, was genuinely pleased, if intrigued, by this flowery courtship. In 1934, at the Congress of Soviet Writers, Karl Radek said amidst great applause, 'In the heart of *bourgeois* England, in Oxford, where the sons of the *bourgeoisie* receive their final polish, we observe the crystallization of a group which sees salvation only in the proletariat.' Such hopefulness undoubtedly stemmed from the notorious gravity with which observers abroad accepted the motions of the Oxford Union. In 1932 the Union had voted by a majority of sixty-seven that 'in socialism lies the only solution to the problems facing this country'. Russians and Communists generally had not then caught on to the fact that there is socialism and there is *British* socialism, by which one might as well say that there is blood and there is red ink, for all that they have in common.

Marxism at the universities had to compete vigorously with such soul-grabbing cults as Buchmanism and Fascism, and there were few undergraduates not fiercely committed one way or the other to the mainly retrograde philosophies thrown up by the collapse of the old civilization. At Cambridge in 1933 the handsome John Cornford, son of Frances Cornford and a future International Brigade victim, successfully led his revolutionary student movement into a Federation of Socialist Societies comprising ten affiliated organizations. The Federation held its conferences in the very house at Clerkenwell Green where Lenin had once edited *Iskra*. At Oxford there was *Outpost* and at Cambridge, *Cambridge Left*, two short-lived but popular 'revolutionary' magazines.

In the great world beyond the quads and courts a desire to clarify the murkiness which had descended upon public life resulted in a publication which successively called itself *New Atlantis*, *New Albion* and *New Britain*. But by far the most influential of all the little Left magazines which came into being by 1934 was *Left Review*, which stood for aggressive communism and a strong party-line where the arts were concerned. It was edited by Montagu Slater, Amabel Williams-Ellis, John Strachey's sister, and T. W. Wintringham.

Humanistic 'pinks' like C. E. M. Joad, Kingsley Martin, Rebecca West, Bertrand Russell and Bloomsbury's Leonard Woolf had their say in a journal called *Plan*, which preached world government, and which contained many ideas which were extraordinary then but which have since found themselves among the more worn platitudes which crackle daily from UNO's inter-com. system.

By far the most entertaining of Pink Press periodicals was Claud Cockburn's cyclostyled and somewhat sinister *The Week*, which began in the spring of 1933 with only seven subscriptions. An *outré* scandal sheet whose sophisticated political gossip, guaranteed straight from house-parties, cocktail parties and embassy soirées, and retailed with a terrible glee, it was reputed to have made Establishment figures very jumpy. Its irrepressible editor was delighted when he heard that *The Week* had become required reading at Fort

Belvedere, but the victims got their own back by refusing Cockburn a passport when he wanted to report the Spanish Civil War for the *Daily Worker*, where he was known as 'Frank Pitcairn'. *The Week* eventually became an influential news-letter.

All this literary activity, some of it magnificent, much of it dull, earnest and breathy, took place against events which began to prescribe a new and awful moral darkness of a kind unknown in Europe since barbaric times. In February, 1934, the Daladier Government fell and Pierre Laval, who had once been a communist but who, by means of an adroit reptilian scuttle, was now so far to the Right that it was only a matter of time before he slithered into the abyss of the new brutalism, came to power. In July that year, the Nazis rid themselves of the devout little Dr. Dollfuss, the Austrian Chancellor. In 1935 Mussolini, far-gone in fantasies about a new Roman Empire, selected quite arbitrarily the medieval African kingdom of Abyssinia for classical enlightenment, a process which opened by bombing grass huts and closed with the mass gassing of young warriors carrying spears. In March, 1936, Germany occupied the Rhineland. A little later that year General Franco landed upon the Iberian Peninsula and with help from the German and Italian Fascists, who were only too pleased to have such a chance of a full-scale military rehearsal for their war of world domination to come, he was able to establish the least interrupted of twentieth-century right-wing tyrannies. As these events succeeded each other, and as civilization floundered and the old diplomacy was neutralized by lies, most of the esotericism went out of the intellectual revolt. It became clear that the salvation of mankind lay in the hands of the common people, and nowhere else. Hugh MacDiarmid lashed 'the precious English comrades', who retaliated splendidly by practising what they preached and going off to fight in Spain. It was a marvellous gesture, sincere unto death in many cases, but a gesture all the same. And darkness is not stayed by gestures, only by light. Enlightenment of this sort was spread by the Left Book Club, a popular encyclopaedist movement of political and economic education which swept the country.

The Left Book Club was founded by Victor Gollancz in 1936. Mr. Gollancz's journey to the literary scene had taken the classical betwixt-the-wars route, a middle-class home, Oxford, schoolmastering, then publishing. A Jew turned Christian Socialist, he brought to the edgy literary ferment of the thirties a compassionate and cultural concern whose unambiguous quality was acceptable to the sophisticated Left-wing intellectual and to the neglected and undervalued man in the dole queue. The Left Book Club was launched at just the right moment and had an immediate and sparkling success. It set out to educate and then to organize ordinary men and women into building a United Front against fascism. The books came out monthly and cost two and sixpence each. They were accompanied by a magazine called *Left Book Club News*, which was soon simply *Left News* and from the very start there was a sense of belonging and, at long last, *doing* which had an extraordinarily heartening effect. It attracted members from all classes and all political parties, and from the more progressive element in the Church.

Gollancz's editorials in the magazine were businesslike, friendly and urgent in tone. In the second number he was writing, and it is a fair example of how he provided a common touch to an enterprise which in other hands might easily have been yet one more aspect of 'coterie' letters:

'I wrote last month [May, 1936], "We have at the moment 6,000 members and expect to have 7,000 before this issue of the Left Book News is published". We had in fact over 9,000 members on the day of publication, and now a fortnight later, have 12,000. Enrolments are flowing in by every post.

'It is clear therefore that, judged merely by numbers, the Club is already a far greater success than was anticipated, not only when it was originally launched, but even on the eve of publication of the first choice.

'. . . last month we were looking for 50,000 as the next figure at which to aim; we are now looking to 100,000. Nor do we believe such a figure to be Utopian. Every experienced publisher can tell, at a very early stage, the kind of success that any new enterprise is likely to have. We have not the smallest doubt that the Left Book Club has struck just the right note to which a vast public up and down the country was waiting to respond.

'There must be no delay, brethren, no people who just read the books and the news and leave it at that. . . . Every member must actively help by enlisting his friends, relations or associates. . . .'

The Selection Committee was made up of Victor Gollancz, John Strachey—whose *The Coming Struggle For Power*, published in 1934, was the prototype of the kind of Popular Front literature soon to be so familiar as Left Book Club choices, and was eventually to be issued by the Club—and Harold Laski. The founder's dream of 100,000 members was not substantiated, the pinnacle being 60,000 members in April, 1939. By this date the Left Book Club was a kind of national institution and over one and a half million volumes of its one hundred or so choices and 'extra' choices were in circulation. Members formed regional groups, discussion centres, and attended meetings. There also existed a number of unusually influential functional groups formed by professional people like doctors, lawyers, schoolteachers, civil servants, artists and poets. The latter group published a communist poetry anthology with poems and articles by Edgell Rickword, Jack Lindsay, Montague Slater and Alan Bush. It was edited by L. J. Isserlis and Philip Manton and was called *Poetry and the People*.

There were signs very early on in the life of the Club that its Progressive platform was being ruthlessly exploited by the Communists and that they often threatened the very independence of the organization.

Douglas Hyde, in his recantation *I Believed*, describes a typical Communist reaction to the Left Book Club. 'When the Left Book Club began early in 1936 it provided me with just the weapon I wanted. To all those who had so often told me that they were of the Left rather than the Right I said "Join the Left Book Club and prove it". To the liberal minded who argued that they liked to read both sides I said, "You can't do so without reading the Left as well as the Right".

'Soon I had dozens of people whom I had regarded as political foes reading a Left book each month and discussing it with me.'

Such eager Communist canvassing is better understood when it is realized that the third issue of *Left Book Club News*, for instance, carried a full draft of the Constitution of the U.S.S.R. and most issues contained the kind of Marxist articles a Left-wing man of the thirties would be most unlikely to have in his home in ordinary circumstances.

Such communist pressures were a great irritant to supporters like Sir Stafford Cripps, Robert Boothby, Sir Norman Angell and other men of good will. Victor Gollancz himself was frequently angered by those who lost sight of the life-or-death broad issues of the

Popular Front for the sake of the Party line, though it was inevitable in the political climate of the thirties that these things should merge in a common haze. Also that such Marxist opportunism should have existed, for no small national Communist Party ever had so respectable, brilliantly organized and popular a vehicle for its propaganda as that provided by the Left Book Club in the Britain of the late thirties. Nearly half the books commissioned by the Club each year were written by Communists and Neal Wood estimated that about a sixth of the membership—6,000 out of 36,000—in April, 1940, were Communists. Communism then had neither the furtiveness nor the déclassé associations it has today and the ordinary Left Book Club member was neither shocked nor bored that his monthly choice and its accompanying magazine should contain quite an amount of blatant Marxism. The image cast by Russia was a sentimental one. Its surface was scratched a little by the Trotskyite trials but wasn't lacerated until the Hitler-Stalin pact.

The success of the Club depended greatly upon keen local support and proselytizing in a given area—as witness the two major universities, where, in 1936, Oxford had only 53 members as against Cambridge's 324. In the Depressed Areas unemployed men worked out a scheme of group membership, with three or four people contributing to the monthly 2s. 6d. and sharing the same book.

The books themselves were distinguished by their immediacy and by their appearance of having a burning authority and hopefulness. They included, *The Acquisitive Society* by R. H. Tawney, *Barbarians at the Gate* by Leonard Woolf, *Civil Liberties* by W. H. Thompson, *Days of Contempt* by André Malraux, *The Labour Party in Perspective* by C. R. Attlee, *Betrayal of the Left* by Victor Gollancz, *Public Speaking* by Sir Richard Acland, *The Road to Wigan Pier* by George Orwell, *Spanish Testament* by Arthur Koestler and *Soviet Communism* by Tom Harrisson.

There were also many 'extra' choices and what Victor Gollancz called, 'a Left "Home University Library" ' which consisted of books on everything from History to Trades Unionism; Religion to English Literature, all of them written by specialists who had been asked to avoid 'a polemical tone'. Prizes were offered in a proletarian novel competition and for a book on unemployment. By the end of 1936 from between 150 and 200 Left Book Club circles had sprung up all over the country. Articles in *Left News* began to draw people's attention to the way civil liberties were being threatened, particularly in the Mosleyite persecution of the Jews in the East End. The facts brought to light were scarifying but the repellent oratory which caused such outrages was defended time after time by the Home Office in the sacred cause of free speech. Perhaps the book which had the most compelling influence was *Spain in Revolt* by Harry Gannes and Theodore Repard. It was a kind of thirties *Lillibulero* which swept young men into the International Brigade. Left Book Club members didn't leave it all to Henrietta Street but assumed responsibilities in their own areas. In February, 1937, the Club was big enough to hold a rally in the Albert Hall, where the platform included Sir Stafford Cripps, Sir Richard Acland, Harry Pollitt, D. N. Pritt and Victor Gollancz. Special trains were booked and the fare from Manchester was 10s.; from Coventry, 5s. 6d. Amongst everybody connected with the Club at this period there was an unmistakable element of relief and gratitude for an invention which effectively broke the ineptitude and the dull nerveless silence. The Left Book Club's impetus was slowed down by the sickening disillusionment brought about by the grins of Ribbentrop and Molotov as they signed their grotesque non-aggression pact, and by the social revolution which began in 1945.

The theatre, an obvious means of disseminating Popular Front ideas and ideals, and a sphere in which poets might cry 'Awake!' with excellent effect, proved to be a harder nut to crack than the bookstalls. Shaftesbury Avenue was glossy as a chestnut through the smooth ministrations of Frederick Lonsdale, Noel Coward and their debtors. The audiences were captive and knew what they liked, and the dramatists dished it out to them, season after season. The naughty scepticism of the twenties was artificially maintained by the *de rigueur* presence of a few 'daring' lines, which were thrown at the audience like hot crumbs by witty young men in dressing-gowns. License and sin rarely made a physical entrance but were near enough to set the senses speculating. The mechanics of the play were compressed into three acts of mellifluous middle-class conversation and the productions, which were frequently excellent in the technical sense, formed a stylized recreation like the pantomime or the annual detective tale from a trusted pen, in which the faithful re-iteration of the tried and familiar brings with it a comforting sense of security. Shaw was still the chief ideas vendor but his arguments, though still relevant and pertinent, had existed for long enough to have their own traditions and were too much like what the public expected of him to move mountains. He amused more than he disturbed. Drury Lane was, for year after year, at the gossamer zenith of pretty British musicals and vast audiences gave themselves up to the sumptuous kitsch of shows like *Glamorous Night* and *The Dancing Years*, and their perennial juvenile lead, Ivor Novello. Noel Coward gate-crashed this flowery clime with *Cavalcade*, a cathartic scrapbook which allowed people a good patriotic cry and its author to make public penance for past frivolity. Cabarets had none of the bite of their Continental equivalents and were dominated by sophisticated monologuists like Tallulah Bankhead, Douglas Byng and Beatrice Lillie. The skies were falling but the attitude of the British theatre was 'no comment'.

It was inevitable that the poets should attack such deadliness. No audience offered a more rewarding reaction to a sudden clashing of cymbals. In 1935 Rupert Doone produced W. H. Auden's and Christopher Isherwood's first play, *The Dog Beneath The Skin*. Doone was an ex-Diaghilev dancer and choreographer, and in the autumn of 1935 he was chiefly responsible for revitalizing a drama-producing organization which, though it had no actual geographical address, was called the Group Theatre. It had been formed in 1932 to promote theatrical experiments which wouldn't have stood a chance in the West End. *The Dog Beneath The Skin* was a dramatic hodge-podge haunted by early Brechtian ghosts, sharply satirical cabaret sketches, profoundly moving classical asides influenced by the Greek drama and lacings of Freud. It was about a modern innocent abroad, the youthful and guileless Alan Norman, who wanders through the thirties' scene looking for the Squire of Pressan Ambo. Alan is accompanied by a faithful dog, who is the Squire incognito, and two journalists who are a mixture of recording angels and 'feeds' for the hero's musings. The journey takes the hero to totalitarian Ostnia, to prisons, brothels, operating theatres, playing fields, hotels, broadcasting stations, barracks and police stations. The wit is sometimes vintage undergraduate and sometimes made thrilling by a sense of political urgency. Some of the protest is more in the nature of cheek than anger, and the whole play, although it generates occasional fury and has one scene of poignant tragedy, cannot absolve itself entirely of the feeling that it was put together in tearing high spirits. J. C. Trewin said that the plays of Auden and Isherwood made him feel that he was crunching along a cinder path in the rain.

'*Dog-Skin*', as Isherwood called it, was followed by the important *Ascent of F6*, the only play from this period of revolutionary drama to retain its exciting power and vitality. Like the previous effort, it showed the cracks of collaboration and Christopher Isherwood even went so far as to confess at a Group Theatre lecture that it had a different ending for each consecutive performance during the first week of its run, but its plea for spiritual integrity towered movingly above its structural defects, like the holy peak of F6 itself, and the audience was rapt. It is about a celebrated mountaineer called Ransom, who is an amalgam of Hamlet, Lawrence of Arabia and an International Brigade poet. He was played triumphantly by William Devlin. The icy, rarified loneliness of the Himalayas was brilliantly suggested by scenery designed by Rupert Doone and used to great effect on a tiny stage. In a later production, in 1939, Alec Guinness played Ransom.

The third play by the Isherwood-Auden axis was *On The Frontier*, which was put on at the Arts Theatre, Cambridge, before a predominantly young and thoughtful audience whose sympathetic reaction added to the pensive survey of its theme, which was war between a fascist and imperialistic state. The date was February, 1939, and now that the sound of swords being sharpened was unmistakable, there was less public concern in the clarion call and a note, as yet no louder than a bat-squeak, of personal anxiety. The Chorus, consisting of factory hands, did not sing with quite the old Anglo-Marxist glamour but the musical background itself, composed by a new talent, Benjamin Britten, was fascinating.

There were other dramatics. *Love on the Dole*, Walter Greenwood's best-selling novel, was staged and received with a great deal of sentimentality by critics and public alike. Wesker and Delany were still light years away and people who went to see plays like *Love on the Dole* did so from the same sense of social duty as might have made them undertake district visiting, not because they thought for one moment that such material—a working-class girl giving her body to the wealthy bookie in order to support her unemployed family—had anything to do with 'going to the theatre'. Jack Jones's *Rhondda Roundabout*, which appeared in 1939, was another attempt

Photo: *Central Press*

'As long as cricket is played with a hard ball there must be contusions . . .'
Larwood bowling against Australia at Nottingham in 1930.

The Reverend Harold Davidson, M.A., during his trial at Church
House, Westminster, March 1932.

I dreamed we both were in a bed
Of roses, almost smothered;
The warmth and sweetness had me there
Made lovingly familiar,
But that I heard thy sweet breath say,
Faults done by night will blush by day . . .

THE REVEREND ROBERT HERRICK, M.A.

to stage a working-class entertainment but its combination of Welsh folksiness and bits of socialistic message made a lumpy mixture which failed to convince.

The current of intellectual rebellion and poetic Marxism which created the Popular Front took many odd turns on its increasingly tardy way to the great Red Sea. Tom Harrisson and Charles Madge, two lively youngsters from Cambridge, drifted along to Pope's conclusion that the proper study of mankind is man and invented Mass-Observation to prove it. Madge combined poetry with a job on the *Daily Mirror* and Harrisson was an anthropologist. They set out to study human behaviour and to analyse all aspects of it, and by 1940 no one was safe from the Mass-Observer, with his pad and pencil and infinite curiosity. He was in the streets, in the pubs, on cottage doorsteps, in the foyers of the packed cinemas, at writers' conferences, in the dole queue and on the country-house lawn. He haunted the summer beaches like Lobby Lud. It was estimated that by the beginning of the war there were something like 2,000 part-time mass-observers who set out each evening and week-end on an insatiable quest for opinions, ideas, likes, dislikes, dreams, aspirations and goodness knows what. The stupendous results were cata-logued and synthesized, boiled down until they were believed to be the essence of the twentieth-century man's thought and action. In 1937 Geoffrey Grigson's *New Verse* contained the sensations of a dozen Oxford undergraduates who had generously placed their naked emotions on the mass-observer's pad for the common weal. Most people—since little happens to 'most people'—rather enjoyed being mass-observed and began to believe that they needed it done to them, like vaccination. And many of the mass-observers found a fearful joy in their rôle of social inquisitor. The generalizations that were made from all this activity were neither sensational nor scien-tific, but it was fun while it lasted. A generation later the same mutual eagerness to ask and answer was to be noticed when the television interviewer thrust his magic wand into the face of the man in the street. Ask a silly question. . . .

The communist flirtation ran little risk of developing to the point of consummation. The intellectual Left and the small solid Red heart of the C.P.G.B. were not made for each other, and they knew it. But they enjoyed and were cynically amused by the affair re-spectively, and the emotional warmth it spread to the proletariat

5

was stimulating and occasionally heady. Certainly it was far better than the slimy chilliness which was like death in life, which existed before the Popular Front emerged. One of the young hopefuls, William Empson, recognized early reservations in the attachment and laughed it off with *Just A Smack At Auden*.

> *Waiting for the end, boys, waiting for the end.*
> *What is there to do?*
> *What's become of me or you?*
> *Are we kind or are we true?*
> *Sitting two by two, boys, waiting for the end.*

In retrospect, the hammer of intellectual Communism in Britain during the thirties can be seen as a melodic symbol beating out a crisp and mainly witty tune and its sickle as a satirical tool with a good cutting edge to it. George Orwell, in *Inside The Whale*, said that 'For about three years, in fact, the central stream of English Literature was more or less under communist control' but as that amiable popularizer of hard facts, Joad, would have said, 'It all depends upon what you mean by "central stream"'. There was a brilliant torrent, fed by many lively tributaries, called the River Auden, and it watered the Desert of Cant and Cowardice, and brought hope to the politically parched. But those who still see it as a flood which affected the whole of intellectual life are still wearing the rose-coloured spectacles of the period—probably for old times' sake.

From all these events, from the slump, from the war, from the boom,
From the Italian holiday, from the skirring of the revolving light
  for one who fled,
From the crowds in the square at dusk, from the shooting,
From the loving, from the dying, however we prosper in death
Whether lying under twin lilies and branched candles
Or stiffened on the pavement like a frozen sack, hidden
From peace by the lamps:
From all these events, Time solitary will emerge
Like a rocket over our mist: beyond the troubles,
Untangled with our pasts, be sure Time will leave us,

said Stephen Spender.
  And it did.

CHAPTER SEVEN

Fall from Grace

. . . they nursed no quarrel, they cherished no feud,
They were strangers to spite and hate;
In a kindly spirit they took their stand,
That brothers and sons might learn
How a man should uphold the sports of his land,
And strike his best with a strong right hand,
And take his strokes in return.

On December 2nd, 1932, the Marylebone Cricket Club began the traditional series of Test matches against Australia at Sydney. Australia, who had held the Ashes since 1930, had a certain unearthly confidence, born of the fact that they also possessed the not quite earthly Bradman. The first Test seems to have been played happily enough, with a resulting win for England by ten wickets. On December 30th the second Test was played—at Melbourne—and this time Australia won by 111 runs. All was sweetness and light. One can search the sporting columns of the English Press vainly for a hint of the typhoon to come. The English team, captained by D. R. Jardine and made up of players whose names still resound like hosannas in the great cricket anthem; Sutcliffe, Hammond, Ames, Larwood, Verity, Leyland, Wyatt, Paynter, Allen, Voce, emerged from the pavilion, each quite obviously the receptacle of honour and virtue. The crowd applauded them with good-mannered impartiality. The heat was very great and hopes were high.

After playing an interim match at Bendigo the visitors went to Adelaide for the third Test. Here, on Saturday, January 13th, 1933, and in glorious weather, began a game which came near to destroying the central mystery upon which cricket is founded and without which it could only exist as one of the dullest pastimes imaginable. To the 30,000 spectators it came near to seeing a cardinal perform a black Mass. Their formal staccato clapping and encouraging platitudes broke down into outraged mob baying. And half-way through the match the Australian Board of Cricket Control sent the Committee of the M.C.C. a cable accusing the English team of unsportsmanlike tactics. If a cable had arrived at Lord's accusing the English Eleven of cannibalism it could scarcely have produced greater horror. When the full nature of the charge was understood England drew back in stunned silence, while *The Times* cleared its correspondence columns of all extraneous matter and waited for the deluge.

Before being wise after the event it is a matter of probity to take a close look at the event itself, even though, as in this instance, doing so merely confirms one's incredulity. Why was such a campaign ever dreamt of, let alone put into action? Wisden, in the exalted language taken for granted by cricketers, says, 'the plan of the campaign was to reduce Bradman to mortal limits'. To the crowd which watched it looked more as if Bradman and his colleagues were to be reduced to mortal remains. As the injured staggered from the field, Woodfull from a blow over the heart with, as Mr. R. H. Lyttelton remarked, 'a thud that was heard in the grandstand and very likely round the ground generally,' and Oldfield from a blow on the head which concussed him, the crowd vented its indignation in sounds never before heard on a cricket ground. Larwood, whose bowling had caused this agony, and Jardine, who had given permission for the bowling, were heaped with personal abuse. The elaborately chivalric structure of the game momentarily rocked and looked as though it was about to cave in, and for a fraction of time it seemed that from these sublime ruins there would emerge a knock-about summer pastime which would be so obviously 'not cricket' that another name would have to be invented for it.

How could such a thing happen? Or, more to the point, how did it?

Play opened at the Adelaide Oval in exquisite weather, on a near-perfect pitch and to a record crowd of nearly forty thousand people on the mounds. Within the first hour England, who were noticeably nervous, suffered the worst revenge they had known since the Sydney Test Match of 1925. Jardine was always uncomfortable as he faced O'Reilly, who it was thought was bowling faster than at any time during the whole of his career. Jardine was out when he made only three runs and the English demoralization continued apace when Hammond was caught out by Oldfield after making a miserable two. Ames then took thirty-nine minutes to make three and although the English batting eventually made a fairly lively recovery, it could have been that the note of sourness, with its Empire-shaking reverberations, crept into the game at this juncture. Leyland and Wyatt rescued the English team from complete disaster and the great Australian crowd, blissfully oblivious of the ferocity latent in its breast, clapped generously. All wasn't well, although on the other hand there was still nothing to indicate a state of affairs which could be called sick.

The second day's play opened before a vast crowd—the biggest ever seen at Adelaide—of some 51,000 spectators. The wicket was described as a batsman's paradise, an uncomfortably ambiguous description in the circumstances. England consolidated the lead given them on the previous day by Wyatt and Leyland, and when the last wicket fell their score was a cosy 341. Australia began badly. Fingleton, McCabe and the great Bradman himself were all out for a total of 34. This would have been worrying enough for the crowd had not Larwood's curious bowling begun to cause a more complex anxiety. He was bumping the balls down most disconcertingly and the easy way in which McCabe and Bradman were trapped was faintly shocking and somehow not quite acceptable. Also it was observed that the batsmen were ducking and dodging as the ball rushed at them. The reason for this was only too apparent when a ball crashed against Woodfull's left breast and he had to leave the ground to receive massage. Uproar then broke out. The enormous crowd stormed and barracked. But Larwood seemed to hear nothing—even when every ball he sent down was booed and jeered, even when, in the twinkling of an eye, he must have sensed that he had suffered a metamorphosis in esteem and was now the Sweeney Todd of the wicket. He bowled on imperturbably. The crowd howled. At the end of this day's strange play the score was, England 341, Australia 109.

The gate was noticeably reduced when play began on the third day; some 15,000 people had stayed away. Those who were present were tense, suspicious and watchful. Larwood began to bowl from the river end and at once employed his body-line bowling. Like Louis XVIII's court, he had forgotten nothing and learnt nothing.

Three times he struck Ponsford on the back with deliveries which got up high and each time the crowd roared its disapproval. The chapter of accidents continued after lunch with Paynter crashing into a fence and hurting his leg so badly that he had to leave the field for a bit. But the grim climax of the day came when Larwood, still practising leg-theory in spite of the arena of hostility which ringed him and threatened his every action, sent a ball down which hit Oldfield on the head. He was helped away suffering from concussion and shock to a crescendo of hooting, booing and every kind of furious noise. At the end of this dreary day the Australian score had roughly doubled and stood at 222.

On the fourth day of this appalling Test match an air of lassitude and withdrawal infected the mounds. The play was dull, the weather was threatening and sultry and Jardine's monumental patience bored the much-reduced crowd into ripples of open derision. As if to flaunt his powers, Larwood showed his bowling superiority by not employing his controversial body-line method against Fingleton and Ponsford, but dismissed them just as easily. Bradman did well and was applauded rapturously, though more because at that moment he personified the old spirit of the game before it was disgraced than for any very great batting brilliance. A dove had circled the wicket as play began, a somewhat satirical bird as it proved, for that evening the Australian Board of Control sent its notorious cable, a communication as sensationally synonymous to the world of sport as the Zinoviev Letter to the world of politics. Addressed to the M.C.C., the cable read:

> *Body-line bowling has assumed such proportions as to menace the best interests of the game, making protection of the body by the batsmen the main consideration.*
>
> *This is causing intensely bitter feeling between the players as well as injury. In our opinion it is unsportsmanlike.*
>
> *Unless stopped at once it is likely to upset the friendly relations existing between Australia and England.*

This cable, sent at a time of passionate indignation and while the third Test was in mid-progress, crashed against the well-bred façade of the M.C.C. and left it gasping, while at Adelaide things had sunk to such a level that they had no parallel in all the history of cricket. The public had to be kept out of the ground when the Eng-

lish team were practising and once, when one of the English
managers tried to express his personal sympathy in the battered
Woodfull's dressing-room there was a violent scene. Jardine, Larwood and Voce (the latter had also been practising body-line
bowling), England's best, were seen down under as a triumvirate of
villainy. Abuse followed them everywhere. The overworked analogy
between the game and national honour fed the scandal and made it
assume grotesque proportions. The Empire watched and waited.
If cricket itself was fallible then surely anything might be fallible.
What in fact had Larwood (and Jardine and Voce) done to bring
such shame on the Anglo-Saxon world?

The Times got in a good word for the defence before the stupendous correspondence began. While the pundits in the shires were
still crouching dazedly over their inkhorns it said:

'In due time, no doubt, the M.C.C. will send a considered and
courteous reply to the cable of protest against what has begun to
be called "body-line bowling" which they received yesterday
from the Australian Board of Control. Meanwhile an attempt to
give some idea of how the matter strikes the average Englishman
may not come amiss. First of all there is nothing new in the kind
of bowling to which exception is now taken. Really fast bowlers
are as rare as truly great statesmen. But they do every now and
then spring up, both here and in the Dominion, and have been
known before now to hit the batsman as well as the wicket.
English players who some years ago suffered many a shrewd knock
from the bowling of Macdonald and Gregory—not to speak of
Jones in his earlier days—have the right to recall their own experiences to those who are now criticizing the tactics of Larwood
and his Captain. Australians know as well as our men that cricket
is not played with a soft ball, and that a fast ball which hits a
batsman is bound to hurt. They also know that, so long as a
"shock" bowler is not bumping down short-pitch balls or pur-
posely aiming at the batsman, his bowling is perfectly fair. It is
inconceivable that a cricketer of Jardine's standing, chosen by the
M.C.C. to captain an English side, would ever dream of allowing
or would order the bowlers under his command to practise any
system of attack that, in the time-honoured English phrase, is not
cricket. To do the Australians justice the grievance at the back of

their complaint is neither the pace nor the direction of Larwood's deliveries. What they probably object to is the array of leg-fielders . . . on whom the English captain relies to increase the effectiveness of his fast bowlers. But in that policy there is nothing dishonourable or unsportsmanlike. . . . After all, the object of every fielding side is to get their opponents out for as low a score as possible. If with that aim in view Jardine has made more use of the "leg-theory" than other captains before him it is largely due to the fashion of the two-eyed stance and the modern batsman's habit of covering the stumps with his leg, thereby preventing the bowler from getting a clear view of the wicket, and incidentally making it more likely that he himself will be hit.'

The Times apologist then doled out tributes and diplomatic advice to both teams and ended his say fretfully with:

'In all probability the present delicate and difficult position need never have arisen but for the irresponsible chapter of elderly critics in the pavilion and in the Press and the craving in some quarters for news-stories. . . .'

This leader was published on January 19th and the following day there was a noticeable hardening of opinion and feeling in favour of Larwood. England had won the Test, but it was a Pyrrhic victory in which it was impossible to rejoice and it was received in this country with the same kind of gratitude which comes to a man when a diseased tooth ceases to rage. The last day's play was gloomy and poorly attended. An X-ray had revealed that Oldfield had a linear fracture of the frontal bone of his forehead. The weather broke. Clouds banked up fast and it became a race between the game and the rain. Larwood, who presumably could not abandon his body-line bowling since to do so might imply an awareness of its savagery, continued with his leg-theory tactics and all ended in bitterness and acrimony.

In Australia there was a certain reaction to all the fuss and a de-cided anger at the uncompromising language of the Board of Control's cable. Ever over-sensitive about what the Old Country thought of them, they began to suspect that the complaint would be interpreted in London as a typical ill-bred colonial whine. The *Sydney Sun* said, 'The Board of Control seems to have become

somewhat confused between the verbs to cable and to burble. . . .'
and it went on satirically, 'M.C.C. might be forgiven, after reading
the appalling suggestions of Imperial disruption, if it replied to the
Board with a request that it packs its several heads in ice.' And the
Melbourne Argus followed *The Times*'s line in putting the whole
business down to irresponsible commentators, and this in spite of
the fact that forty thousand Aussies were there to know the reason
why. As an Australian living in London pointed out, 'It must be
perfectly obvious that thousands of spectators and the Board of
Control, all eye-witnesses of the play, *thought* that such tactics were
being deliberately adopted, otherwise, why the protest? Has an
optical illusion on a gigantic scale been performed?'

There followed an upsurge of violent reminiscences. And a gruesome showing of scars. H. B. Cameron, the South African captain,
boasted that he had been knocked out by Larwood at Lord's in 1932
and P. H. Shaw reminded the world that the marks on his limbs
reminded *him* that cricket was played with a hard ball. Very old
cricketers came out with tales which competed fiercely with the
worst excesses of the Colosseum, so what were those post-war
colonials whimpering about? And Lord Buckmaster's recollections
of actually what did happen on the classic village greens of England
dismissed the white and emerald idyll with contempt.

'. . . Leg bowling', confessed this Uncle Matthew-like peer, 're-
vives old memories and old desires. Pitches like billiard tables and
spectators numbered in thousands make people forget what cricket
used to be. Fifty years ago this new danger was a common incident
in every match played outside the few places where groundsmen
guarded the turf. Fast bowlers—*quorum parvissima pars fui*—were
regarded as essential and were often, as I was, most erratic. I have
often seen a ball pitch once and then bounce straight into the
backstop's hands.

'Nor were these eccentricities confined to local grounds. I remember on one occasion the first ball of a match slung with immense violence straight at the big black beard of W. G. Grace. Did
he object? Certainly not: he simply hit it out of the ground and
waited for the next.

'In the country there were some pitches renowned for their fiery
qualities. On one of these I recall a game in which Ranjitsinhji took
part. Two benches from the village school provided the grandstand

and on these were seated the squire, the local doctor—whose patients were long-suffering and few—the publican and some countrymen.

'Ranjitsinhji was cleanly bowled by the village postman, who wore his official uniform, and all the four innings were finished in the day. As for the leg balls and head balls and body balls, they formed the feature of the match, which no one seemed to enjoy more than Ranjitsinhji himself. The world has been made smooth for the game and its lords, but is it a better game?'

Such words were salt in the Australian wounds. Had they made—were they making too much fuss about the whole affair? Small boys saw the matter quite simply. A new game appeared on the streets in England. The requirements for it were a rubber ball, a biscuit tin and a bat. The bowler, always addressed as Larwood, bowled at the batsman, who had to prevent himself from being touched by the ball, either by swiping it with the bat or by dodging. Should the ball touch him he had to lie flat on the road and then be carried off by his friends. This game wasn't called cricket.

A. A. Milne tried to bring a little humour to the situation by calling it 'the laugh of the year . . . that batsmen should break the hearts of bowlers by protecting the wickets with their persons, and that when at last the bowler accepts the challenge and bowls at their persons, the outraged batsmen should shriek that he isn't playing cricket!' Most people who heard this view of the matter were obliged to believe that it was a poor year for laughs.

Immediately after winning this calamitous Test there was an attempt by the managers of the M.C.C. team to force their way back into the old grand vocabulary of the game where the crude sounds of the Adelaide Oval had no place. 'Members of the M.C.C. and the English team had no desire to enter into public controversy,' the statement said, 'for they deplore the introduction of any personal feeling into the records of a great game. . . .' Nobody in Australia took much notice of this; they were waiting now in a crippled silence for the boomerang from Lord's. While all intuitively knew that body-line bowling was wrong, there was also a general agreement that the wording of the Australian cable protesting against it was, to put it mildly, unfortunate. The M.C.C. Committee's reply came on January 24th and was all the Australians dreaded that it would be.

We, the Marylebone Cricket Club, deplore your cable. We deprecate your opinion that there has been unsportsmanlike play. We have fullest confidence in captain, team and managers and are convinced that they would do nothing to infringe either the laws of cricket or the spirit of the game. We have no evidence that our confidence has been misplaced. Much as we regret accidents to Woodfull and Oldfield, we understand that in neither case was the bowler to blame. If the Australian Board of Control wish to propose a new law or rule it shall receive our careful consideration in due course. We hope the situation is not now as serious as your cable would seem to indicate, but if it is such as to jeopardize the good relations between English and Australian cricketers, and you consider it desirable to cancel the remainder of programme we would consent, but with great reluctance.

(signed) Findlay, Secretary.

The M.C.C. Committee, presided over by Lord Lewisham, had spoken. Here was majesty. Here was straight rejection of the scarcely mentionable charge of 'unsportmanslike'. And here was a careful avoidance of the trouble spot—body-line itself. Before a fresh wave of cricket jabberwocky had time to obliterate the main argument, Mr. R. H. Lyttelton forced people to face facts.

'Cricketers all over the world are in a fever about the cricket now being played between the picked elevens of England and Australia,' he declared grimly. 'In the Third Test match just concluded Mr. Woodfull got a very severe blow over the heart from a ball bowled by Larwood. It was the most deplorable event in the most disagreeable match that has been played since the game began. . . .

'From the reports that have reached us it appears that Larwood bowled a ball either on the leg stump or perhaps straight to the batsman. This particular ball kicked and hit Mr. Woodfull a terrible blow. . . . This could not have been the case were it not due to the fact that it was a direct hit straight to the body and hit it because the batsman was facing the bowler and therefore exposing the head, heart and other vital organs. This method of play is most dangerous, and that is probably due to the fact that modern wickets have been brought to such perfection that a ball very seldom kicks.

'Now the question is, How would W. G. Grace in his prime have played Larwood and any fast bowler? He would have stood firm on the right foot, with his left shoulder well forward: to certain balls well pitched up he would have played forward and smothered, but never was W.G. guilty of adopting the two-eyed stance, or in other words exposing the full face of his body to the bowler, and never in his life was he dangerously hit.

'As long as cricket is played with a hard ball there must be contusions, but if the modern batsman would adopt the methods of W. G. Grace by abandoning the two-eyed stance and learning to play forward and smothering the ball there would be very few accidents.... It is now up to the batsmen to kill the two-eyed stance.'

This sweet reasonableness brought a more constructive attitude to the whole affair. The Australians began to recover from the faint sense of shame they had felt about the Board of Control's cable. Some of the English at least were recognizing that they had a case, even if they were presenting it clumsily. The smooth wording of the M.C.C.'s reply had to be admired. Immediately it arrived, Mr. Jeanes, the Board's secretary, conferred with the South Australian delegates for about an hour and then made a telephone call to the chairman, Dr. Robertson. All that the public gleaned from this was that if the English packed up and went home at this stage of the tour there would be a loss of some £45,000 in gross receipts.

The Australian Press's reaction was confused and irritable. It ranged from the mild servility of the *Melbourne Argus*—'the M.C.C. are under a misapprehension which, in the circumstances, is quite pardonable ... they don't appreciate the good will, the comradeship which the visit of an English team evokes . . .' to some good old Australian plain-speaking in the *Melbourne Herald*—'it is a pity that the protest, however clumsily worded, was not received in England with a greater effort of understanding. The cable did not come from an irresponsible source.' And it added stoically, 'It must now be considered that the protest has completely failed and that if the English captain considers that bodyline bowling is the right tactics at Brisbane and Sydney, then our batsmen will have to do their best to stand up to it.' As for the *Sydney Sun*, it saw the M.C.C. reply as pure Limey upper-class winner-take-all stuff—'With one shrewd thrust M.C.C. has changed the question, "Shall leg theory continue?" to "Shall Tests continue?" Thus the Board is out-manœuvred and would be well advised to withdraw for the time being with all the grace it has at its command.'

But the Board didn't withdraw. It met behind closed doors and then sent this reply to London:

We Australian Board of Control appreciate your difficulty in dealing with the matter raised in our cable without having seen the actual play. We unanimously regard body-line bowling, as adopted in some of the games in the present tour, as opposed to the spirit of cricket and unnecessarily dangerous to the players.

We are deeply concerned that the ideals of the game shall be protected, and have therefore appointed a committee to report on the action necessary to eliminate such bowling from Australian cricket as from the beginning of the 1933–34 season.

We will forward a copy of the Committee's recommendations for your consideration, and it is hoped for your co-operation as to its application to all cricket. We do not consider it necessary to cancel remainder of programme.

The reply staggered the M.C.C. They had not expected anything like so positive an attitude, and as an authority which had always considered itself the last word on cricket it found the unequivocal statement that body-line bowling would in future be illegal in Australia audacious, to say the least of it. Nor could the independent and chilly tone of the reply be ignored. Also—and here was the sting—although there was no more mention of that ultimate gamesmanship obscenity 'unsportsmanlike', the cool declaration that a method of bowling which had been sensationally adopted by an English captain would in future be banned in Australia made it starkly clear what Australians thought about it. Even the *Melbourne Herald* was shaken by the tough line taken in this second cable and called it a pistol held to the heart of the English authorities.

The M.C.C. was now on the defensive. Did the Australians still believe that Jardine and Larwood had been unsporting? *They simply had to know.* Nobody could breathe, eat, sleep or think until they did. The M.C.C.'s second cable was a trifle overwrought. It noted with pleasure that the Australians weren't thinking of cancelling the programme and then it came to the point. '*May we accept this as a clear indication that the good sportsmanship of our team is not in question. We are sure you will appreciate how impossible it would be to play any Test Match in the spirit we all desire unless both sides were satisfied there was no reflection upon their sportsmanship.*

When your recommendation reaches us it shall receive our most careful consideration and will be submitted to the Imperial Cricket Conference.'

While these messages came and went the English team were moving about in Australia under a nightmarish cloud of obloquy and suspicion. Some individuals thought that their personal honour was at stake until the Board of Control publicly retracted its haunting accusation and they wanted the Fourth Test to be abandoned. The team went so far as to ask E. T. Crutchley, the British Representative in Australia, to plead for them. The Governor of Queensland, Sir Leslie Wilson, tried to lessen the tension by remarking tartly, 'that it was a serious symptom when people take cricket too seriously'. He didn't say a symptom of what. The Board of Control allowed dishonour to swing like Damocles' sword over the heads of the Englishmen right up to the moment before the Fourth Test opened at Brisbane on February 9th, when it announced coldly, 'We do not regard the sportsmanship of your team as being in question. . . . It is, as indicated in our cable of January 30th . . . the particular class of bowling which we consider not in the best interests of cricket. . . .'

So that was that. Or was it? Not quite.

Larwood went in for body-line bowling again during the Fourth Test and the crowd jeered again, but the jeers were soon silenced by the brilliance of the Australian batting. Soon it became so good that it defeated leg-theory and Larwood. It was captivating and courageous and it forced the crowd to discipline itself, and the Fourth Test became the happiest match of the whole tour. England beat Australia by six wickets and regained the Ashes, and when the King's telegram of congratulations arrived both victors and vanquished felt like cheering, just for normalcy's sake.

The body-line controversy spread from the Adelaide Oval to every anglicized acre of the earth and was compulsory conversation wherever the English met. But other things were happening in the world during this three weeks' wonder, events which were to put Larwood's game of cricket on a par with Francis Drake's game of bowls. For on January 31st Adolf Hitler broke Hindenburg's long resistance to him and became Chancellor of the Reich and Captain Göring took control of the police in Berlin and over more than half Germany. The full meaning of this was only faintly comprehended —even when the Reichstag was burnt down twenty-seven days later, even as the Oxford Union was provocatively debating whether it would fight for King and Country, and deciding that it wouldn't. England and Australia, each emerging thankfully from the sudden darkness which had overtaken them, were wholly given up to the luxury of cricket evolution. Letters flowed into the Press, though only 99% were about the two-eyed stance and leg-theory. One was from Mr. Neville Chamberlain to the editor of *The Times* and hoped that it might be of interest that in walking through St. James's Park he had noticed a grey wagtail. . . .

CHAPTER EIGHT

The Rector of Skiffkey

Monday is parson's holiday.
                    DEAN SWIFT

'I am parshial to ladies if they are nice I suppose it is my
nature. I am not quite a gentleman but you would hardly
notice it but cant be helped anyhow.'
                    MR. SALTEENA—*The Young Visiters*

'WHAT is truth?' asked jesting Pilate. What indeed! might have
replied that nimble divine, Harold Francis Davidson, M.A., Rector
of Stiffkey with Morston, whose application of the truth as it
appeared to him was to provide a ribald anti-clerical entertainment
throughout the whole of 1932, the year of the yo-yo. When human
conduct reaches a certain point the ordinary laws cannot apply.
Where one insists upon applying them there is set in motion a comic
process in which retribution slips on its own banana-skin, as it were.
For Church and State to conspire together so elaborately to exact
a penalty from the Rector was a hopeless gesture from the very
beginning. That much is plain now. They might as well have tried
to lasso a Chagall cow and drag it from its pasture among the stars.
The Anglican Church is an elastic institution and had it not been for
a little Miss Judas it is doubtful if the Rector of Stiffkey's stretching
a few points would ever have been noticed. The parish was a different matter. When the storm broke, the village may have been
staggered by the fury of it but not at all surprised that there should
have been a storm eventually. Villages know.

Stiffkey, which the locals call 'Stewky', is a pretty place near the
Norfolk coast, and its only claim to fame before 1932 was the fine
house built by Sir Nicholas Bacon, Keeper of the Great Seal to
Queen Elizabeth I. The Rector was inducted into the living there
in 1906 when he was thirty-one years old, and he had lived with his
wife and five children in Stiffkey Rectory, a handsome structure,

for twenty-six years before the extraordinary events of 1932 caused him to remove himself to a barrel in Blackpool.

The Reverend Mr. Davidson's downfall—he would never have it so—was girls. Not *a* girl, not five or six girls even, not a hundred, but the entire tremulous universe of girlhood. Shingled heads, clear cheeky eyes, nifty legs, warm, blunt-fingered workaday hands, small firm breasts and, most importantly, good strong healthy teeth, besotted him. A single human life was all too short for him to savour such a universe and his awareness of this allowed him to encounter at least a thousand girls during the twenties alone. And this on his own estimate, not his detractors'. Quite early on in his sacred career he hit upon an exciting solution to what otherwise might have been an insoluble problem; he would make girls his special ministry. And so he set about it with a single-mindedness which in any other circumstances should have brought him a deanery.

Sunday found him bustling into the pulpit of St. John with St. Mary, Stiffkey. Monday found him rushing to Wells-next-the-Sea to catch the London train. If either he or the Church itself had thought that dull Stiffkey was a safe address for an Agapet, a reliable exile for an early twentieth-century Herrick, they must have quite forgotten that love will find a way. The most efficient way back to Paradise, or Piccadilly, as the prosecution called it, was by the London-North-Eastern line and the Rector took it with alacrity. He went to London first thing Monday morning and returned to Stiffkey last thing Saturday night, not just often, but regularly every week for years and years.

The next thing about the Rector, his kind of girl, as it were, can be partly explained by his times. He was born in 1875 when Mr. Gladstone was picking up fallen women on the Duke of York's Steps, to take them back to Mrs. Gladstone, soup and concern. A child of the rectory himself and related to twenty-seven other clergymen, he knew that *bourgeois* churchmanship and fundamental Christian ethics took care to have nothing in common which might cause embarrassment. The Rector sought to remedy this, to lessen the gap, as it were. His error, or one of his errors—there were so many—was to see every young girl from fifteen onwards on the skids, and being torn between preventing her from falling any further and from rescuing her when she had fallen as far as a girl can tumble. Eventually, his attitude seemed to be, let them fall if they must. And if they don't, give them a little shove. What was there to worry about? Most of them were so low already that they wouldn't be able to fall very far and, anyway, where in the world would they find charity like that of the unfortunate sisterhood? Good girls knew where they were at once with the little rector from the word go, and bolted. Bad girls sank back into the sleazy bed-sitters he discovered for them, heartily relieved that there was nothing to fear, such as salvation, for instance. Styling himself the 'Prostitutes' Padre' and working out a plausible analogy between his vocation and the Magdalen's repentance, the Rector of Stiffkey began to lead a life in London which passed all comprehension.

London is all things to all men but even allowing for this there can be few men who saw London as Harold Davidson saw it. As the train fled from Norfolk in the small hours of Monday morning, his heart would soar, his blood would race. As Romford and Ilford flashed by, he might fancy he already heard it, the siren song of the Nippies, the ineffable harmonies created by starched linen crackling over young breasts and black-stockinged calves in chubby conference just below the hem of the parlourmaid's frock. As Stratford disappeared, an inexhaustible plethora of A.B.C.s, Express Dairies and Lyons' teashops would come sharply into focus and his eyes would grow dreamy at the thought that he would soon be present in one of his marble-tabled temples where, all unbeknown to him, the staff knew him as 'the mormon'.

Some people in London are blackballed at clubs or made *persona non grata* at courts and embassies, but the Rector of Stiffkey's fate was to be turned away from teashops. He challenged this rule once by arriving at such a teashop with a bishop, but the bishop was served and he wasn't. He was philosophical about this persecution; there were always rebuffs to reform and, mercifully, there were in the London of the twenties a quite unparalleled number of teashops. Moreover, the pavements between the teashops were agog with girls tottering along in shiny art silk stockings, their pretty baby faces clownish with cosmetics beneath the mysterious shadows of the cloche hat, their handbags not often containing more than two and sixpence, for times were hard. The Rector plunged into this ever-flowing girlish flood, intoxicated by its sweet cheap scent, not over-much worried by its skin but wild when spikily painted lips parted to reveal good white teeth. He was potty about teeth.

'You said she had pretty hair, skin and teeth?' asked the prosecution.

'I never said skin,' said the Rector.

Council for the Prosecution then looked at his notes and murmured, 'You are quite right; you did not say skin.'

'I know I am right,' said the Rector in the tone of one who never erred in essentials. Skin meant nothing to him.

While in London he rarely, if ever, went to bed. All day and all night until it was time to hurry back to Stiffkey for Matins, he waded deeper and deeper into girlish streams. He spoke to them, smiled at them, kissed them and kept them, but muddled himself up so cosily between adoring them and saving them that the difference soon escaped him.

In late 1931 the girl of girls, Miss Rose Ellis, his proto-penitent from as far back as 1920, irrupted. There was a chain reaction of ingratitude and before his bishop or anyone else had taken the first step to investigate the scandalous nature of his life, the Rector began to defend himself against Miss Rose Ellis in the newspapers. The sensation was immense. So was the congregation at Stiffkey Church on Sunday, February 7th, 1932, when 500 people arrived to sing Evensong and hundreds more swarmed devotedly in the graveyard outside. They came on foot from miles around, by bicycle from Norwich and special excursion buses from places as far away as Bournemouth.

A week later Miss Rose Ellis made a public recantation. Eight glasses of port wine plied to her by a ruthless inquiry agent in a saloon bar had wrung these untruths from her. She was sorry and ashamed. But by this time the Rector had contracted with the *Empire News* to tell *his* version of the story and didn't see why his chance of authorship should be lost just because Rose had changed her mind, and so he Told All. Friends and the bishop's legal advisers hurried to beg him to say no more and to point out the folly of all this publicity, but they found him very divided on the subject. He had stood up in the pulpit at Stiffkey and seen a great multitude reaching from the lectern right out into wintry Norfolk itself and it struck him as an excellent opportunity to preach about love. He became exultant. He wrote more articles, preached more sermons, threw himself into the thing and became very famous.

The law and the Bishop of Norwich could not share these views and made legal history by prosecuting the *Empire News*, the *Daily Herald* and the Rector of Stiffkey for contempt of a consistory court. Thus, still before anything had occurred officially, the Stiffkey affair was already established as a *cause célèbre*. When the trial opened, on March 29th, Stiffkey was as notorious as Babylon and its incumbent as celebrated as Al Capone. With poetic justice and some consideration for what it might cost to bring scores of London girls to Norfolk, the Norwich Consistory Court decided to sit in the Great Hall of Church House, Westminster. The Rector, who had little sense of time and was to be conspicuously late for his manifold tribulations at every stage, dashed to his place a few minutes after the proceedings had begun. The charges, after so much juicy gossip, left everybody feeling distinctly cheated, though not for long.

The defendant had been guilty of immoral conduct for ten years from 1921 to 1931 with a woman named. He had made improper suggestions to a waitress in Walbrook. He had kissed a girl in the Chinese restaurant in Bloomsbury. And for five years he had habitually associated himself with women of loose character. The Rector denied all the charges and then sat quietly watching the Bishop's Counsel, Roland Oliver, K.C., Walter Monckton, K.C. and Humphrey King. His own Counsel sat near-by. The galleries of the Great Hall of the Lower House of Convocation contained quite a fair number of spectators, but were not crowded. Among them sat Mrs. Davidson, the Rector's patient wife. Nobody present that cold March afternoon dreamed that they would still be present in June. Nobody guessed that the thin line between jurisprudence and entertainment was to become invisible. Nobody mentioned lions.

But before the day was out it was plain that ecclesiastical justice being seen to be done under the quizzing-glass of Fleet Street was legal folly. But such folly! Yo-yos were laid away, the Dartmoor riot forgotten and the semi-literate and the wholly sophisticated alike settled down to read an extraordinary serial which might have been called, 'A thousand and one nights in darkest London, thank goodness'. Presiding over the Court was the Chancellor of Norwich, Mr. F. Keppel North, and he was the first to fear and in some ways regret the probing of this hornets' nest. The Rector of Stiffkey regarded him blandly. The shrill humming set up in the world on account of his odd ministry was not unwelcome. He heard the astounded Mr. Oliver tell the court the pattern of his life for the past decade or so, and he smiled.

He had been Rector of Stiffkey since 1906. He had married and he now had five children. His stipend was £800 but a bankruptcy and a flair for financial disasters of all kinds had reduced this to about £400 a year. The only time he ever spent in his parish was on Sunday; all the rest of the week he was in London. So eager was he to be in London that it was nothing for him to leave Stiffkey in the small hours and arrive in town by dawn, and so reluctant was he to return to Norfolk that often brother clergy in the neighbourhood of Stiffkey would be telephoned very late on Saturday night to say that the Rector had been unavoidably delayed and would they please take the services for him? This went on for many years. It was not his occasional whim; it was his regular habit. In London the Rector's activities were unevenly divided between searching for a Mr. Gordon, who owed him a thousand pounds—sometimes a quarter of a million pounds, and certainly an apology—and in making friends with girls. The point the Court had to prove was, were these friendships innocent? And this was the sole reason why the court was sitting.

A number of things occurred to the prosecution, grumbled Mr. Oliver. Why, for instance, did the rescue work include taking all these girls to theatres, to cinemas, to meals in restaurants and—to Paris? And, how did a man who was an undischarged bankrupt since 1925 and who had a country rectory full of children over a hundred miles from the capital, and only £400 a year, *do it*? Also, why did not the Rector's charity include young men as well as young women? To discover some of the answers to these questions a firm of private detectives had followed the Rector on and off for about six months. And things had rushed to a climax after one of his girls, Barbara Harris, had written to the Bishop of Norwich.

The Rector had met Barbara Harris, the first witness and the last angel, through means he had invented, perfected and made fool-proof. He saw her at Marble Arch, he walked round and round her in wonderment and then, in his most gentlemanly way, he had begged her to forgive him and tell him. Was she—could she be— surely she must be—Miss X, the film actress? Barbara, who was a highly experienced sixteen-and-a-half, found such an approach dottily intriguing. Very soon afterwards, she and her Indian lover were sitting up in bed in their pyjamas entertaining the Rector to tea when he happened to call about two in the morning. They got on fine. The Indian was a policeman and he told the Rector fascinating tales of temple girls. 'God,' the Rector told Barbara, 'did not mind sins of the body, only sins of the soul.' And he went on to urge her to improve her mind with literature, such as the Works of William Shakespeare and *Damaged Goods*. 'Have ideals,' he advised her in a letter from his study in Stiffkey, 'and you will become ideal yourself.' On the day she found out that he was a parson, for he had concealed this from her, his advice took on an added urgency. 'Let me warn you in the words of Psalmist, "to set a watch over the door of my lips so that I offend not with my tongue." '

During the prosecution's cross-examination of Barbara the Rector was seen shaking with laughter and had to be called to order by the Chancellor. Mr. Davidson said that he wasn't laughing at the witness's answers—which only left the prosecution's questions as the source of his amusement, and it was true they would have entertained a cat. Mr. Oliver began to dislike Mr. Davidson very much indeed from this moment.

Barbara's story continued. The Lower House of Convocation became frowsty with her bed-sitters and bizarre with her lovers, but she herself, now at the ripe age of eighteen, seemed pleasant enough. She described her digs and jobs. She told of a journey to the Rectory at Stiffkey with Rose Ellis. This was during the summer of 1931, when the Rector had a brainwave and had solved the Sunday problem, as it were. On July 29th he had put Miss Barbara Harris and Miss Rose Ellis, the last and first of his loves, on a train for Wells-next-the-Sea. He said he was going to give them a country holiday, which was something neither of them very much wanted. When they reached Stiffkey Rectory they found to their disgust that it was not only full of Mr. Davidson's big family, but paying guests besides, and that they were expected to do housework. So furious were they with this arrangement that they at once began to walk back to London, sleeping under hedges and running all sorts of risks, such as catching colds or getting blisters. A kind man had eventually given them a lift in a motor-car and taken them all the way. The Rector immediately hurried back to town and made his peace with Barbara and soon afterwards resumed his amiable régime of hurrying from her side on Sunday mornings to catch the 5.5 a.m. train which got

him to church in Norfolk just in time to hare into the vestry and
robe for Matins. The private agents were worn out with his ways,
particularly with his indifference to whether it was day or night. He
drifted almost ceaselessly two and three days at a time through the
packed streets of the West End, he paid calls after midnight, he
cashed cheques in friendly pubs, in one of which he was greeted
with 'Hello, you old thief! How are all the girls?' He spoke to
countless strangers, none of whom seemed in the least bit offended.
Clothes and class meant absolutely nothing to him. His hands
patted shoulders, waists, clung to other hands. His eyes recognized
no social barriers. He offered no guard and expected none. He was
entirely disarming and he made the disarming of others his chief
business. All this naturally led him into spheres where the normal
social taboos had never properly taken root and which he genuinely
believed to be full of pagan innocence. But neither Barbara Harris,
nor Rose Ellis, nor Miss Nellie Churchill, who rather came it with
a refained accent, nor the Rector himself was concerned with
innocence, and well they all knew it. But by manipulating the convention of innocence they were able to amuse themselves for years.
They met their Waterloo when their version of innocence had to
compete with innocence viewed as an absolute. This became the
central dilemma of the trial, for the Rector stuck fervently to his
beige conception of purity. It was a shade much favoured by the
girls he knew, since they could not wear white. They were not unprincipled and neither was he. Let him who was without sin go out
and cast the first stone. Since the Rector's life, subsequent to his
removal from Holy Orders, was nothing more nor less than a
dedicated vocation to force the world to comprehend what he meant
by 'innocence', and since he was certainly the last Christian to be
eaten by a lion for the sake of his beliefs, it would be fatuous as well
as uncharitable to deny him principles. It has to be remembered
that the extraordinary Mr. Davidson was not ruined by his trial.
He was roused. The suppressed Thespian of Stiffkey, released from
the restrictions of his cloth, donned the motley with prodigious
effect. If the world insisted that he had turned the pulpit of Stiffkey
into a sideshow, then he would turn a sideshow into a pulpit. Nor
would he be the first to do so. Supposing Diogenes or St. Simon
Stylites had lived in 1928, would they have been a don and parson
respectively? Of course not. They would have joined Bertram

Mills's Circus. Did such dreams as these sustain the Rector on the last day of March, 1932, in the Great Hall of Church House? For it was certain that something sustained him. It was he who smiled and his nostrils which did not wrinkle as the court forked over the steamy humus of his past.

He listened as the prosecution insisted on being shocked and surprised by things which had never remotely shocked or surprised him. The inquiry agent had tracked him down to a Chinese restaurant in Bloomsbury and had seen him kiss and embrace Barbara. What was surprising in that? What was surprising to *him* was that men could sit among the cruets and cream buns of restaurants and teashops and *not* kiss girls.

Barbara was a very special girl and his feelings for her had got quite out of hand. Conventional girlish treats, such as taking her to the *Folies Bergère* in Paris, were not for her. She was witty, rising eighteen and she dazzled him. They gipsied together through a warren of rooms in the West End. He was her 'uncle', her 'guardian' and sometimes just her very good friend. He bought her clothes. He even told her about Mr. Gordon, his peregrinating pot of gold. Finally he told her what it had never been necessary to tell all the others, that he would divorce his wife and marry her. Or so she said. In and out of this romance, tangling it up into a grossly complicated knot, were Barbara's youthful Indians and the Rector's Rose, the latter no longer eighteen but thirty, and faithful like Cynara in her fashion. It was Rose who had got sloshed on the inquiry agent's port and said too much.

It now became the object of the prosecution to tie labels on Barbara and Rose for the sake of clarity. Rose, being thirty, was Bad. Barbara, being eighteen, was Good, but Betrayed. But no sooner had these labels been safely fixed than the two girls began tearing them to bits for all they were worth, Barbara, with the immortal candour of the harlot, Rose with a certain bleak logic. Rose had, after all, outlasted a thousand girls and had known the Rector for ten years. She was truly sorry for her part in the débâcle. Hopeless she may have been by any of the rules governing Church House, Westminster, but not hopeless to the angels.

Barbara was a different matter. In the first place she gave the sentimental protection of her age the brush-off. Mr. Levy, for the defence, who quite expected contrite sobs and pathos, found a ready

conversationalist whose terrible honesty and frightful lies were
equally reprehensible, since his witness used them according to
which she thought might entertain the court most. Her real name
was Gwendoline and she had made love with many men, including
some Indians. No, she hadn't had V.D. but once she thought she
had. Silly me, she implied cheerfully. Banking on her good nature,
Mr. Levy launched a crucial question. And kind, girl-saving Mr.
Davidson had intended to take her away from All This?

'No,' said Barbara.

'He tried to get you a situation?'

'He pretended to try,' said Barbara.

She told how the Rector had introduced her to titled people,
though goodness knew why, since none of them ever helped her
although they were very interested to hear all the details of her life.
Nobody helped her. Nobody ever had. Mr. Davidson had said that
she should be an actress. She had left school at fourteen and from
then on she had helped herself. When she had not got a job she
stayed in bed until eleven or more in the morning. She liked all the
men she had known. She was always happy. She liked reading. She
would have liked to marry one of her Indian boys but he had returned to India and quite vanished but she still liked him.

'I suggest to you that you wrote to Mr. Davidson because he was
kind and useful to you?'

'He was kind and useful,' said Gwendoline-Barbara.

'Do you usually keep friendly with people who try to rape you?'

'If they come in useful,' said Gwendoline-Barbara.

The Chancellor had to interrupt here to make a moral observation about staying in bed until eleven in the morning, which struck
him as the worst thing he had ever heard in his life.

Barbara trumped this enormity with a story about her lover, the
Strong Man. The Strong Man did feats in the gutter to theatre
queues and she went to live with him. He was young and kind. She
told him that the Rector of Stiffkey was her uncle and he believed
her. The Rector always wore his clerical collar when he met the
Strong Man. All three of them got on well together. The Rector had
taken her to the home of a Mrs. Beach, who was married to an
actor. Mrs. Beach was to teach Barbara to dance. He had tried to
reconcile her with her family, but had fallen for her sister, a housemaid of twenty-two. He had got her various jobs which she had been

obliged to abandon after the briefest trial because of the number of gentlemen who asked for her on the telephone of any house she occupied. What a tiresome invention! Barbara implied. Inconsequentially, she added Mr. Davidson had given her a black eye.

'Why have you not mentioned this before?'

'I wasn't asked.'

'Mr. Davidson is rather different from many people?'

'Yes.'

'Kind hearted spasmodically?'

'Yes.'

'People who are quite strangers to him he will greet by putting his arms on their shoulders?'

'Girls,' amended Barbara mordantly.

She became precise. No, Mr. Davidson had never mentioned the Prodigal Son. No, it wasn't a wicked lie to suggest that he had suggested that she should enter a brothel; he had suggested it many times.

And in February she had felt compelled to write from her very latest address, Providence Place, Shepherd's Bush, a long letter to the Lord Bishop of Norwich. It was 'very hard to be good when once you have been bad', she told the Bishop and after many appalling revelations concerning the Rector of Stiffkey's evangelism she signed herself off 'in all sincerity'.

After this the grumpy Mr. Oliver for the prosecution began the impossible task of putting Barbara together again after she had so obligingly desiccated her own character and left it more or less useless as a weapon with which to belay the Rector or to save him. Barbara had got the hang of the law by now. Somebody asked you a question to which there was a right answer and the answer they required. It was her business to make a good guess at the latter. She did her best. She went so far as to tell them her joke about appendicitis. A Scotsman had asked his girl whether she would like to see where he was operated on for appendicitis and had pointed to St. George's Hospital. The Chancellor said he had never heard a joke with less joke in it.

Landladies began to arrrive. They processed in and out of the witness-box noisily announcing their respectability. Barbara's housemaid sister came to attest that she had heard the Rector call Barbara the 'Queen of his heart'. Major Philip Hammond, a

Stiffkey churchwarden, took the stand to protest bitterly that the Rector hadn't shown up at an Armistice Day service and a London chemist came to add his naïve view that the reason why the Rector chased waitresses—even to their cloakroom behind the restaurant—was to hurry up the service.

And so the case built itself into a fantastic edifice of prelates, waitresses, strong men, hunting churchwardens, amorous Indian youths, publicans, landladies, dentists, titled female do-gooders with a passion for facts, the *Folies Bergère*, bathing suits, photographs, train journeys, Mr. Gordon and every possible variation on the popular prurient theme of 'virtue exposed'. The Press had a field day—or rather a field year—for there was scarcely an issue of any newspaper appearing between February and October 1932 which did not contain something about the Rector of Stiffkey. Very soon, the Chancellor was forced to announce that the Court would be obliged to sit continuously and indefinitely. Far from being aghast at such a prospect, the Rector showed positive signs of relief. Sometimes he laughed aloud, to the great irritation of the Chancellor. And sometimes his gaze would stray to the disastrous Barbara in open admiration. She was unique. There seemed no end to the distance she could fall.

A landlady told of her friendship with the Rector. He was different from the ministers she had been used to. He moved in a galaxy of girls. They came to his room at all hours of the day and night, and because of them she had given him notice no less than six times. Yet she liked him. She and her husband had driven the Rector all the way back to Stiffkey for an ordination but even then he had sat in the back of the motor with a pretty actress. They had had their photos taken on the Rectory lawn. The Chancellor took one look at the prim group.

'Does Mrs. Davidson always go about like that?' he asked in wonder.

'She refused to be taken and put leaves over her face,' explained the landlady, as if this was the most ordinary thing in the world.

The Chancellor became hypnotized by this photograph. Yet another dimension was being added to the Stiffkey affair.

'It puzzles me . . .' he said helplessly.

The reason for taking a London actress to Stiffkey was explained.

It was to prevent her from joining the Roman Catholic Church, but although the Rector had travelled all the way back to town with his arm round her waist, she *had* joined the Roman Catholics, and what was more, she had become a nun. The landlady, momentarily transported to rural Norfolk, took the opportunity to have a heart-to-heart with the Rector's wife. She heard how Mrs. Davidson and her children muddled along in profound resignation to a never-ceasing accompaniment of duns and girls.

Day after day passed, and still the witnesses arrived at Church House and told the same stories with different names in them. After two weeks it didn't seem as if anything fresh could be added. The kind witnesses spoke of friendly pats and the unkind ones of pestering. Mr. Levy complained that, 'the word pestering seems to be like a gramophone record in the mouth of every witness', to which Barbara replied that 'she did not know another word that fits so nicely'.

On April 6th there was a different consternation. The funds for the defence began to run out. With great magnanimity, the prosecution offered to hand over £250 of its money for this purpose, to the faint depression of the Chancellor who hoped that lack of funds might hurry things up a bit. He pulled himself together to hear the testimony of a Mr. Inglebert Thole of the Arrows Detective Agency. Mr. Levy was frivolous with Mr. Thole. How many cigars had the Rector smoked? How many times had he sneezed? Mr. Thole, who had no wit, tried to remember. His colleague, a Mr. Percy Butler, was more graphic. He had seen the Rector talking to strange girls everywhere. He had seen him write letters in the Charing Cross Hotel, take taxis, tubes, visit pubs and, needless to say, take in on the way quite a lot of teashops. He had followed the Rector and Barbara to the Piccadilly Theatre, where they had seen a play called *Folly to be Wiser*. This was one of the Rector's favourite shows. By nine o'clock the agent was whacked hollow and the Rector disappeared from view, with many happy hours still before him.

The following day began with the Rector showing a rather grand reluctance to accept charity from the prosecution in relation to the £250 it was willing to hand over for his defence, and with Mr. Oliver rapping him severely over the knuckles. 'Mr. Davidson is entirely wrong in thinking that the offer is made as a favour to him. It was made in what was conceived to be the best interests of

British justice. Who made it doesn't signify in the least. It has been refused. The result is that this case, which should have been finished in a reasonable time, will now drag on for many many weeks. . . . May I mention that while it goes on Mr. Davidson goes on exercising his sacred functions. . . .'

This was true enough. Stiffkey, once so remote and quiet, was now the centre of a deplorable pilgrimage. Sensation-lusting multitudes bore down on its little valley every week-end and packed the church, the churchyard and the lane beyond. When the Rector preached he mistook this gaping audience for a congregation. It was the first of the countless open-mouthed crowds which from henceforth were to mill around him until the day of his death. Not that he cared. When the trial was adjourned he used his notoriety to get funds. On May 19th he returned jauntily to Church House to hear the defence offer the following highly intelligent analysis of his character.

'Mr. Davidson's friendship starts not after years of acquaintance-ship, but immediately; in fact almost before acquaintanceship begins. He likes his fellow creatures and expects, rightly or wrongly in many cases, that they will return this feeling. It is not unusual for him to kiss women. His kisses have been paraded before you as signs of guilt, but you will hear from many that he is quite accus-tomed to kiss. . . . It is a stupid thing to do, and may lead to all sorts of suspicions on the part of evil-minded people. You will find he kisses his landlady, his landlady's daughters, his maids, not in a sensual or sexual way; it is a kiss on the cheek or on the forehead. It is the usual gesture for him when leaving someone he likes or if they have done something for him. . . .'

Mr. Levy filled in the big blank spaces of the Rector's life with some unsuspected facts. How he had not been able to go to the university for lack of funds and had gone on the stage instead. How he had eventually earned his own university fees by acting. Ordained in his late twenties, he at once set about his mission for saving the hordes of youthful nobodies which drifted across the metropolis. He had scarcely begun this work when he was suddenly inducted into the living of faraway Stiffkey. Undaunted, however, by this fate he turned his attentions to the young in Paris and during 1910, '11, '12 and '13 he went to Paris *once a fortnight* without fail. He served with the Navy during the war and then, in 1919, began his work among

London's teeming girls. Mr. Levy's speech began all right but half-way through it could not sustain its reasonable edge. The facts simply refused to be accommodated in rational lodgings. The effect was bizarre to everybody except the Rector, to whom the recitation sounded plain dull. He listened patiently, even sweetly, to the defence and prosecution in turn and it was only when the latter dared to attack the mysterious Mr. Gordon that he showed any asperity. He had met Mr. Gordon in 1919 and had helped him during his bankruptcy in 1922.

'Quite frankly,' said Mr. Oliver disparagingly, 'I am suggesting he is just a sort of swindler.'

'I am being charged with sexual immorality, not financial im-morality,' declared the Rector. This brought a great burst of applause and the police began to hustle people out of the public galleries. But Mr. Oliver wouldn't drop the money business and it was some time before the Court settled down to matters which the Rector found less harassing, such as being barred from the Overseas League for chatting to the telephone girls in their den. That day's proceedings concluded snidely with the prosecution muttering, 'I care nothing for delicate circumstances,' and the defence snapping, 'I'm sure you don't.'

The Rector found the persistent fogginess of the prosecution irritating. This time it was about such normal matters as going to theatres twice in one day, taking taxis and eating out in West End restaurants immediately after writing to a duchess to tell her that his family was starving at Stiffkey and that they had no coal. He told the Court crossly that 'I generally take one day off a week, like the Bishop of London, who always takes Friday off'. Nor could he understand how, because a girl was a tart, she was necessarily beyond the pale.

'She must have been an abandoned little creature,' said Mr. Oliver of Barbara.

'Abandoned morally,' said the Rector, 'but she had remarkable qualities of character.'

Mr. Oliver wanted the Rector to hold up a photograph of himself posing with a naked sixteen-year-old. He was dreadfully shocked. Really, it was disgraceful! The court had no shame. The descriptions of how the subpoenas were served did nothing to lessen the levity. 'A man came in, ran upstairs and pushed it down Mrs. P's neck.

The landlady fished it out and stuffed it down the young man's neck.' Sighing during his examination, the Rector shook his head and said, 'As a clergyman one spends one's whole life in bedrooms. . . .'

He had written to his bishop,

'For years I have been known as the Prostitutes' Padre—to me the proudest title that a true priest of Christ can hold. I believe with all my soul that if He were born again in London in the present day He would be found constantly walking in Piccadilly. He suffered the cruellest slander, but this did not deflect Him from solicitude for the fallen, and His attitude to the woman taken in adultery and still more His close friendship with the notorious harlot of Magdala . . . has always been my inspiration and comfort in the difficult work I have humbly undertaken in His name. . . .'

Five super-sensational days later, the defence clung to these scriptural precedents with both hands.

'Time after time in the New Testament kissing has been enjoined upon the Church. . . .' 'Greet him with an holy kiss. . . .'

But the prosecution left both kisses and Holy Writ alone and concentrated on the 'black-hearted' Barbara and divers other matters, none of them salubrious. On June 6th, after twenty-five days of unabated and unprecedented clerical scandal, the court adjoined, the Chancellor to work on his summing-up and the Rector to work out an ingenious plan to raise cash. But first of all there was the welfare of Stiffkey itself. Alas for prophets in their own country. When he got there he found another clergyman just about to take the service. However, Mr. Davidson soon sent him packing, though not before this clergyman had made a speech. The next day there was consternation over all Norfolk and the Archdeacon was seen wringing his hands and murmuring, 'hectic conditions'. The Archbishop of Canterbury, Dr. Lang, had already protested at the verbatim reports of the trial and the terrible publicity. When, towards the end of June, the Rector of Stiffkey was granted an application to give dramatic recitations in Birmingham to an audience not exceeding 2,000 people, the Church authorities realized with a groan that their troubles were only just beginning.

On July 8th the Rector was found guilty on all five charges. He listened to the verdict impatiently and then, snatching up his silk hat, he ran at full speed down the length of the Great Hall of Church

House, down the stairs and out into Westminster, for there was much to be done and not a moment to lose. He appealed to the Privy Council. His appeal was dismissed. He presented a private bill to the Privy Council and took it to the office himself, but nobody could look at it as they were all just about to go home to tea. He dashed to the office again the next day but they said he needn't have hurried because the Privy Council wouldn't be sitting again until October. Five days later, he heard from the Bishop of Norwich that he was not to hold services at Stiffkey after August 25th. Like all his tweenies and Nippies, he had been given a fortnight's notice. He was severely shaken by this.

It was then that the Rector of Stiffkey turned cynic, and left cold-hearted Norfolk for Lancashire, to throw in his lot with Diogenes. Diogenes, whose friends called him Dog, sat in a tub and believed that one should be free from shame, free from emotion and free from all useless conventions. Not having any honour to begin with—his father had defaced the coinage—he refused to acknowledge the existence of honour. 'Get out of my light,' was all he had to say to Alexander the Great when he called on him. Neither the Archbishop of Canterbury nor the Chancellor of Norwich came to Blackpool to see the Rector sitting in his barrel on the promenade, muttering, 'desperate ills require desperate remedies', but roughly 3,000 other people did and he was fined for obstruction. His barrel was sandwiched between a fasting girl and a flea circus. He sat in it for fourteen hours a day, hoping to get about £2,000 for all the appeals which lay before him.

October came, and with it a chilly notice from the Privy Council dismissing his private bill appeal. The Rector was feeling unusually bitter because only a few days before, when he had called on Major Hammond, his churchwarden at Stiffkey, the Major had turned him right-about-face on the front steps and booted him down them. Life indeed was hard. On October 14th he saw himself as the subject of the whole of the first leader of *The Times* and took heart. The Major had been fined twenty shillings but his own fame was priceless.

A week later, on Trafalgar Day, the last great set-piece of the Stiffkey drama was staged; the place, Norwich Cathedral itself. Early in the morning the great doors were locked and the Beauchamp Chapel was arranged like a little court, with a red-covered table in the centre and hard chairs placed in rows all around it. The Close

Photo: *Radio Times Hulton Picture Library*

Spell-binding in Trafalgar Square. 'Red' Ellen Wilkinson at a great Peace Demonstration held a few days before Munich.

Sir Oswald Ernald Mosley, 6th Baronet. Black shirts at 5/- each and the clean smell of blood.

was mute, the first leaves were falling. East Anglia cringed in the gritty October sunshine. The shades of the Lady Julian, Old Crome and Sir Thomas Browne rustled mournfully and the bell of St. Peter Mancroft tolled plangently, for the Rector of Stiffkey was to be unfrocked.

Promptly at a quarter to twelve, the time arranged for the horrible little ceremony, the Bishop of Norwich, the Chancellor, the Registrar, the Dean, the Archdeacons, the Canons and their solicitors came in solemn procession to the Beauchamp Chapel fully robed and, in some instances, wigged. The Registrar then read out the following telegram.

> *Have motored through night to be present today eleven forty-five. Have been slightly delayed. If late please allow a few minutes grace. Hope see you* [the Bishop] *and Archdeacon about business matters afterwards. Harold Davidson, rector of Stiffkey.*

Shuffling, its majesty scarcely impaired, the procession departed but had no sooner disappeared than distant cheers announced the break-neck arrival of a small muddy car in the Close. And its wheels had hardly slithered to a standstill when out leapt the Rector of Stiffkey in a silk hat and accompanied by his sister and a friend. The three of them rushed into the Cathedral and the Rector took a seat immediately opposite the Bishop's throne. The solemn procession returned, the Bishop striding along somewhat wrathfully with the aid of a magnificent gold and silver crozier. Everybody stood while the Apparitor called, 'Oyez, Oyez, Oyez, all persons cited and admonished to appear at this court and answer to your names as you shall be called. God save the King.' The Rector's name was then called three times and he answered, 'Here.'

The Bishop then prayed, 'Prevent us, O Lord, in all our doings . . .' and was answered with a volley of fervent Amens. And then, making no more ado, and simply picking up a paper, he began to pronounce sentence.

This was too much for the Rector, particularly after such a long drive. He was accustomed to justice taking its time. He sprang to his feet and shouted, 'May I be allowed to say anything before sentence is passed?'

The Bishop and his solicitor bowed nervously towards each other and then Dr. Pollock said, 'Yes, if you please briefly.'

6

The Rector then stood very straight, glared hard at the Bishop, gripped the table and said, 'I wished before you pass sentence to say that I am entirely innocent . . . it is the Church authorities which are put on trial, not myself . . . and I shall work for the rest of my life for the reform of the procedure under which these courts are conducted. . . . There is not one single deed which I have done which I shall not do again with the help of God. . . .'

He then sat down and the Bishop rose. Holding his crozier in one hand and a large piece of paper in the other, he read in a flat sad voice,

'In the name of God, Amen. Whereas the Judge and Chancellor of our Consistory Court has notified us that the Reverend Harold Francis Davidson, M.A., Clerk in Holy Orders, Rector of the parish churches of Stiffkey and Morston, has been found guilty of immoral conduct, immoral acts and immoral habits . . . we, Bertram, by divine permission Bishop of Norwich . . . pronounce, decree and declare that the Reverend Harold Francis Davidson ought to be deprived, and we do deprive thereof by this our definite sentence. . . .'

He then sat down, signed the document he had read, rose again and pronounced the Blessing in an atmosphere so frozen that the ancient wastes of the Cathedral seemed to ache with silence. There was a pause and then he added, almost conversationally, 'I shall now move to the High Altar.'

But no sooner had he said this than the Reverend Harold Davidson was on his feet and haranguing the throne. He threatened more appeals and a competent judge. He then led the way to the High Altar himself, forcing the Bishop and the clergy to process behind him. In the chancel he broke away and took a front seat. A second or two later the sumptuous ecclesiastics swayed past, what feelings they had quite concealed by gorgeous vestments. The Bishop prayed; Mr. Davidson prayed. Then, standing before the High Altar of Norwich Cathedral the Bishop deposed the ex-Rector of Stiffkey from Holy Orders because he had caused grave scandal.

'Now, therefore, we, Bertram, by divine permission . . . do hereby pronounce, decree and declare that the said Reverend Harold Francis Davidson, being a priest and a deacon respectively, ought to be entirely removed, deposed and degraded. . . . We hereby, by the authority committed to us by Almighty God, the Father, Son and Holy Ghost, remove, depose and degrade him. . . .'

It was done. The Bishop prayed about human frailty, pronounced the Benediction, then crumpled to his knees. But not so the ex-Rector of Stiffkey. He jumped up and cried in a high imperious voice which rang through the entire Cathedral,

'I am very glad that the deposition service has been added because I know that there is a right under the Clergy Discipline Act to address an appeal to the Archbishop of Canterbury within one month, *and this I shall do.*'

But the Bishop seemed not to hear. His procession re-formed and passed into the vestry.

*

Five years passed during which Harold Davidson should, by every law of social retribution, have sunk conveniently out of sight. But the lurid waves which had washed him from the pulpit at Stiffkey were not destroyers and once he showed signs of coming to terms with them, they began to keep him afloat. Diogenes continued to sustain him in other ways. He recognized that humanity is divided between the entertained and the entertainers, and that he belonged to the latter. He joined the great company of buffoons. He learnt to live on his shortcomings as well as with them. The campaign to clear his name, very real at first, declined with gimmicky tricks until it became an *outré* side-show in which goggle-eyed holidaymakers would cram themselves to see a real live Sunday newspaper sensation.

But by 1936 his position was that of a once famous music-hall turn whose act was on the wane. The 'Rector of Stiffkey' was billed in increasingly outlandish circumstances and during the summer of 1937 it was announced that he would lecture in a lion's cage at Skegness.

The cage was part of Skegness Amusement Park and it was busy August with the trippers pouring through the town. Mr. Davidson had signed a contract to appear with one lion, but when he reached the cage he found there were two, a male and a female. He questioned this but courageously went ahead with his act. The lion-tamer opened the cage and he slipped between the huge Freddie and his mate, who rested towards the rear of the den. And thus, in scarcely credible terms, the little clergyman from Norfolk and the lion acted out the classical Christian martyrdom to the full. He fought wildly, gallantly, but Freddie killed him in full view of a gaping mob. Eventually, the lion-tamer showed immense bravery and managed to get his body away from the animals and out of the cage. She was a sixteen-year-old girl named Irene.

CHAPTER NINE

Jarrow

'The night cometh, when no man can work.'
ST. LUKE

'When you are unemployed, which is to say when you are
underfed, harassed, bored and miserable, you don't *want* to
eat dull, wholesome food. You want something a little bit
"tasty" . . . Let's have three pennorth of chips! Run out and
buy us a twopenny ice-cream! Put the kettle on and we'll have
a nice cup of tea!'
GEORGE ORWELL—*The Road to Wigan Pier*

THERE has to be some selectivity in disaster. A small part of it has
to be personalized as a first move towards an accurate comprehension of the whole. It was Anne Frank's Diary and not the Eichmann
trial statistics which measured in valid terms the monstrous per-
versions of Hitler's Germany. The calcined human shapes discovered at Pompeii are final in their eloquence and say all that there
is to say on the pathos and horror of natural disaster. The casualties
of the First World War were so great that grief itself became cloudy
and amorphous and had to be focused on a single anonymous victim
before it could be understood.

All the events of the inter-war years took place against a huge,
dingy, boring and inescapable backcloth—unemployment. By 1935
it had existed for so long and had proved to be so irremediable that
it came to be regarded as a normality. The chronically unemployed
had learned how to make a pattern of idleness and had become conditioned to hopeless poverty. The streets in which they lived
breathed an apathy which in the worst areas was a kind of nerveless
peace. Paint flaked from woodwork, doorsteps were ritualistically
whitened, delicate undernourished children in darned jerseys and
clothing-club boots flocked to see Shirley Temple and Tom Mix

on Saturday afternoons for twopence, young men, many of whom
had reached their mid-twenties without ever having a job, walked or
bicycled in groups over the neighbouring hills and meadows; older
men crouched on benches on their allotments and gossiped. The
women suffered in a different way. It was they who were exhausted
by the constant preoccupation with mean economies, they who
under-ate so that the children had sufficient, they who answered the
door to the debt and rent collectors, the Means Test spies and seedy
touts of all kinds—for the extreme scarcity of money and the
meaninglessness of time filled the slums with hawkers and spongers
—and they who preserved the maleness of their menfolk when everything conspired to turn them into so many little cloth-capped
negatives in the dole queue.

The strange thing is that it was both their plight and their salvation that no one came to their aid. Humiliated, degraded and
intimidated by the Labour Exchanges, the Means Test, the Poor
Law and the police, the British unemployed were a vast malleable
force which only needed a leader for it to become a threat. When it
marched on London, as it frequently did, like a dark, singing worm,
there was an immediate but quite unnecessary tension. The worm,
grudgingly allowed its civic rights, would be met and escorted
through side-streets if possible to Hyde Park by foot and mounted
police, where it would chop itself up into smaller—and safer—
pieces and listen to Wal Hannington or Aneurin Bevan. Occasionally it was entertained by Oswald Mosley and the British Union
of Fascists, a predominantly middle-class movement which was big
enough on November 1st, 1936, for its leader to boast that it would
put up a hundred candidates at the next general election. But the
unemployed remained unbeguiled. The oblique violence inherent
in the B.U.F. movement offered nothing to those who had been hurt
enough without wishing to hurt others, and as for the B.U.F.'s other
main ingredient, jingoism, this was quite ludicrously unappealing.
So the unemployed resembled a torpid hippo sinking deeper and
deeper into the silt left behind by outdated industries and the refuse
of a defunct economy. Sometimes a Shinwell or a Bevin would prod
the vast beast and it would quake—would even rumble—and mayors
would search hurriedly for the riotous assembly act. Sometimes an
irritant such as the hated Means Test would make it turbulent and
dangerous. But always, inevitably, it would slip back into its

acceptance sloth and the first estate of the realm would breathe again.

The curious thing is that the one man whose understanding of, and compassion for, the unemployed were founded on the richest patriotism was himself the victim of inertia. Stanley Baldwin's indolence was a miracle in his own day and is a legend in ours. His languor was contagious. How much it influenced his Cabinet colleagues it is difficult to say. He made it all too plain that once a man had received his seals of office he would be the last person in the world to say how they should be used. 'His Majesty's ministers are co-equal,' he maintained, adding, 'Luckily they are not co-eternal . . .' before slipping off to sleep on the Treasury Bench. He lost no sleep even at the height of the two main crises of his career, the General Strike and the Abdication. He shrank from new thought, particularly new thought which had by-passed the Attic groves. 'The intelligent are to the intelligentsia what a gentleman is to a gent,' he said. The hustings left him in such a state of mental nausea at the vulgarity of it all that he always settled his mind with Horace before retiring. His idea of a busy day, says G. M. Young, his friend and biographer, was not to read the official papers, not to talk to politicians during luncheon and to write his personal letters in the Cabinet Room during the afternoon. All this would have been scandalous had he not almost broken his heart at the sight of two millions of his fellow countrymen reduced to rags and bones. He brooded on 'unemployment which was eating away the energies of the nation and breeding dangerous thoughts'. The British belief that war must only be declared when the nation is least prepared to wage it may have had something to do with Baldwin's belated reaction to the Fascist dictators, but the stagnant remedies he brought to heal the terrible disease of unemployment were shameful and, considering his quasi-mystical passion for England's green and pleasant land, enigmatic. It was in his nature to find Hitler too frightful for words and Europe a bore, but he loved England as Shakespeare loved it. Yet he let it rot.

Wages began to fall and prices to rise in 1920. 'In April, 1920, all was right with the world. In April, 1921, all was wrong,' said R. H. Tawney. Trade unions were forced to stop their idealistic schemes for nationalizing industry which had received such an exultant shot in the arm through the success of the Russian Revolution and turn their energies towards getting pay rises for their members. Strikes began to paralyse the antiquated coal industry and the plain economic issues of the times were clouded by the sentimentality of the miners on the one hand and the barefaced greed of the coalowners on the other. Neither could see the need for change in the industry. When, in 1920, the miners demanded a reduction in the price of coal and increased wages the Bishop of Durham declared that 'England has ceased to be a constitutional monarchy and is making its first advance towards the dictatorship of the proletariat.'

Class issues which had lain dormant all through the necessary brotherhood of the war and which in many instances might have withered away were viciously revived on both sides. The triumph of Bolshevism heartened the Left in the same way that the French Revolution heartened Wordsworth. The Right sought old remedies for new fears, and these shocked and sickened the disbanded soldiers who had been promised everything, from fair shares to a demi-paradise. Instead, they found themselves herded once more into the back-to-back ghettoes of the Industrial Revolution. They saw vitality and style return to middle-class life and their own lives reduced to a bewildering prospect of human negation.

Throughout the twenties the number of unemployed in Britain never dropped below the million mark and the sight of seedy men wearing scraps of uniform, tramps surging into the casual wards of country towns evening after evening, thin, worried-looking women and obviously under-fed children, became so common that they caused no more emotion than the beggars do in Egypt. Nor was the blight confined to cities. Agriculture had been declining ever since 1870 but the war had temporarily halted this and things looked actually rosy in 1920, when farmers were offered government protection from the vicissitudes of foreign agriculture. Then, in 1923, wheat, which had reached so high a price as 80s. 10d. per quarter, fell to 42s. 2d. Other prices followed suit. The slump had arrived. The Government now couldn't afford to honour its commitments and the Agriculture Act of 1920, so full of hope and promise, was repealed. Farm labourers' wages fell from 42s. a week to 30s. and less. The land was neglected and hikers would wander through shaggy fields and enjoy the picturesqueness and false peace of dilapidated barns. Hedges thickened into copses and copses into small woods. Field verges broadened until the patches of corn and sugar-beet were islanded by the last rich opulence of wild flowers, birds and insects the countryside was to know before mid-century sprays were to make such things legendary. There was tragedy in the tied cottage, a different type of tragedy from the terrace house in the Distressed Areas. The farm labourer had been used to having part of his pay in kind—house, milk, wood, fruit, vegetables—and these things vaguely continued. Also his relationship with his employer and all classes in his village was intimate and personal, and these things did not change greatly, even if his wages did. But the unemployed miner or shipyard worker was in a very different position. The economics of these trades made it necessary that such men should be employed in small armies, that they should be housed in packed lanes of slums and that their relationship to the bosses should be one which was dominated by a fearful respect. The knowledge that there could be ten or more thousand idle men a mile or two from his house un-nerved many a coalowner, who often behaved heartlessly out of fright.

The average unemployed man could not relate his personal suffer-ings to the economic condition of his time and he felt betrayed. The years passed and in some areas a generation of young men grew up which had never known work. The North and South of England be-came curiously divorced and when marchers from the coal counties came to London in futile protest after protest at the terrible neglect which denied them their very existence as men, they seemed like foreigners. One of the few people who tried to fill this artificial and cruel breach with warmth and understanding was the young Prince of Wales. His actions were seen as unconstitutional criticism of the government and were much condemned. The first march of the unemployed on London took place as early as October, 1920, when a multitude of workless ex-servicemen attended a group of Labour mayors who were petitioning Lloyd George. This demonstration was broken up with great violence by foot and mounted police.

In 1921 it became obvious that unemployment insurance bene-fits based on the assumption that a man would only be out of work for a few weeks would have to be subsidized and the Unemployment Fund was allowed to borrow £30,000,000 from the Treasury. This became the 'dole'. From the dole there sprang the bureaucracy necessary to administer it and from this bureaucracy, a regiment of nosy little clerks who were to be the Torquemadas of the most re-sented inquisition the British working-class was ever to suffer—the

appliers of the Means Test. The Means Test was a policy of economic prurience which degraded both victim and administrator
alike and the moral distress it brought innocent people was out of all
proportion to its usefulness. Nothing was more perfectly designed to
goad otherwise reasonable men to revolution and it was only because
of the outsize decency of the ordinary man that it never did.

The family Means Test was imposed in 1931, after the financial
panic of that year. It meant that, after an unemployed man had exhausted his insurance stamps he was turned over to a Public Assistance Committee which demanded to know details of all monies
going into his house. Even if his son had a 3s.-a-week paper-round
or if his wife had managed to put a few pounds by into the Post
Office, he had to declare these details and the Public Assistance man
would vary his dole accordingly. The family Means Test was enforced with great exactitude and its officers would stand in the front
rooms of poverty-stricken homes asking endless deeply personal
questions, while their prying eyes flickered over the furniture, the
clothes, the pets and the food of the family being interrogated. Tale-
bearers thrived. A child from a 'Public Assistance' home might be
seen with a new overcoat or a bicycle, and the Means Test man
would arrive to ask where these things came from. Resentment of
the Means Test caused some of the most inflammable working-class
demonstrations of the thirties, and even at the dread hour when
Churchill took control of the nation in 1940 one of the first demands
the Labour leaders made as a condition for joining the war-time
coalition was that the family Means Test should go. It partly died in
the Determination of Needs Bill of 1941, and thanks chiefly to
Ernest Bevin. After the war and the social revolution brought about
by the adoption of the Beveridge Report, the Means Test seemed to
belong to a far more distant past than the thirties.

In 1930 unemployment figures ceased to be merely bewildering
and became terrifying. Up and up they crept, in a high tide of
human desuetude, until by the end of the year they reached the unprecedented total of 2½ millions. The Labour Government watched
the tide incredulously and then was washed away by it. All the
industrial parts of the country were paralysed. The whole of Wales
and Lancashire was numb with wretchedness. J. B. Priestley likened
Stockton-on-Tees to a theatre kept open 'merely for the sale of
drinks in the bars and chocolates in the corridors'. Walter Greenwood

in *Love on the Dole*, described the nothingness to which life had descended.

> 'He was standing there as motionless as a statue, cap neb pulled over his eyes, gaze fixed on pavement, hands in pockets, shoulders hunched, the bitter wind blowing his thin trousers tightly against his legs. Waste paper and dust blew about him in spirals, the papers making harsh sounds as they slid on the pavements.'

During 1932 the dole for a married couple and their three children was 29s. 3d., but this was always liable to be subjected to the Means Test. 'The test,' said George Orwell in *The Road to Wigan Pier*, 'was an encouragement to the tattle-tale and the informer, the writer of anonymous letters and the local blackmailer; to all sorts of un-neighbourliness.' And 'it stimulated petty tyranny and insolence on the part of Labour Exchange clerks and managers,' said Walter Greenwood. 'The weekly visit to the Exchange would bring the sudden curt announcement by the clerk: "They've knocked you off the dole." '

Eventually, unemployment became a way of life. There was something akin to genius in the manner with which millions of men and women didn't go to pieces or to the barricades, but settled down, in Orwell's phrase, to 'living on the dole'. This peace or resignation wasn't easily come by. The almost sedate quiet of the distressed areas was the quiet of bewilderment and exhaustion. For more than ten years there had been a ceaseless attempt to catch the government's eye, as it were. And to capture the imaginative sympathy of the middle class and to force it into action. Pamphlets, plays, commissions, deputations, letters to the Press, sermons, threats, pleas and, most of all, marches had been employed to make the authorities stir. Vast rallies of men from Rhondda and Glasgow blackened Hyde Park, and on one occasion their irritation led them to darken the carpets of the Ritz Hotel. They sang 'Tipperary' and 'David of the White Rock' and 'The Red Flag'. They wore their medals and stood accusingly outside Buckingham Palace. Some contingent or other of them was as expected a sight in the capital as were the Beefeaters. 'The unemployed . . .' people said as they passed, but without deep emotion. For these were, after all, only the latest version of the poor who, according to scripture, would always be with them.

It took Jarrow, an industrial Lidice, to break the deadlock and Ellen Wilkinson to see that it was a clean break.

Jarrow is unique among all the inhabited places of England in that at two distantly separated dates in its history it became identified with the ultimate light and some of the worst darkness known to the human spirit. In the eighth century it was the fulcrum which Bede used to preserve art, literature and Christianity when Britain and all northern Europe were temporarily blacked out by the barbarians. It was the chink in the darkness through which the divine light never ceased to stream. Bede lived at Jarrow for over sixty years. Towards the end of his life his cell was the only place left where the twin flames of Hellenism and Christ's doctrine of love unwaveringly endured and the hamlet became one of those spots, like Delphi, Little Gidding or the Mount of Olives, which are sacred. Nothing changed at Jarrow for over eleven hundred years, then a mining village grew up on the banks of the Slake. In 1852, by the opening of Palmer's Shipyard, this harsh village was transformed into the most horrible of all the horrible industrial hells of the nineteenth century.

When Augustus Hare went to Jarrow to visit his friend Edward Liddell and his wife in 1876 he found this saintly clergyman 'amidst a teeming population of blackened, foul-mouthed, drunken rogues, living in rows of dismal houses, in a country where every vestige of vegetation is killed by noxious chemical vapours, on the edge of a slimy marsh, with a distance of inky sky, and the furnesses vomitting forth volumes of blackened smoke. All nature seemed parched and writhing under the pollution. . . .'

Jarrow during the Dark Ages had Bede and the first stained-glass windows in Britain; Jarrow during the nineteenth century, when the churches were packed to the doors, had Charles Palmer and the first British armour-plate industry. Palmer's Yard made floating batteries for the Crimea and iron ships, screw colliers and, later, liners for the big shipping lines. Ellen Wilkinson said that Charles Palmer was one of the first men to grasp the idea of making an industrial plant an organized, integrated whole and that the Yard at Jarrow was, in the late nineteenth century, a triumph of planning. To this belching enterprise, from all over the North and from Ireland, came the 'hands', the faceless labour, in their thousands. In 1851 the population of Jarrow was 3,500, and in 1921 it was 35,000. All these people lived in stinking darkness, near sickness and obscene poverty.

Yet when the slump hit Jarrow in the early thirties and Palmer's was liquidated the fearful human dereliction which followed caused people to look back to these days with longing. Almost overnight Jarrow became a place which was not only made to feel it was spiritually expendable but also physically non-existent. There were many industrial areas as badly stricken by unemployment but none suffered Jarrow's unique isolation. It was as though the town had been amputated and cast into the oblivion reserved by history for its enormities. The skies, scarcely seen for eighty years, cleared above Palmer's Yard and the only sound to compete with the unfamiliar noise of the marsh birds returning to the filthy Slake was the ring of the breakers' hammers as the cranes and machinery were dismantled. This very quietness was scarifying in itself. A profiteering concern called National Shipbuilding Security Ltd., notorious in the thirties for the way it bought up its slump-hit competitors with no thought for the many thousands of ordinary people involved, and which acted with the cold unfeeling consent of Walter Runciman at the Board of Trade, had moved in. When it moved out Palmer's Yard, Jarrow's Moloch for nearly a century, was left stark and useless. Neither the Government nor the businessmen gave any sign of a secret awareness that things might soon be very different and that shipping would soon have to be built at a furious pace. Many of the artisans of Jarrow had invested small savings in Palmer's, which was to them the universe, a harsh world but a safe and everlasting one. None of these savings was honoured or returned and some were as much as £300—an enormous sum for a working man to have scraped together between the wars. After National Shipbuilding Security had made its bid, Runciman, the coldest fish in mid-thirties politics, turned down his thumb and then the Government, the country and, some of the Jarrovians thought, God Himself, all behaved as if Jarrow was no more.

'Red' Ellen Wilkinson, the Joan of Arc of Jarrow, and its M.P., summed it up in a Left Book Club best-seller, *The Town That Was Murdered*.

'Charles Palmer started Jarrow as a shipbuilding centre without considering the needs of the workers. They crowded into a small colliery village which was hurriedly extended to receive them. They packed into insanitary houses. They lived without social amenities. They paid with their lives for the absence of any preparation for the growth of such a town. And in 1933 another group of capitalists decided the fate of Jarrow without reference to the workers. . . .'

For the next three years Jarrow was the Ultima Thule of the slump. When the student of human wretchedness reached this place he knew that he had reached the very pit of the Depression. There was help of a kind. Prosperous southern towns took to 'adopting' stricken communities in the distressed areas and Jarrow received pastimes for a social club and other small comforts that were on a par with a leper being waved to. Sir John Jarvis, a local industrialist, was more practical. He introduced one or two new trades and established them in part of the gaunt hollow of Palmer's Yard. He also did all he could to fill the void left by the death of Palmer's and at first was the only person outside the huge shuffling ranks of the workless who gave them hope and linked them with the outside world. It was Sir John Jarvis who revealed, in letters to the Press, to friends, and in speeches, the lies and distortions behind the greedy policy to make Jarrow defunct. This excellent man failed as anyone must fail who tries to play the good squire to a town of nearly forty thousand people. And, anyway, the rôle of liberator had already been ear-marked by fate for Ellen Wilkinson, a character who might have come straight out of George Bernard Shaw.

Red Ellen rose classically from the nonconformist working-class home to scholarships, degrees, local government, the Communist Party and the Labour Party to the Ministry of Education. It was platforms, platforms all the way, but Ellen seemed to dance on them. She was small, pretty, red-haired and crackerjack with vivacity. She understood the need for glory in life. She had a pert femininity which was almost that of the great music-hall artist and she had no fear at all. She became the Member for Jarrow in 1935 and lost not a moment after the votes were counted before she set-to ringing all the bells of hope in that living grave. In January, 1934, she had led a march of about 300 men and women to the neighbouring town of Seaham, where Ramsay MacDonald was visiting his constituency.

It wasn't a very long march but the bearding of the Prime Minister in a cosy drawing-room by a throng of polite men and women, some of them far from young, who had tramped over fifteen miles in a great storm just to make him *see* Jarrow, somehow caught the imagination of the Press, used as it was to unemployed marches.

'What good do such marches do?' Red Ellen asked herself after the Prime Minister's supremely fatuous remark as the deputation trudged from his fireside into the rain—'Ellen, why don't you go out and preach socialism, which is the only remedy for all this?' But although unemployed marches were ten a penny, this particular stolen march on the discomfited MacDonald both amused and interested people. There was another factor also which manifested itself at this time, and this was Jarrow's cool dignity and dramatic stoicism in the face of protracted disaster. The forsaken town had turned in upon itself like a family in misfortune and its inhabitants had become purged of rancour and even physically cleansed of all signs of the demeaning effects of their rough occupations. The photographs which appeared in the Press reflected a new kind of man and woman, ascetic, contained and enduring. The Greek tragedy of the place caught the popular imagination and at once it was decided to organize the unemployed march of all unemployed marches and shame the Government into action. Before this happened there were further conventional deputations to the heartless Walter Runciman. When Runciman said that Jarrow must work out its own salvation it was the last straw in official cruelty and in July, 1936, plans for the great crusade were put into action.

Big crowds—practically all Jarrow—saw them off. But before they had taken a single step everything possible was done to impress upon the country and upon the marchers themselves that what was happening was unique. This was to be no sorry shuffling rabble of malcontents but a dignified official delegation to Parliament. The original idea for the march came from a Jarrow councillor, David Riley, a descendant of the poor Irish which had crowded into Tyneside during the boom days. This was in the summer of 1936. All through August and September letters were written—on the Town Clerk's writing paper, so that they were bound to receive proper civic protocol—funds were collected, boots were repaired and a great banner was stitched. The banner stated 'Jarrow Crusade' in large unequivocal appliquéd letters. All class, political and religious factions in the town came to varying degrees of temporary truce for the occasion. Candidates for the municipal re-elections agreed to pair and not fight each other's seats. Two hundred men were chosen out of the many hundreds who volunteered and on Monday, October 5th they set out on the high road for London, nearly 300 miles away. Their objective was to reach the capital by the time the new King Edward opened Parliament. The king's sympathy for the unemployed was well known. What was quite unknown, at least to all these humble, stricken men who had reason to put more faith in princes than politicians, was that this particularly hopeful king would make his first and last journey to Westminster with a heart so filled with his personal anxieties that there would be little room for theirs and with only a few more weeks of his reign left to go.

Malnutrition and idleness gave the marchers a refined, almost delicate, look. Their slight bodies were covered by dark, clothing club suits and each wore a roll of mackintosh across the chest and over the shoulder like a bandolier. Except for Councillor Riley, who marched the length of England in a bowler hat, the men wore cloth caps. They marched gravely in step to the sound of mouth organs and with the diminutive Ellen Wilkinson at their head. The Mayor and Mayoress of Jarrow led them for the first stage of the journey, a distance of twelve miles. Before setting off they had all attended a huge undenominational service in the parish church and had received the blessing of the Bishop of Jarrow, Dr. Gordon, that most kindly man, an action which was to goad the Bishop of Durham into a fury of criticism. The progress of the marchers was grave, almost sedate. The miseries of the depression had made them unnaturally reserved and reflective. At the rests Ellen Wilkinson and the medical students who had offered their services to the crusade cut away rough home-knitted socks from blisters and nursed bodies reacting strangely to the unfamiliar violence of discipline and action. But both blisters and peakiness belonged only to the initial stages of the march, and not many days had passed before fresh air and the sheer delight of being necessary brought a transformation to the wan faces that was little short of miraculous. By the time the men got to Sheffield they had lost their humiliated look and had instead a certain nervous poise. Some had plodded by the Somme and the Marne. Some would soon be in the Western Desert. Their perky ranks straddled the peace. Their official expenses for a month on the road were £2 a man which, as Ellen Wilkinson said, was more than any of the other marchers had ever had.

Meanwhile, news of this very special march and of all the hopefulness it contained had spread and produced an epidemic result. On the same morning as the men of Jarrow set out, 400 Scotsmen, accompanied by a retinue of cooks, cobblers and tailors, left Glasgow with the intention of linking up with various other large contingents of the unemployed from the distressed areas in order to achieve the biggest yet demonstration against the Means Test. Nor was marching as a form of social protest confined to Britain but broke out in all parts of the world, and on October 6th, 1936, the most tragic and macabre of all marches took place in Manila, when 300 lepers walked out of their hospital and journeyed in grim ranks to the Presidential Palace demanding 'liberty or death'. Nor were the Mosleyites backward in keeping up with this restlessness and their massive forays into the East End began to take place almost nightly, bringing the strongest objections from borough councillors and priests, whose streets and parishes were submitted to disgusting scenes of violence and Jew-baiting. In Germany, the cult of the Wandervogel, a kind of folk-singing woodcraft society with undertones of homosexual love which had developed among students as far back as the 1880's, was channelled by Baldur von Schirach into the Hitler Youth. The spirit of the *Jugendherbergen*, before it took on its sinister Nazi affiliations, drifted to Britain and inspired the more youthful of the workless to take to the lanes and mountains. The huge sales of J. B. Priestley's *Good Companions* testified to the enormous romance of the open road. A picaresque literature grew up which contained carefree footloose doctrines. Heroes like *Anthony Adverse* and the ruffled vagabonds of Jeffery Farnol's novels made insecurity a virtue and the simple life, preferably alfresco, was extolled by best-sellers like *Tales From an Empty Cabin* by 'Grey Owl'. It was the heyday of Hobson's choice, of learning to actually *live*—as apart from merely existing—without money. Youth Hostels were founded in 1931 by the National Council of Social Service and by the end of the thirties there were 297 hostels sleeping half a million hikers and bikers a year. This wanderlust occasionally got out of hand, as in the case of the young brothers who stole a little trawler called the *Girl Pat* from her moorings at Grimsby on April Fools' Day, 1936, and sailed her for 8,000 miles all over the world with only a school atlas to help them, before justice caught up with them. Their action was a colourful snook cocked in the face of some of the most soul-crippling officialdom ever experienced by ordinary men and women. During this year, too, there took place the first British march against the Dictators, when scores of idealistic young men volunteered for the

International Brigade in Spain, while their Nazi opposites in London tarred Epstein's *Day* and blued his *Rima*. The scene was one of personal commitment and decision, general apathy and governmental cowardice and hesitation. This was the climate through which the 200 men of Jarrow marched, carrying in a heavy oak chest, which they took turns to haul, a petition to Stanley Baldwin, that bedtime titan in a world that was gradually finding its feet.

In an article in *Time and Tide* written by Ellen Wilkinson during rests and halts on the march, she describes the weary column's arrival in the October evening streets of Chesterfield, Mansfield, Nottingham, Loughborough, Leicester and all the way to London. How,

'Sometimes we came in from the dark road to beautifully set tables, napery and crockery and bright lights. Immediately the men smartened up. When it was not possible for them to wash before tea, they surreptitiously combed their tousled hair and rubbed soiled fingers on their handkerchiefs. But in those towns . . . mercifully few . . . where the tables were bare boards, and tea was poured from buckets into our own mugs, the men who had appeared so smart and alert at the well-set tables, suddenly looked "poor-law", and just as grubby as their angry M.P. who still had to smile and return thanks for the bread and marge. . . .'

The medical students, supplied by the Inter-Hospital Socialist Society at the rate of two a week, fixed up a clinic each evening in the casual wards, halls, etc. where the marchers slept, and cared for the half-starved bodies and neglected teeth. But some of the Press refused to be beguiled by the general goodness and worthwhileness of all this and commented primly on the Jarrow authorities for 'exposing the miseries of the men on the road' and for 'sending hungry and ill-clad men across the country on a march to London'. Ellen Wilkinson rushed off to the Labour Party Conference in the middle of the march, where she expected sympathy and understanding, and where she got the cold shoulder. 'I went from the warm comradeship of the road to an atmosphere of official disapproval,' she said.

The reception of the marchers was varied to the point of being bizarre. In some places it was a case of watch out, the beggars are coming to town, and in others it was the most imaginative love and hospitality. The Co-op boot repairers at Leicester worked all night for nothing in order to mend the men's decrepit footwear. Territorial officers at snobbish Harrogate looked after the marchers with the utmost kindness and generosity. At Barnsley the mayor ordered the public baths to be heated. The men slept in their clothes and usually on bare floors but they shaved daily and somehow contrived to look fresh and clean. Dinner was cooked by the wayside on a field kitchen and on one particularly dreadful day, during the twenty-mile stretch between Bedford and Luton, it rained without ceasing and the water crept through the mackintoshes until every man was soaked to the skin. The small frail Ellen never faltered through all this.

On the 15th of October, when the marchers had been on the road for ten days and were receiving, contrary to either the Government's hopes or expectations, a royal treatment from the Press and public alike, the Cabinet decided to discourage all marches as they came very near to being breaches of the peace, but even *The Times* flared up at this and reminded the Government sharply that the marchers had begun their great journey with the blessing of the Bishop of Jarrow, had attended service in Ripon Cathedral *en route* and that they were the legitimate deputation of an English town on its lawful way to Westminster.

Two days later an appalled Ellen Wilkinson learned that the Bishop of Jarrow had made a public disclaimer that the march had his support, though he had felt it his Christian duty to pray for God's blessing on the marchers themselves. The Bishop's retraction was answered by the Archdeacon of Northumberland in a superb re-statement of the marchers' purpose published in *The Times*. And at the same time it was learned that when the Special Areas (Development and Improvement Act) came up for renewal in the new Parliament, the Government intended to include it in the Continuation Bill, which meant that once more the tragic problem of the distressed areas would not be examined in detail, but would be passed over in a general kind of fashion.

The last week of October, 1936, saw a dramatic heightening of the restrained anarchy as the forces of reaction and what looked like the first stages of a great Popular Front movement wooed the torpid politicians. On October 22nd more than a thousand Blackshirts marched through Bethnal Green in state. A drum and pipe band headed the procession and the great company of foot and mounted police which escorted it were noticeably part of the parade. On October 25th two more marches began, one of Means Test protestants from all over South Wales and the other made up of blind men who were angry because the war blind were given preferential treatment to civilian blind. As these huge processions of strangers swept into towns and villages they presented a great many practical difficulties to the inhabitants who, on the whole, behaved extremely well. Rotarians and ex-servicemen's associations were generous and made up for the near-Dickensian state of mind which still ruled the roost in many workhouses.

Hensley Henson, the Bishop of Durham, and Ellen Wilkinson argued the pros and cons of marching from violently opposite points of view, or so it seemed. However, a close examination of their letters shows that they were both terrified of the same danger, the end of liberty. The Bishop maintained that marching involved substituting for the provisions of the Constitution the methods of organized mob pressure. 'If generally adopted, as there now seems great likelihood that it will be if it be now encouraged, it may bring us before the winter is out into grave public confusion and danger. . . .' Ellen reacted violently to this. She told the Bishop and all who thought as he did that to stigmatize as 'dangerous' a legal petition to Parliament was perilous at a time when constitutional rights were being threatened on every side. The wrangle cleared the air a bit. Those with only the rudiments of political sense could now see that the Jarrow Crusade was more than an industrial complaint, it was an uncompromising but simple restatement of part of the ancient common law of England.

As the marchers neared London and rumours grew that the Government did not intend to receive them there was a sudden stepping up of public sympathy, most of which reflected a correct patriotism. Bedford was particularly warm and received the Jarrow men with a mixture of official courtesy and personal hospitality which did much to bridge the chasm which existed between the South and North of England.

On November 1st they entered London during a cloudburst and singing 'The Minstrel Boy' to their mouth-organ band, while a single drum throbbingly kept the step. Ellen, visibly worn out and helping herself along with a walking-stick, led them through empty Mayfair, down Regent Street, where small groups of spectators and

Pressmen stared from shop doorways, past Charing Cross and so to the inevitable soup kitchen. They had arrived. London was neither welcoming nor hostile; it was merely the sprawling immensity which had seen everything and which was incapable of astonishment. After the highly individual towns and cities on the route with their comprehensible reaction, tepid or otherwise, and usually the latter, London seemed negative. As they plodded through the ornate streets of the West End which showed no sign of hard times, the marchers felt the old dread insignificance return to them and began to realize in a dull way how impossible it was for those who lived in such a place to have any conception of what it must be like to be virtually left to rot in a black proletarian warren. A reluctant rearmament programme had severed the North and Wales from the South. The unemployment figures for Middlesex were 4·3 per cent of the working population; in Glamorganshire they were 33·4 per cent. The Government's refusal to put new arms factories in the stricken areas was little less than a vote of no confidence for tradesmen whose hands were white with idleness. The atmosphere at the soup kitchen in Garrick Street was tense and protective. The men felt like foreigners and now realized how worthless it had been to send all those individual spokesmen, letters from the Town Clerk and even Ellen to speak for them in the past. Not so Ellen. She continued to breathe and flash enthusiasm and optimism and the next day, from the public galleries in the House of Commons, the marchers in their dried-out but shapeless clothes watched her present the petition. The document, in its oak box, had gained a sentimental mystique during its long journey. It contained 12,000 names. In it resided all the dignity, suffering, accusation, hope and longing of what *The Times* called a forlorn community. . . . Ellen, metamorphosed overnight from a cheerful dripping vagabond into a pretty woman of considerable importance, rose and spoke. The House smiled indulgently; it liked Ellen and on the whole it liked drama. The bony, weather-reddened faces of the workless stared down like sparse carvings from the gallery.

'I ask leave to present to this honourable House the petition of the people of Jarrow,' said Ellen in a clear, slightly irritable voice which soon changed to one of impish charm. 'During the last fifteen years Jarrow has passed through a period of industrial depression unparalleled. . . . Its shipyard is closed and its steelworks have been denied the right to re-open. Where formerly 8,000 persons, many of them skilled workmen, were employed, only a hundred are now employed on a temporary scheme. The town cannot be left derelict. . . .'

When she had finished, Sir N. Gratton-Doyle presented another petition, this one signed by nearly 70,000 Tynesiders on behalf of Jarrow. Ellen then asked the Prime Minister how many resolutions he had received from public bodies, corporations and individuals regarding Jarrow since July, that is, since the march was first planned.

The whole thing then sank into a strange unfeeling clamminess as Stanley Baldwin told Ellen that he had received 66 resolutions and 8 letters from public bodies, and 1 telegram, 5 postcards and 8 letters from individuals. The buck was next passed to Walter Runciman and the amazed marchers listened while the President of the Board of Trade solemnly told the House that the unemployment position at Jarrow, while still far from satisfactory, had improved during recent months. When a member protested at this, Runciman shut him up with the remark that if the question was put on the order paper he would consider the matter. The member, who was the Liberal-National Mr. Magnay of Gateshead, wouldn't stop here and pressed Runciman to say whether the ban on Palmer's Shipyard prevented the Admiralty building ships there. What was to stop the Government putting two years' work at the Yard? (This was the real issue—why, when one had a great yard and thousands of skilled workers, and one needed more ships in a hurry, *why was Jarrow ostracized*?) Everybody knew why, of course. National Shipbuilders Security had bought and dismantled the Yard, and in effect Jarrow itself, for reasons of private profit. When Sir Samuel Hoare pompously talked of the Yard 'being disposed of' there was satirical laughter from all over the House. When a Welsh member asked the Prime Minister whether it was in the public interest that a private company should be free to barter away the livelihood of the whole population of a district like this, Baldwin refused to answer. And that was that. The result of three months' excited preparation and one month's march had led to a few minutes of flaccid argument during which the Government speakers had hardly mustered enough energy to roll to their feet. But when the bewildered unemployed trooped downstairs they found everything surprisingly changed and jolly, for it was teatime. Ellen did her best to cheer them up and the faces which had registered nothing during the questions now beamed warmth and friendliness as cups and cakes were pressed on the guests.

On Guy Fawkes Day the men left King's Cross by special train for Jarrow, where a great welcome was awaiting them. But the important little gods at 'the Labour' remained implacable and unaffected by all this, and the Unemployment Assistance Board in Jarrow promptly deducted from four to eleven shillings from the marchers' allowances on the grounds that while they were on the march they could not be available for work, had work turned up.

Ellen's best-seller, *The Town That Was Murdered*, which she wrote for Victor Gollancz's Left Book Club, came too late to help Jarrow, for it was then 1939, and things were different.

CHAPTER TEN

Thugs, Trunks and Things

'Something will come of this. I hope it mayn't be human gore.'
SIMON TAPPERWIT IN *Barnaby Rudge*

NINETEEN THIRTY-FOUR, the year of blood, the year when the abattoir came into use as an ante-chamber in the chancelleries, the year of Grand Guignol politics, of assassins, of follow-your-leader.

In America there was gang war, as the repeal of the prohibition laws threatened the standard of living of the bootleggers. In Indianapolis John Dillinger was lying in state in a funeral parlour while 5,000 sightseers paid homage to his naked body and counted the bullet holes. Some were seen to file past over and over again, just to make sure. On July 25th they buried him in a borrowed suit. $10,000 had been offered for his corpse and his family had been rightly scandalized. Was a man who had stolen a cool half million to be sold like a pauper? Reverently, while Franklin Roosevelt held the greatest ever inter-state police conference, they lowered Dillinger into consecrated ground to rest beside his mother.

In Austria, on the same day as Dillinger's funeral, two young men, Otto Planetta and Franz Holzweber, shot Doctor Dollfuss and left the little Chancellor to bleed to death on a sofa. Six days later, and exactly three hours after hearing their sentences, they were hanged in Vienna. 'Heil Hitler!' they cried on the gallows. Had they not reason to be joyful? Would they not meet in heaven and would not Horst Wessel be of the company? In Berlin, the trial of the three killers of the Nazi proto-martyr, who had so bravely moved to a notorious Red district of Berlin in order to teach the new faith, was proving to be something of an embarrassment. To unconverted ears it sounded uncommonly like a group of noisy young men fighting over a tart.

But better a girl than a boy. On June 30th the Führer's austere morality discovered that it could no longer endure Captain Ernst

Röhm, and the Führer did the only clean thing. He murdered him. Röhm was asleep in bed on the Night of the Long Knives, some said not alone. He was awakened and given a gun and told to commit suicide. He could not, so they shot him. The next day Germany learned that its new head of state, the Leader who had leapt into President von Hindenburg's jackboots before even the old warrior had been trundled away to his tomb in Prussia, had organized and carried out the assassination of ninety people, and all in a few hours. The rest of the world heard the news with shocked incredulity. But the Führer did not blanch or apologize. He waited for two weeks and then he rose in the Reichstag and shouted to the amazed assembly,

'For twenty-four hours on June 30th I was the supreme court of the German nation in my own person: I gave the order to shoot the main culprits and I ordered that the mutineers should be shot down. . . .'

The madness could have received some kind of check at this point. For a silent split second it even seemed that it might. Then tyranny received its mandate in wave after wave of tumultuous applause. Germany had chosen its saviour. More cleanliness followed. Richard Strauss helped to hound Furtwängler from his post and from the country: Karl Barth was dismissed. Two men divorced their wives on the grounds that they were one-fifth Jewish. But six million other men, women and children continued to catch buses, study for examinations, have dinner, make love, read books and go for walks, whilst their elected government invited tenders for crematoria and discussed unusual disposal problems with sewage experts.

Nineteen thirty-four, at midsummer, was rotten in a way no year had ever been before or since.

In London, Oswald Ernald Mosley, sixth baronet, a tall, handsome young man in his mid-thirties, offered himself to England as a St. George *noir* and all that year it was often touch and go whether England might accept him. Dressed from throat to toe in vigorous tight black clothes—'a visible expression of the businesslike but straightforward spirit which marks this up-to-date movement', as a *Daily Mail* reporter put it—the extraordinary person who had married Curzon's daughter and who had not so long ago crossed the floor of the House to sit with the socialists, was now so far to the Right that ordinary Tories were obliged to look out of the corners of their eyes to keep track of him. Not so Lord Rothermere, who faced

that direction fairly and squarely, as he thought. Not so Lady
Houston, who was not above shopping for the government she preferred and who would, if necessary, have brandished her cheque-
book in heaven. Not so the thousands of hearty chaps of both sexes
from all over the country who paid 5s. each for a black shirt, not so
the generals who rushed from their furious retirement in the shires
at the smell of (clean) blood; not so the 'Biff Boys', the cohorts
specially trained at Mosley's H.Q. in Chelsea to preserve the right
of free speech with their fists.

The new movement venerated King George V, hoped for great
things of the Prince of Wales, used the Union Jack as though it were
a club emblem and was swept into real unqualified adoration by the
National Anthem. It skirmished nightly in the great cities. People in
drab backstreets would become tense and fearful as the dark,
strutting processions arrived and the police and the civic authorities
would seem to lose their lawful power. Then the Reds, who in 1934
had every reason to believe that they were fighting for their lives,
would surround Mosley, who was himself concentrically ringed by a
huge double belt of Biff Boys and policemen, and the trouble would
begin. Mosley was a brilliant orator when he liked, but all too often
his meetings lacked words and were careful try-outs of force. The
drill was always the same. A heckler would shout out a question,
then the spotlights would discover him and hold him blinking until
a group of Fascist stewards dragged him away for his beating.
Women Fascists were trained to deal with women hecklers and were
taught to slap instead of punch. After each assault Mosley would give
a little homily on the need for Fascist methods to preserve free speech.

On June 7th, 1934, the B.U.F. gave a terrifying display of power,
when they took the whole of Olympia for a 'private' meeting, thus
excluding the police. The sadism at the meeting reached an erotic
intensity. Seven hundred and sixty policemen were on duty outside
and yet there was no one to stop the extraordinary public beatings-
up inside the vast building. A group of visiting M.P.s of all parties
were outraged by the sheer audacity of it. Baldwin's private
secretary, Geoffrey Lloyd, was appalled by the spectacle of men and
women being deliberately injured at a public meeting.

'I saw case after case of single interrupters being attacked by ten
to twenty Fascists. Again and again, as five or six Fascists carried
out an interrupter by arms and legs, other Blackshirts were engaged

in hitting and kicking his body. I saw several respectable people who merely rose in their places and made no struggle, treated with unmerciful brutality. It was a deeply shocking scene for an Englishman to see in London.'

Who went to watch the Blackshirts? *The Times* thought that a very large proportion of the onlookers were 'people of middle age who wore neither blackshirt nor badge: people with a tired expression and wrinkled brows: some of the people who bore the strain of the war and the cost of the peace. There seemed to be few people of the professional classes. They were those who have tired of passing through difficult times in which hope has been strained. And they seemed to be looking for the reason beneath this resurgence of youthful enthusiasms and militant spirit, lest they should have missed a chance of deliverance which these in their inexperience had miraculously found. In so big a crowd there was miraculously little cheering. The impression one gained was that the inquirers, who feared that they had become back-numbers, had neither found the secret nor caught the enthusiasms.'

The people who watched Fascism, in fact, were the same people as the not inhumane but near-moribund spectators who could watch their neighbours being collected for Belsen. 'If what happened at Olympia could happen at a time when Fascists held such little power, what might be expected to happen later on?' asked Isaac Foot. Similarly, when a British Minister of the Crown, Sir John Simon, felt it necessary to publish his ancestry in the Press to give the lie to rumours that he was of Jewish descent, again what might not happen later on? Hitler himself, after all, had only been in power for eighteen months.

So the darkness intensified. The smell of violence clogged the summer air. People who up until now had appeared rational, now solemnly discussed the indecent fantasies of race purity. Should Jews be castrated or should they be banished to Madagascar, where international warships should police the waters for ever to prevent their escape? Such questions were posed, not by maniacs, but by patriots, political hostesses and even by some churchmen. The line was, that society was sick and needed some surgery. To hell with sentiment! Humanism was pansy, so to hell with that, too! In July a Blackshirt threw a four-year-old child through a plate-glass window in the East End and no charges were preferred against him.

This particular year *Der Stürmer* circulated in Britain and was purchased for as much as £1 a copy. Julius Streicher had owned and edited this weekly since 1923. It was obscene and insane, but it was read with a considerable degree of sophisticated interest and amusement. While its 'Jewish Ritual Murder' number was being hawked in high places, a Brighton cinema manager was fined £5 for showing the film *Poil de Carotte*, chiefly because it was in French. This particular year saw a lavish exhibition of anti-God posters from the U.S.S.R. on view in St. James's Street. The National Portrait Gallery, entering into the spirit of the times, described its portrait of the Duke of Cumberland as 'The Hero of Culloden'. Aleister Crowley frowned satanically from all the Sunday papers, having been summoned for pinching Betty May's letters, and a steady stream of wife stranglers and husband poisoners jostled for precedence on the page. All in all, it was a lurid extravaganza of a year and the only wonder is how the normal domestic outrage, so essential to Anglo-Saxon sabbatarians, managed to get a look in.

*

Perhaps it was the classically Tussaud-like proportions of the Brighton Trunk Murders which so enraptured the public. Perhaps they fulfilled the British requirement of crime as a salutary entertainment, which was something which Fascist excesses consistently failed to do. The British are not, on the whole, sadistic, but they have always found much amusement in the processes of retribution. Sybil Marshall, in *An Experiment in Education*, tells how she once met an old woman who took her into her cottage to show her the shawl in which her great-grandmother had been married. 'They were married at the church here in the morning,' she said, 'but after that they didn't know how to spend the rest of the day. So they walked into Cambridge to see a man hung.'

In the last weeks of 1934, while civilization slithered, Mr. and Mrs. Everyman thronged to Lewes Assizes to see a little twenty-six-year-old waiter hanged. The material for Norman Birkett's legal homily was so seamy that no self-respecting Biff Boy would have been seen soiling his fist with it. The circumstances which gave rise to it were morbid and bizarre. In fact, the Trunk Murders were to have everything—except murderers.

On June 18th, 1934, the left-luggage attendant at Brighton

Station sensed that all was not well in his office. A large new brown canvas suitcase, left in his charge on Derby Day, was beginning to proclaim its uniqueness. For a 12s. 6d. suitcase 'such as might be purchased anywhere', its eloquence was very terrible. The attendant wavered, stroked the plywood battens which held the case together and then called the station-master, who at once called the police. When the trunk was opened they saw a fat brown paper parcel tied up in yards and yards of new Venetian blind cord. Inside was what at first looked like the torso of a plump middle-aged woman, for such is the ungallantry of death.

That same evening, the attendant at the left-luggage office at King's Cross Station found a suitcase containing two still very pretty legs. They had been deposited on June 7th, the day after Derby Day. At the time the King's Cross attendant found the legs he had not heard of what had happened at Brighton, but immediately afterwards there was tremendous activity throughout the left-luggage offices of England. But no head and no arms were discovered. Nor were they ever found. The effect of this crime on police and public alike was sensational, nor was the drama in any way lessened when Sir Bernard Spilsbury, seeing through the motley of corruption, pronounced the victim to be a meticulously well-cared-for girl of perhaps twenty, with light brown hair and long and beautiful toes, the latter having been pedicured only a few days before dismemberment.

The year 1934 was a great time for missing girls and the fate of this little *inconnue* of five-feet-two-inches—and five months gone with child—touched every imagination. A fate worse than death was expected for such girls. But this! The murder brought the speculative genius of the Press, the Newgate passions of the public and the full resources of Scotland Yard into a single concentrated obsession. The monster had to be found, if only because he alone was likely to produce the head, which was something everybody simply longed to see. But the girl's identity was never known and never will be. She had been dead for about three weeks. The brown paper shroud bore a single clue, the word 'ford' in blue pencil. They thought it was the last syllable of a place-name, only which place? It was never discovered. The police worked hard for two or three days and then came up against a blank wall, after which they threw the whole affair open to the public. Anybody's guess was preferable to no guess at all. Such a death, it was maintained, could not be discreet. It prescribed mess, smell and noise. Brighton was asked to describe any strange occurrences during the past month which came into these categories and this had the result of Chief Inspector Donaldson of Scotland Yard receiving a dossier on the town which suggested that a massacre had taken place in it round about Whitsun. He put this wearily on one side. It was the first of an avalanche of 'helpful' correspondence which was eventually to drive him from the uproar of Brighton police station to the rococo peace of Brighton Pavilion.

House agents and landlords handed in long lists of empty proper- ties where such grim work might have been done without interrup- tion, and these were all thoroughly searched. Scores of runaway girls were rounded up and returned to their provincial homes, much to their disgust. All day long, for weeks, people brought the Brighton police blunt instruments and bundles of women's clothes, until the police station began to look like a crook's jumble sale. On June 26th a young man found a human skull on the beach, drifting in a wash of cigarette cartons and scraps of bathing costume, but he did not retrieve it as he thought it had nothing to do with him. Epithets used for the murderer now changed from 'brutal' to 'cunning' and the ghastliest crime was now being called the perfect crime.

By the end of June they were digging up the race-course and examining all the jerry-built shacks which had spread like a pebble- dash pox round the coast of Britain since the war. Meanwhile, a report that the toenails had been painted was indignantly denied by the authorities, who were now assuming a very gentlemanly attitude towards their bits of girl. Similarly, when it was rumoured that the second toe on each foot was longer than the big toe, a statement was instantly issued to say that, far from being in any way abnormal, the toes were so perfectly formed that they gave the impression of being longer than usual. Hope was raised when it was thought the toes might have been part of a Miss Daisy Johnson from Cardiff, but were soon dashed when Miss Johnson appeared alive and well.

By the end of July the police had received 6,000 helpful letters, most of them prudently signed *Pro Bono Publico*, and the Detective- Inspector in charge of the case had collapsed with the worry of it all and had to be taken to hospital. It was shortly after this that the Chief Inspector fled to the comparative serenity of the Royal Pavilion. And on August 12th the officers from Scotland Yard put the whole affair back into the hands of the local police and went home. After all, it *was* 1934 and Trunk Murder Number One was not the only crime to be solved. The girl with the pretty toes had defeated them. She remained as she had been when the lid first rose on her in the baggage-room, headless, armless, nameless—a victim of what? Of whom? No one ever learned the answers. Moreover, the sad little victim was even to be denied the singularity of her fame, for on July 15th Trunk Murder Number Two came to light.

Some days before this happened, the police had checked up on the raffish human flotsam which eddied in and out of Brighton's crevices, and had interviewed a dark little man whom they knew as Tony Mancini, but whom Brighton knew as Jack Notyre or Tony English or Tony England or Mr. Swinley or Antoni Luigi or Mr. Watson or, it seemed, as anything which happened to come into the young man's head when somebody asked him his name. His quite elegant real name was Cecil Lois England.

The police went to Mancini's basement flat in Kemp Street, a dull little working-class thoroughfare conveniently near to Brighton Station, and there they found a trunk containing an entire corpse. As in Trunk Murder Number One, the tray of the trunk was missing. There was an immediate hunt for Mancini, who had disappeared, and who was last seen carrying a portmanteau. A few hours later he was picked up on a road near Blackheath, arrested and charged with the murder of Violet Saunders, a dancer.

'All I can say, sir,' said the nervous young man, 'is that I am not guilty.'

And all the world could say, and did say long before he reached the dock, was that he *was* guilty. His guilt was pronounced so vehemently and so often that Mancini's forthcoming trial soon took on the status of a formal legal convention, and although there was nothing to connect him with the first Trunk Murder, the Press and the public had made up its mind that he might as well be hanged for both crimes and be done with it.

Cecil England, alias Mancini, was a flashily handsome youngster of twenty-six who wore plenty of grease on this thick black hair and whose chief delight was to dance. He was born in the East End and had floundered through his teens and a few petty crimes before meeting Violet Saunders, who was sixteen years his senior. He was a good lover. His mixture of physical slightness, amorousness and dependent affection brought out the protective side of otherwise world-hardened older women, and they loved him. He had a child's feckless gaiety which allowed him to dance nightly in cheap cafés for hours at a time and with little thought for the morrow, and when the terror caught up with him he was to show a child's fear. The irony was, that the only breast to which he might have turned in his extremity was that which lay unspeakably comfortless in the big black trunk. Though who would believe this? Who would believe anything Mancini said? In his mind, too, the verdict was foregone. Guilty or Not Guilty were no more than words in his experience of justice. They had got him; he would swing. It was simple as that.

The trial opened nearly six months later, on December 10th, at Sussex Assizes, by which time Mancini had been so besmirched and vilified in the Press that the scared Italian-looking youth in the dock and the monster in the newspapers who bore his name seemed to have no relationship. But the big legal guns which had been brought in to battle for his life—Quintin Hogg and J. D. Cassels for the prosecution; Norman Birkett and John Flowers for the defence —did much to reassure people that here was evil out of the ordinary. There was an all-male jury. Great crowds queued for the public seats. The few who reached them heard Mancini plead Not Guilty and saw him standing in the dock with a look of dull resignation on his white face.

They heard how he had come to Brighton the previous autumn with Mrs. Saunders, who was known on the stage as Violet Kay and who was the other half of a dancing act called 'Kay and Kay', her partner being a man named Kay Fredericks. When they reached Brighton, Mrs. Saunders had shown signs of being in great fear and she was always packing her clothes and saying to her young lover, 'Come on, we must move.' So they moved many times. In March they came to rest in a basement flat in Park Crescent, where Mancini told his new landlord, Mr. Snuggs, that he was a gentleman's clothes-presser. Mr. Snuggs knew the couple as Mr. and Mrs. Watson, liked them and found them to be on entirely affectionate terms. In May, Mancini got himself a job as a waiter at the Skylark Café. It was the first job he had had since coming to Brighton in the autumn and all this time Violet had kept him and looked after him. On May 7th, two days after Mancini had begun work, Violet paid Mr. Snuggs his rent, and that was the last time he saw her alive. That

Norman Birkett, K.C. leaving Lewes Assizes during the Mancini trial, December 1934.

Photo: London News Agency

Cecil Lois England alias Tony Mancini.
'Strange as it may seem, I used to love her . . .'

Photo: Radio Times Hulton Picture Library

Edward VIII of Great Britain, Ireland and the British Dominions beyond the Seas, King, Emperor of India—

Photo: Keystone

—and Mrs. Ernest Simpson, late of Baltimore.

Photo: Keystone

same afternoon a man had been seen driving the car belonging to an elderly man named Mr. Moores, and this car had stopped at 44 Park Crescent and the driver had got out and spoken to Violet as she lounged in the doorway of the basement flat. This man was the very last person to see her alive.

A few days after this, Mancini gave a friend of his at the Skylark Café all Violet's clothes and told her that Violet had left him and gone to Paris. Also at this time, Mancini went to a dealer named Wood in Brighton Market and bought a big black trunk. He told the dealer that he needed the trunk because he had got himself a job in France. He continued to work at the Skylark Café and amongst his customers were a nice Mr. and Mrs. Barnard who lived in Kemp Street, near the railway station. On May 14th, just a week after Violet had been last seen, Mancini went to live at the Barnards' house in Kemp Street. He arrived with another young man very early in the morning and between them they lugged a very heavy trunk into his new room. They had brought the trunk across Brighton on a hand-cart. He told the Barnards that his 'wife' had gone away with his 'uncle', meaning old Mr. Moores. Once settled, he began to dance. He danced compulsively, excellently, ever-lastingly, in a jazz dive called Aladdin's Cave. He danced there sadly on the evening of the day he had spent at the police station, when he told his partner that he had only four more days of happiness left to him. Male gossips from the Cave were to describe how they had heard Mancini talking violently about his 'wife', how he had 'bashed her from pillar to post', etc., though, as it turned out, there wasn't a sign of a bruise on her body.

For two long months Mancini slept in a little bed by the side of Violet in her trunk. He even entertained his friends in the same room and blamed the smell on to the landlady 'because she wouldn't let him open the window'. The glassy-eyed court heard how Mrs. Barnard had discovered fluid dripping from her lodger's luggage and hastened to the Skylark Café to tell him about it. 'Don't worry,' said Mancini, 'it's only French polish,' and he came home and mopped it up.

Mancini was on the early morning train to London when Chief Inspector Donaldson and Inspector Pelling entered 52 Kemp Street and opened the black trunk. There she was, no *inconnue*, no fair-footed waif but, on the contrary, an ageing creature all too well

7

known, Violet Saunders, a woman who had abandoned her coal-miner husband for the bright lights and the wild freedom which had followed the Armistice. Kay of 'Kay and Kay', where the world was concerned, but now nothing easily describable to the policemen staring down at her. Her brother, a meat-porter, identified her. He said he knew her by her long thin hands. It was again a case of extremities.

Sir Bernard Spilsbury gave the cause of death as shock following a fracture of the skull. His presence was to spice the affair. He and Pierrepoint, the public hangman, were high on the list of those who diverted the age.

When Mancini was arrested on the main road from London to Maidstone, he said, 'Yes, I am the man, but I did not murder her. I would not cut her hand. She has been keeping me for months.'

They found blood on his clothes, blood in the cupboard of his previous lodgings. All this and more made up the case for the prosecution and the thoughts of everybody were on how the wretched young man in the dock would take the death sentence, when they heard a quiet, silvery, concise voice with an almost theatrical carrying-power asking questions. Norman Birkett said very little at first but even at his first sentence the helter-skelter self-assurance of the prosecution began to waver and lose its impetus. He forced Mr. Snuggs to change his genteel tone, and did so without offending Mr. Snuggs.

A man had been seen going down the basement flat. He was tall and he wore a trilby hat. This was about the end of April and the man stayed for about an hour. Mr. Snuggs had also seen 'uncle', who came to the flat in a chauffeur-driven car. 'Uncle's' name was Charles Moores and he was an elderly bookie. But although Birkett could not get Mr. Snuggs to say that a man called 'Darky' and a man called 'Hoppy' had visited Violet, he had proved his point. While Mancini was away, waiting or dancing, odd males drifted in and out of 44 Park Crescent. Kerslake, the chauffeur, added a strange new note. On May 5th, only a few days before Violet's disappearance, 'Uncle' had been certified by the Brighton Relieving Officer and had entered a mental home. When he, Kerslake, had seen Violet on the day of her death, or the assumed day of her death, she had shaken so much and had looked so ill that he thought she had been drinking. As he came away he saw another man descend the basement steps.

The court was almost painfully still now. Everything was changing. The assumptions of the past five months lay in ruins. For all that, the white-faced prisoner continued to look like a cornered animal, though now not such an interesting animal. Birkett continued mellifluously to sow doubt, wreck assertions, challenge glibness. Then he began the super-human task of restoring to Mancini a few decent rags to cover his moral nudity. A five-month newspaper campaign had left him a monstrous scarecrow. Turning to Mr. Barnard, the much-bothered landlord of the Kemp Street flat and someone who had every justification for being furious with Mancini for bringing all this trouble to his premises, Birkett asked softly, 'You have no complaint to make about him?'

Mr. Barnard then saw his ex-tenant as he was and replied, 'No. All the time he was living with us he was a perfect gentleman.'

A dancer came from Leicester Square to tell of her eleven-year friendship with Violet. She liked Violet's young friend and had often danced with him. She had always found them on the most affectionate terms. Kay Fredericks told of his and Violet's partnership, not only as 'Kay and Kay', but as lovers. They had parted after three years and he had not seen her for a further two years. Since the break-up of their affair and their act he had lived at the Headquarters of the British Union of Fascists, where he was employed as a photographer.

A bombshell descended shortly after this evidence. Dr. Roche Lynch, the pathologist, said that he had found no trace of blood on the hammer which the prosecution was assuming to be the murder instrument, that Violet had been dead too long for him to know her blood group and, most sensational of all, that her body contained morphine, which, after so long a time, could only indicate that she had taken a distinctly greater quantity of the drug than the normal safe dose.

Mancini's two statements were read out. The first was the lie about Violet going abroad with Moores. The second was without doubt the bleak and wretched truth.

'I got frightened. I knew they would blame me and I could not prove that I had not done it. I had not the courage to tell the police what I had found so I decided to take it with me. I bought a trunk. She was a prostitute. There were always men coming to the house all night. I did not kill her as God is my judge.'

Chief Inspector Donaldson told the court why Mancini was frightened of the police. His convictions for petty theft sounded trifling in comparison with his present trouble, but he and Violet, who had been convicted for prostitution, were the sort of people who would never go to the police. The Chief Inspector added that most of the stories filling the Press were untrue.

Sir Bernard Spilsbury, always a star turn, revived flagging sensation by dramatically holding up a human skull. The court was dazzled by it. Mancini looked deeply shocked. It was, however, merely a skull from a medical school and Sir Bernard was demonstrating. Holding out a piece of bone he told the court that it was the exact piece which had formed the depressed area in Violet's fractured skull.

Birkett: 'How long have you been in possession of the small piece of bone which has been produced here *for the first time on the third day of the trial*?'

Sir Bernard: 'Since the first examination.' [i.e. five months]

Birkett: 'Did it not occur to you that the defence might have been informed?'

Sir Bernard: 'I am afraid it did not occur to me.'

Birkett: 'Let me get this perfectly plain. You appreciate that *no doctor for the defence* was present at the post mortem?'

Sir Bernard: 'I did not think anyone was in this case, certainly!'

Birkett: 'For a piece of bone which has been in existence all this time to be produced on the third day of the trial does put the defence in some difficulty?'

Sir Bernard: (muddled and shaken) 'I did not think it would take anyone long to examine it and come to conclusions. . . .'

Birkett: (swiftly) 'You will concede at once that there are many other possible theories available for the death of this woman?'

Sir Bernard: (very quietly) 'Yes.'

Birkett then began to make and substantiate a series of perfectly valid hypotheses for Violet's death. He made them with extreme courtesy, attacking no man's honour, merely proving to everybody present that a woman who drank, drugged and received, amongst other lovers, an elderly mental patient; who moved because she was scared and who, at the time of her death, was living at the bottom of a dangerously steep flight of area steps, could die from one of many reasons. He attacked the Press: 'It is not merely unjust and un-

English, it is a crime akin to murder that when a man is charged, and before he is charged, statements of that kind should be made.'

When at last he questioned Mancini, the court was tense. Mancini, it was certain, would let his advocate down. How could he not? The tension grew until it became well-nigh unbearable and when it was at bursting point, Birkett asked a question which took the prisoner by surprise, jolting from his lips the last thing people expected to hear.

'During the whole time you lived with her as man and wife, how did you get on together?'

'Strange as it may seem,' said Mancini, 'I used to love her. We were always on the most affectionate terms. There were no quarrels.'

'Did that cover the whole time?'

'Yes, every second that she was alive.'

The jury was out for two and a quarter hours. When the foreman announced the verdict, Not Guilty, the court looked stunned and Mancini put his hand to his pale face in an arrested, incomprehending manner and remained frozen in this attitude until the judge, Mr. Justice Branson, said, 'You are discharged.' Mancini then bowed his head slightly, climbed from the dock and walked out of the court with his light dancer's step.

The verdict was received by the public with sullen incredulity. Its mood was not unlike that of a Colosseum mob on those sparse occasions when the emperor gave the thumb-up sign.

Shortly afterwards, Chief Inspector Donaldson took a well-earned holiday in Scotland and on his way home he stopped his car at Moffat, and sat on a little stone bridge above the burn to have a smoke. He saw the waters sweeping between the rocks and under the bridge and was at peace. Tucked beneath the bridge, and well out of sight, was a large pile of parcels—Dr. Buck Ruxton's wife, in fact—but the Inspector knocked out his pipe, started his car and drove from the spot in blissful ignorance of this latest development of ladies-as-luggage. And in Parliament Captain Cunningham-Reid formally inquired of the Home Secretary if he was satisfied that the existing regulations of railway cloakrooms were adequate to prevent the growing use of these places for the concealment of dismembered bodies. The Home Secretary thought they were.

CHAPTER ELEVEN

Wallis, of All People

ON January 20th, just five minutes before midnight, King George V died at Sandringham House and his widow, whose sense of duty had never at any time been jeopardized by sentiment, instantly turned from the deathbed to kiss the hand of the young man at her side. He was embarrassed but she was right. The following morning Britain and the Empire contemplated the features of King Edward VIII. They were the most familiar features—blue eyes, *retroussé* nose, wistful mouth—in the whole world, and the Press was unanimous in declaring that kingship became them. The new King was forty years old but an unparalleled expenditure of celluloid had arrested the years in his case, and his subjects, hallucinated by a photogenic fairy-tale which had begun in 1911 at Caernarvon Castle, watched tenderly as a slight blond youth ascended, with what appeared to be becoming reluctance, the remote eminence from which death alone could release him. Or so it was believed.

The new King flew from Norfolk to his Accession Council in St. James's Palace in an aeroplane, so creating the first of a series of precedents which were to land him in a dilemma usually reserved for the characters of Dornford Yates. That afternoon, in the Banqueting Hall of St. James's, a hundred Privy Councillors swore allegiance to the High and Mighty Prince Albert Edward Christian George Andrew Patrick David, their only lawful Liege Lord. But all the new King saw was a large group of elderly men wearing on their faces the expression of the last reign and hiding in their hearts some astounding suspicions.

The next day Garter King of Arms, attended by Heralds, Pursuivants and Trumpeters, came out on to the balcony and proclaimed the new King-Emperor. Watching the pageantry from a little disused room in Friary Court was Lord Beaverbrook's sister-in-law Helen FitzGerald and a small pin-neat American woman with smooth dark hair. Suddenly the King came into this room and was greeted with confused curtsies. The Guards Band played the National Anthem and the strange group was imprisoned in the huge sumptuous noise, after which King Edward touched the arm of the spruce little American, whose eyes now glittered with unshed tears, and said, 'Wallis, there will be a difference, of course. . . .'

Not many hours later King George's body was drawn through the streets of London on a gun carriage and was followed on foot by the new King, who looked extremely worried, rather than grief-stricken. The Imperial Crown rested on the coffin. Suddenly the mass of jewels quavered and came apart, and the great Maltese cross on top of the Crown, which consisted of a square sapphire framed in two hundred diamonds, toppled to the ground. The King watched it flash past his feet and lie in the gutter with split-second symbolism before, with no appreciable faltering of step, a sergeant-major scooped it up and put it into his pocket.

It was barely a month after King George's body had vanished from view on silent rollers at Windsor that King Edward made it plain to the Court and to the country that he intended to have his cake and eat it too. He would be King but he would also, when it suited him, be private. At first nobody demurred. George V, it was recalled, had spent much of his reign living the life of a country squire in Norfolk and the new King's desire for privacy was equally understandable. But when this privacy was seen to be gardening in a grubby shirt, and sometimes in no shirt at all, immolation in an architectural folly called Fort Belvedere in a distant corner of Windsor Great Park, walking to appointments from Buckingham Palace in the rain, eating little dinners in London flats, not going to church, making short shrift of a morning of loyal addresses by receiving a number of distinguished delegates *en bloc* and generally simplifying life, voices were raised in alarm. What worried the old guard was that there were no precedents for the King's behaviour. Was he like his grandfather? Hardly. Edward VII was cheerfully fleshly. He was an opulent man never very far from fat diamonds, rich gravy, champagne and generous women, whereas his grandson enjoyed the mock-virgin pallor of Syrie Maugham's white rooms, being one of the boys, using his hands, cutting the cackle and substituting the matey gesture for the Royal condescension. Was he, though God help them there, like George IV? Not remotely. Prinny was a man of remarkable taste who had a mysterious passion for blowsy dowagers. King Edward had no taste in the truly aesthetic sense and in his friendships with women he preferred a certain brittle containment. Physically fragile himself and only five feet six inches tall, he seemed to be always pushing away the overwhelming things of State, the huge dignities and dignitaries, the 'suitable' women and the enormous houses in a continual gesture of *noli me tangere*. It worked quite well during the long prentice years when he was Prince Charming. He was allowed his flippant magic because it worked. For nearly the whole of the twenties he wandered among the Dominions and Colonies on a dazzling progress in which his boyish impromptus were recognized as Empire-binders of a spectacularly successful kind. He mixed but remained ever separate; it was the secret of his triumph. Successive governments cashed-in shamelessly on the Prince of Wales's popularity and more and more tours were arranged for him. Then, in April 1930, when he was thirty-five, occurred a curious conjunction of feeling and event which can now be recognized as the first soft notes of the overture to the drama of 1936. The Prince suffered some kind of disenchantment in his role of Empire spell-binder and became introspective and vaguely bewildered. The possessive hands which he so dreaded had become very pressing during George V's illness in 1928, when the King had nearly died, and had never quite withdrawn. His mother talked tactfully but frequently of suitable princesses. His youngest brother George seemed also to have been involved in this wave of benevolent criticism and stampeded to the Prince of Wales's side. Prince Edward's desire for a place where he couldn't be got at now became something of an obsession. He had to retrieve all that was left of his true identity from the most successful journalistic legend of the century. None of the rented houses he had rested in between voyages would do for his purpose. He needed a retreat with an uncompromisingly inviolate quality—and found it in Fort Belvedere.

The Fort was a Grace and Favour oddity on the Sunningdale edge of Windsor Great Park and in April, 1930, it fell vacant. The Prince at once asked his father if he might have it. 'What could you possibly want that queer old place for? Those damn week-ends, I suppose,' said the King. The Fort had been built by George II in 1750 as a military look-out post and it had been used by troops returned from quelling the '45. It still had a line of four-pounder guns left there by Butcher Cumberland. Wyatville had added a tall tower and on this Edward flew the flag of the Duchy of Cornwall—even when he was King—to make it clear that it was a private house. Eventually, 'the Fort laid hold of me in many ways. Soon I came to love it as I loved no other material thing. . . .' Shortly after it was furnished and renovated the young Prince George moved in with him and only left when, in 1934, he married Princess Marina.

The stage being set, it was now the time for the play to begin. The chief characters were so utterly isolated that had their mésalliance depended upon the art of fiction rather than the accident of fact it is doubtful whether it could ever have taken place.

On July 21st, 1928, a young couple were married at Chelsea Register Office. Each had been married before and the wedding was quiet. They went to Paris for their honeymoon and came back to house-hunt, settling in 12 Upper Berkeley Street. Ernest Simpson was an English shipbroker who had spent most of his business life in the States. His wife, born Bessie Wallis Warfield, was a sagacious Baltimore woman of little real culture but plenty of the kind of charm which pays the biggest dividends outside its national habitat. At first the only other person Mrs. Simpson knew in the whole of London was her husband's sister, Mrs. Kerr-Smiley. The middle-class friends to whom Mrs. Kerr-Smiley introduced her vivacious sister-in-law were quiet conventional people to whom Mrs. Simpson's fresh unguarded transatlantic talk sounded so unusual as to be clever. She gave little dinner parties and served American food; she played bridge and listened with an immediate hypnotic interest to the accompanying title-encrusted talk.

'Seeing a key to the British riddle, I formed the habit of reading most of the London newspapers. I studied them from front to back; and there was one organ of the British Press that instantly absorbed my curiosity—the Court Circular. . . .'

The approach to the Court Circular came about like this. The Simpsons tended to find their easiest social relationships amongst the officials at the American Embassy. The First Secretary was Benjamin Thaw, who was married to Consuelo Morgan, one of the celebrated Morgan sisters, the others being Mrs. Vanderbilt and Lady Furness. Lord Furness was a shipping millionaire with a house at Melton Mowbray where the Prince of Wales was often to be found. One day in November, 1930, the Thaws rang up the

7*

Simpsons to say that they couldn't join the Furnesses for the week-end because Benny Thaw's mother had been taken ill. So would Wally and Ernest go in their place? The Prince of Wales was to be present. Wally wavered but Ernest said, 'Of course we'll go. All that is expected of you, darling, is that you be yourself.' In the swaying train from St. Pancras to Melton Mowbray, Benny Thaw, who it appears had not gone to his sick mother after all, taught Mrs. Simpson to curtsy and at seven o'clock that evening she did it to a small fair man in very loud tweeds. Their first conversation was about central heating.

In 1931 Mrs. Simpson borrowed Lady Furness's feathers and was presented at Court—in spite of the anti-divorcee rule. On January 30th, 1932, came the summons to Fort Belvedere. The party included Lady Furness and the Thaws. They found the Prince doing embroidery on a sofa, an art his mother had taught him, he said. It was an enchanting week-end with the Prince wearing the kilt, taking Turkish baths, billhooking the shrubbery and dancing to 'Tea for Two' on the gramophone. Mrs. Simpson was shattered. She had expected a cross between the activities of the Hell-fire Club and the Tower of London, and had found instead a decorous and determined innocence. She played up to it gamely and then found herself swept helplessly into the Berkshire charade. The Prince came to her little dinners in Bryanston Court, and then adopted the habit of dropping in at all hours. Early in 1934, Lady Furness was called back to the States for business reasons and before she sailed she confided her anxieties about the Prince to her very good friend Mrs. Simpson. The conversation ended with Wallis saying, 'Oh, Thelma, the little man is going to be so lonely,' and Lady Furness insisting, 'Well, dear, you look after him for me while I'm away. See that he does not get into any mischief.'

Lady Furness was much shaken when she came back from America and saw what had happened. 'Wallis of all people!' she said. And that was the general verdict—Wallis of all people.

Twenty years later the Duchess of Windsor was to provide as candid a comment on what to most people was an incomprehensible love affair as any that were written before or since.

'The only reason to which I could ascribe his interest in me, such as it was, was perhaps my American independence of spirit, my directness, what I would like to think is a sense of humour and fun, and, well, my breezy curiosity about him and everything concerning him. Perhaps it was this naturalness of attitude that had first astonished, then amazed, and finally amused him. Then, too, he was lonely, and perhaps I had been one of the first to penetrate the heart of his inner loneliness, his sense of separateness. Beyond this point my speculations could not carry me; there was nothing else that was real or tangible to nourish them.

'I had no difficulty in explaining to myself the nature of the Prince's appeal over me. Over and beyond the charm of his personality and the warmth of his manner, he was the open sesame to a new and glittering world that excited me as nothing in my life had ever done before. . . . It seemed unbelievable that I, Wallis Warfield of Baltimore, Maryland, could be part of this enchanted world. It seemed so incredible that it produced in me a happy and unheeding acceptance. . . . All I can say is that it was like being Wallis in Wonderland.'

*

In November, 1934, Prince George left Getting-Away-From-People-House, as his brother called Fort Belvedere, for his marriage, and Peter Pan, as Mr. Simpson called the Prince of Wales, was left alone. In May, 1935, King George and Queen Mary celebrated their silver jubilee amid scenes of unparalleled affection. The Simpsons were invited to the State Ball at Buckingham Palace and it was here, as she danced with the Prince before his glacial parents, that Mrs. Simpson felt the first tremors of the earthquake to come.

For the few months that were left of the old King's reign the Prince and Mrs. Simpson behaved as exemplarily as the situation would allow them to. It was always *Mr.* and Mrs. Simpson in the Court Circular and although there were signs at Bryanston Court that the charming bookish husband was beginning to feel the indignity of the role he was bound to play in order to preserve so delicate a *status quo*, it was none the less his gentle poise which was the chief provider of the freedom his wife and the Prince of Wales were to enjoy all through 1935. For him, too, there was no precedent. What was a chap to do when he came home from the office to find the heir to the greatest empire the world had ever seen taking pot-luck with his wife? Only bow himself out to his room on the pretext of finishing off some important work, which is what he did. 'Until now (one evening Mr. Simpson had banged the door), I had taken for granted that Ernest's interest in the Prince was keeping pace with mine,' Mrs. Simpson was to declare naïvely.

If Mr. Simpson chose to have an understandably blind eye concerning the matter, there were others who did not. Indeed, could not. The Prince of Wales, for twenty tentative years the 'world's most eligible bachelor' and the white hope of a fragmented generation which escaped the massacres in France, was suddenly seen to be tenderly attached to a diminutive American woman with a bitten-back smile and a monumentally complacent husband. Although the British Press maintained an absolute reticence concerning the matter, United States and Continental newspapers suffered no inhibition whatsoever in getting out their biggest, blackest type. Facts and rumours poured in and Miss Ellen Wilkinson, forcing the pace, demanded to know why the magazines she received from abroad had large holes cut in them.

When the Prince became King the situation was well out of hand and he tried to face up to it realistically. There was now a considerable nucleus of people in politics and society who knew what the average person still had no inkling of, that Mr. Simpson's enigmatic wife must—since what was there to prevent her?—become the Queen of England. Whoever the King married became Queen automatically. This fact was not hidden from Mr. George Allen, the King's solicitor, when he asked, 'Are you quite *sure*, Mrs. Simpson, that you want a divorce?'

Meanwhile, the King began to slash away rather recklessly at the conspiracy of silence which hedged him in, just as he once bill-hooked the stagnant laurels at the Fort with his own hands in his determination to open that private prospect to sweetness and light. He took Wallis to meet the Duke and Duchess of York, driving her to Royal Lodge in a new motor-car. Realism had been called for and had apparently been proffered, for Wallis was to write, 'I left with the distinct impression that while the Duke of York was sold on the American station-wagon, the Duchess was not sold on David's other American interest.'

Neither was Stanley Baldwin, when he met Mrs. Simpson about a month later after the King had told her, 'It's got to be done. Sooner or later my Prime Minister must meet my future wife.' Mr. Simpson was present.

So much now had to be done—and swiftly, before the tempest

broke. On July 9th the King gave another Wallis-launching dinner party at his old home, York House. Sir Samuel Hoare was present and remembered Wallis, 'not only for her sparkling talk, but for her sparkling jewels in very up-to-date Cartier settings'. This time Mr. Simpson was not present. Moving from the matrimonial home to the Guards Club he was no longer obliged to play gooseberry.

About three weeks after this dinner party the King, feeling more confident about things than for months past, sailed off for a holiday cruise in Lady Yule's yacht, the *Nahlin*. The party included the Duff Coopers, the Herman Rogers and Wallis. The cruise of the *Nahlin* constituted the last wild fling in the rebellious idyll which had begun at Fort Belvedere in 1930 but the ship's determined gaiety was trammelled by skeins of melancholy not unlike those which subdue the lovers in Watteau's *Embarkation for Cythera*. This foreboding did not inhibit the King-Emperor from appearing on the bridge of the *Nahlin* almost naked as the yacht slipped through the close confines of the Corinth Canal, to the fascination of thousands of Greeks and the horror of the Duff Coopers. Everywhere the *Nahlin* docked it was besieged by photographers and reporters as the scandal was fed to an already glutted American and Continental Press. There was one photograph in particular which told everything, Wallis with her hand on the King's bare arm, a gesture which carried with it plain for all to see, not an ordinary indiscretion but a settled, enduring relationship—and, moreover, a relationship which had already endured for some time. The hand was not that of a mistress but that of a wife.

British citizens in the United States now thought it about time that the Government at home had some idea of what was happening and shoals of letters containing Press-cuttings poured into Downing Street. Nothing happened because the House was in recess and Stanley Baldwin himself was in Aix, taking the waters, a habit from which only something such as the Second Coming was likely to deter him.

After the cruise Mrs. Simpson went to Paris and there she read about herself in the newspapers for the first time. She was deeply shocked. Back home in London, the King dined with his mother who then began the superb series of non-sequiturs with which she armed herself to face the music to come. 'Didn't you find it terribly warm in the Adriatic?' she asked.

While the *Nahlin* was cruising, Mr. Goddard, Mrs. Simpson's solicitor, had commenced divorce proceedings against Mr. Simpson at Ipswich, a court chosen for its obscurity but which also meant that Wallis would have to live within its jurisdiction for a few weeks. So a cottage was discovered for her at Felixstowe. The hearing, at which she was represented by Norman Birkett, took place on October 27th with only two women spectators, the judge's wife and a friend. The judge frightened her by his apparent hostility and she was even more frightened when he hesitated before saying in a bitter voice, 'Very well, decree *nisi*.' She drove back to London and to the new house she had taken, 16 Cumberland Terrace, feeling soiled and sad. The case was barely reported and appeared in the most insignificant print, this being the result of a 'gentlemen's agreement' organized by Lord Beaverbrook and the Hon. Esmond Harmsworth at the request of the King.

The King spent the previous week-end—'those damn week-ends'—at Sandringham but he had no sooner arrived than a message came asking him to meet the Prime Minister immediately and secretly. On Tuesday Stanley Baldwin arrived at Fort Belevedere at ten in the morning and asked the King for a whisky-and-soda, after which he smoked his pipe furiously. Gradually, after pointing out to the King the danger in which the Monarchy stood, he came to the gist of his visit, which was that Mrs. Simpson should be prevailed upon to withdraw her divorce petition. The King's reply was adroit to trickiness. He had no right to interfere with the affairs of 'an individual', he said. It would be wrong to attempt to influence Mrs. Simpson just because she happened to be a friend of the King's.

So as things stood the King's Coronation, at which he was to swear to uphold the Church and Defend the Faith, was fixed for May 12th and the future Queen of England's second decree absolute was due towards the end of April. The Press pullulated with what it knew and still must not say, and the King opened his first and last Parliament. And on November 13th, as he was about to take his bath at Fort Belvedere, where he still insisted on living in spite of the fact that Queen Mary had at long last moved her stupendous collection of bric-à-brac from Buckingham Palace to Marlborough House, he received a letter from his new Private Secretary which staggered him by what he regarded as its effrontery. This was the letter.

Buckingham Palace,
13th November, 1936.

Sir,

With my humble duty.

As Your Majesty's Private Secretary, I feel it my duty to bring to your notice the following facts which have come to my knowledge, and which I *know* to be accurate:

1. The silence of the British Press on the subject of Your Majesty's friendship with Mrs. Simpson is *not* going to be maintained. It is probably only a matter of days before the outburst begins. Judging by the letters from British subjects living in foreign countries where the Press has been outspoken, the effect will be calamitous.

2. The Prime Minister and senior members of the Government are meeting today to discuss what action should be taken to deal with the serious situation which is developing. As Your Majesty no doubt knows, the resignation of the Government—an eventuality which can by no means be excluded—would result in Your Majesty having to find someone else capable of forming a Government which would receive the support of the present House of Commons. I have reason to know that, in view of the feeling prevalent among members of the House of Commons of all parties, this is hardly within the bounds of possibility. The only alternative remaining is a dissolution and a general election in which Your Majesty's personal affairs would be the chief issue, and I cannot help feeling that even those who would sympathize with Your Majesty as an individual would deeply resent the damage which would inevitably be done to the Crown—the cornerstone on which the whole Empire rests.

If Your Majesty will permit me to say so, there is only one step which holds out any prospect of avoiding this dangerous situation, and that is for Mrs. Simpson to go abroad *without further delay*— and I would *beg* Your Majesty to give this proposal your earnest consideration before the position has become irretrievable. Owing to the changing attitude of the Press, the matter has become one of great urgency.

I have the honour ...

Alexander Hardinge.

P.S. I am by way of going after dinner tonight to High Wycombe to shoot there tomorrow—but the Post Office will have my telephone number, and I am of course entirely at Your Majesty's disposal if there is anything at all that you want.

This letter infuriated the King and dismayed Mrs. Simpson. He saw in it some collusion between his Private Secretary and his Prime Minister and promptly decided to tell his troubles to Walter Monckton, an old Oxford friend, instead of to Hardinge. Mrs. Simpson panicked to the extent of saying that she thought the advice in the letter was right and that she ought to leave the country. The King wouldn't even think of such a plan and there was a scene in which he ordered her to do no such thing—'I won't have it.' After positively begging Beaverbrook to return home—he was Arizona desert-bound on the *Bremen* in search of asthma relief—in order to postpone the Fleet Street conflagration, the King sent for the Prime Minister.

Baldwin arrived, only a different Baldwin. This time there was no whisky-grabbing, only plenty of finger-cracking and plain words. Baldwin told the King that whoever he married would become Queen. It was as simple as that. This was the first time the word 'marriage' had been used and it rolled between them like a mine between a sturdy puffing tanker and a pleasure craft. When Baldwin said, 'I believe I know what the people would tolerate and what they would not' the explosive sphere was flipped expertly into the King's path. The King paused and then by a single bleak sentence brought the Prime Minister to heel. 'I am going to marry Mrs. Simpson and I am prepared to go,' he said. Baldwin later described this as the ice being broken but the King was nearer the truth when he said that the interview left him feeling like Eliza on the icefloe.

This meeting had a poignant effect on the King. Just being able to say so immensely sacrificial a thing as giving up his Throne for his lover put him back in his own eyes on the chivalrous eminence from which he had conquered the world in the old Prince Charming days. The scandals of the present faded and Baldwin said that 'his face wore such a look of beauty as might have lighted the face of a young knight who had caught a glimpse of the Holy Grail. No reasoning or pleading by family or friend could penetrate that rapturous mist. He was alone with his vision. . . .'

That evening the King told his mother of his decision. She heard it through the mask-like calm of her now undentable façade and the great misery she felt was all the more harrowing for its being denied the ordinary human outlets. The next morning, when she received the Prime Minister, she took shelter behind a rough Georgian homeliness. 'Well, Mr. Baldwin,' she said, 'this is a pretty kettle of fish.'

The King then saw his three brothers. The Dukes of Gloucester and Kent provided the extremes of reaction which he anticipated, the former feeling little and not pretending to feel more, the latter feeling everything and still to his own mind not feeling enough for this adored brother. There remained the Duke of York. He, poor man, was so overwhelmed as to be for a time quite outside feeling— little or much. All his life he had been passed over by what brother David was to call the 'Royal show'. It had become the thing for cameras to turn away when he approached. A convention of privacy had been observed for so long where he was concerned that to the country at large he was almost meaningless. The nervousness in his wide-eyed and bony face was so near the surface as to evoke an un-flatteringly obvious consideration for it in the faces of those who met him. He also possessed a slight speech defect which had been much commented on by those who had not heard it. He and his pretty Scots wife lived in Piccadilly in circumstances that, when compared with those of the Prince of Wales, amounted to semi-retirement. Now it was proposed that he should wear the Crown. He was filled with dread. Constant tact from others had had the effect of making him too modest and he had quite lost sight of his own merits, if he ever knew them. He was, in fact, ideally suited for the British Throne. But there is little to show that King Edward understood this when he allowed the Crown to pass to such a flinching head and much to show that although he shared the common belief in his brother's frailty he did not allow this to influence him when it came to burdening the helpless Duke with kingship.

Friends now took the principal characters in the great drama aside to proffer various kinds of ingenious advice. Duff Cooper told the King that as Mrs. Simpson's decree absolute could not be granted until April, the whole matter should remain 'abstract' for five months, the plans for the Coronation got on with and the tempera-ture accordingly lowered. Esmond Harmsworth took Mrs. Simpson to Claridge's and explained to her what 'morganatic' meant. Would she mind being Duchess of Lancaster, say, instead of Queen? She thought it 'strange and inhuman'.

The King, however, now beginning to seize on any suggestion that could release him from the *impasse*, let Harmsworth go to Downing Street with his blessing. Then came the King's big mistake. By telling Baldwin that he was willing to submit the morganatic marriage proposal not only to the British Cabinet but to all the Dominion Cabinets as well, he knew that he would have to act on their 'advice'. Beaverbrook returned the next day and saw at once the error in letting the morganatic marriage question be decided at Cabinet level. *His* plan was a brilliant romantic Press presentation of what he called the 'King's Case'. Both Duff Cooper and Winston Churchill were to be in different degrees associated with the 'King's Case' but while these plans were yet embryonic the Prime Minister acted. Mrs. Simpson was with the King at Fort Belvedere when the heavens burst.

The signal for the flood which was to wash the King away came from where it was least expected. No one, certainly not Stanley Baldwin, terrified the King more during his unique tribulations than Geoffrey Dawson, the editor of *The Times*, whose behaviour during the Abdication crisis would have done credit to Sir Francis Walsingham. How far his pen was levered to dislodge his King is still conjectural but even if one has to leave the reckoning at its editor's known activities it shows that *The Times* had during the thirties an authority which was little short of scriptural. All through the last days of November King Edward waited and trembled for the appearance of the awful first leader he had reason to suspect was already written and set up. And November passed and nothing appeared.

And nothing might have appeared for ten or more days had not Dr. Blunt, the Bishop of Bradford, told his diocesan conference that he wished that the King 'would show more positive evidence of his awareness of the need for Divine guidance. . . .' All the Bishop meant was that the King should attend Church regularly. He had never heard of Mrs. Simpson. All he was concerned with was the use of the Coronation service as a symbol of national spiritual resurgence. The Church of England in 1936 was in the doldrums because of the way its teachings had managed to accommodate the blood lust of the militarists during the First World War. The Archbishop of Canterbury and saintly men like Dr. Blunt saw in the coronation of a popular young King a wonderful means to reconcile the cynical to a Church which had learnt a lot since 1918. The key figure in this spiritual awakening was, of course, the King himself. Much of Archbishop Lang's subsequent behaviour, with its apparent lack of ordinary charity and barely suppressed fury, can be attributed to the fact that he saw a woman wrecking the best opportunity the Church was likely to have in his lifetime for rehabilitating itself in the affections of ordinary people. The Bishop of Bradford knew nothing of any woman. All he knew was that mentions of the King at Matins were few and far between.

It was unusual to criticize the King at any time but in the unnatural silence of the 'gentlemen's agreement' even the mildest reproach was inflammable. The destruction of Prince Charming by the same machine which had invented him was a repellent business. Having put him together, the Press knew how to take him apart, and this it did while the world gasped. The country was bewildered and angry that things had reached so extreme a pass before it had been given the least hint of the business. The King's popularity was tremendous. Who were the Press lords and the politicians that they should keep this near-perfect King's love from his subjects? the people asked. And they turned avidly to their newspapers to treat tolerantly their monarch's boyish infatuation with a post-war Lily Langtry, for this is what they expected. What they saw was utterly incomprehensible.

A severe, governessy face stared back at them. It was unassuming, unbeautiful and unquestionably the face of 'a lady'. By looking hard it was possible to see that the King's friend was elegant and probably wise. The gossip columnists did their best to build her up to consort level but always the delicate structure toppled the moment they added the salient truth. The lady was one and a half times divorced. If only Mrs. Simpson had *looked* like a woman who had two husbands and was contemplating taking a third it was just conceivable that there might have been a generalized good word for her. But she didn't. She looked instead like a woman whose impenetrable natural dignity was at odds with her history, and the conjunction of the two states, incontrovertible in either case, made her appear sinister. The Duke of Windsor, after twenty years of marriage to her, was to write, 'In character, Wallis was, and still remains, complex and elusive. . . .' A pretty-faced nobody in the same situation would have received kinder treatment.

By December 4th the Press was overflowing with her pictures but even at her most informal she remained, to the public at large, inscrutable. Her house in Cumberland Terrace was stoned and she awoke to find herself notorious. The King, anxious for her safety, took her and her chaperoning aunt, Mrs. Merryman, to Fort Belvedere, where the scene was like the most extreme kind of comedy-thriller, with the King calling himself 'Mr. James', loyal unto-death telephonists clinging sleeplessly to switchboards, cars doubling out of the tradesmen's entrance with the King and gliding out of the front gates with the cook, and everything in a state of unadulterated drama. On Thursday Mrs. Simpson was driven from the country, ostensibly by Lord Brownlow in her own Buick, in actuality by the ferocious Press. She and the King's equerry crossed to Dieppe, that sanctuary-post for so many generations of defaulting Anglo-Saxons, and drove the 650 or so miles to Cannes in circumstances nearly as harrowing as those of Marie Antoinette during her flight to Varenne. At Lyon she heard for the first time the description of herself which was to pursue her for the rest of her life. A man caught a glimpse of her as she shrank back into the car and shrilled convulsively, '*Voilà la dame!*'

' "*Voila la dame!*" ' she wrote. 'For a long time that curious cry was to reverberate in my memory. This, I reflected bitterly, was what I had been finally brought to—no longer Wallis Simpson, no longer just another woman, but *the* woman. I was marked.'

Back home the King was taken to task severely for not being his age. Forgetting that it alone was responsible for 'H.R.H. Peter Pan', the Press insinuated that the King was too old for the love game. Dominions newspapers were particularly severe on this point. 'It is almost inconceivable,' scolded a New Zealand paper, 'that in less than a year of the death of King George, the Throne should be shaken to its foundations by indiscretions which age, experience and cognizance of his exalted office should have warned King Edward to avoid . . .' and the dreaded first leader in *The Times* went out of its way to remind the King that 'he had reached middle age without the blessing of a happy marriage', while the Melbourne *Argus* declared that 'Australians are astounded at being required to look at their idol from an entirely new angle'.

The King's defenders ranged from Winston Churchill, whose passionate interpretation of history lent his grief a classic quality, to

Sir Oswald Mosley and his egregious cockney Nazis, who marched up and down Whitehall with a portrait of the King chanting,

One, two, three, four, five,
We want Baldwin dead or alive.

The Beaverbrook-Rothermere Press came out for the King in frankly sentimental terms and many private individuals, such as a Miss Lucy Houston, who hawked her own pamphlet through the West End ('The King's Happiness Comes First') did their bit. Among the arguments for keeping the King, at least until after his coronation, was one which pointed out that a Yorkshire pottery firm would have at least a quarter of a million mugs left on its hands if he left the Throne now.

While all this was going on the Crystal Palace burnt down at Sydenham and Queen Mary, sensible of the value of an ordinary gesture at an extraordinary time, drove out to see the iron and glass miracle which had so perversely gone up in flames. This cheered everybody up enormously.

Still believing that there must be a hard core of genuine affection in the dismally collapsing tinsel image of himself, the King decided to challenge his people's love. If it was only a fraction of what they had declared it to be over twenty adorative years would they not take his side against the chilly forces of his ministers? He decided to broadcast to the nation and plead like an ordinary man for the simple cause of being able to marry the woman he loved. His words, which he intended to have polished by Winston Churchill, would cut across the sophistries of priests and politicians and the wave of devotion they would inspire would reduce the whole issue to manageable proportions. Excited by this idea, he left Fort Belvedere for Buckingham Palace for his fifth meeting with Mr. Baldwin. The Prime Minister did not care for the imaginative element which was beginning to creep into the King's proposals, but he said nothing. After grudgingly allowing Winston Churchill to be the King's adviser he said he would have to discuss the broadcast suggestion with the Cabinet. He then drove away from the Palace. So did Edward, never to set foot in it as monarch again.

The next day found the King of England virtually a prisoner in a mock Gothic folly in Windsor Great Park. All consideration and restraint had gone and an army of photographers and reporters besieged the Fort. The papers arrived and the King and Walter Monckton pored over them. *The Times* and *Telegraph* reflected the official attitude but the King and his friend were thrilled to see that such unlikely weeklies as the *New Statesman* and the *Tablet* supported the marriage. Again hope rose and when news came in that great crowds were singing the National Anthem and 'For He's a Jolly Good Fellow' outside the Palace there was a heady moment when the battle seemed almost won. But in the afternoon it became plain that all was lost, crushed irrevocably by Baldwin in a statement to the Commons.

'Suggestions,' said the Prime Minister blandly, 'have appeared in certain organs of the Press . . . that if the King decided to marry, his wife need not become Queen. These ideas are without foundation. There is no such thing as what is called morganatic marriage known to our law . . . the lady whom he marries, by the fact of her marriage to the King, necessarily becomes Queen. . . . The only way in which this result could be avoided would be by legislation dealing with a particular case. His Majesty's Government are not prepared to introduce such legislation.

'Moreover, the matters to be dealt with are of common concern to the Commonwealth as a whole, and such a change could not be effected without the assent of the Dominions. I am satisfied, from inquiries I have made, that this assent would not be forthcoming. . . . I have no other statement to make.'

This was the end of the 'King's Case'. Everything was now pellucid, bitterly and mortifyingly so. The King was still smarting from the nerveless and unanswerable logic of the Prime Minister's speech when its author drove up to the Fort in the too-small car which Edward found so ridiculous. He brought with him a précis drawn-up by Sir John Simon which told the King what he might and might not do. So was salt rubbed in the Royal wounds. After this, thinking that the audience was at an end, the King began to rise but was checked by a gesture from Mr. Baldwin. There was one other thing. Could the King give the Government his decision without delay, if possible during the week-end?

His *decision* . . . when only that morning he had indulged in the sweet morganatic pipe-dream! The King needed all his strength to say, 'You will not have to wait much longer, Mr. Baldwin.'

The King hardly slept that night. After breakfast he told Walter

Monckton to go to London immediately to warn the Prime
Minister that when he came to the Fort that afternoon 'I shall
notify him formally that I have decided to abdicate'. The King also
begged a favour—that a second Bill should be submitted to Parliament with the Abdication Bill, to make Mrs. Simpson's divorce
absolute immediately, so that he could go straight to her and be
married. When Monckton had left, the King sent an agent to
Switzerland to find a hotel near Zurich. 'For me the golden thread
of my inheritance had snapped.'

At ten o'clock on December 10th, 1936, King Edward, the Dukes
of York, Gloucester and Kent, Sir Edward Peacock, Walter
Monckton, Ulick Alexander and George Allen met in the drawing-
room at the Fort. Fifteen documents lay on the table before them.
Each document said the same thing.

> *I, Edward the Eighth, of Great Britain, Ireland, and the British
> Dominions beyond the Seas, King, Emperor of India, do hereby
> declare My irrevocable determination to renounce the Throne for
> Myself and for My descendants, and My desire that effect should be
> given to this Instrument of Abdication immediately.*
>
> *In token whereof I have hereunto set My hand this tenth day of
> December, nineteen hundred and thirty-six, in the presence of the
> witnesses whose signatures are subscribed.*

The King signed his name fifteen times neatly—almost casually—
and then went out into the garden. At Mr. Baldwin's suggestion
that he might like to add something personal for Parliament to hear,
the King wrote two little notes, one commending his brother and
the other exonerating Mrs. Simpson from taking any part in per-
suading him to abandon his Throne. When the time came the
Prime Minister read out the first note and totally ignored the
second.

Mr. Baldwin's speech was a masterpiece, a marvellous performance. He made it after question time to a packed and utterly silent
House. He had few notes and the novelist *manqué* in his nature
warmed to the unique drama he alone could unfold. His great
audience listened spellbound. When he sat down emotion seemed to
have drained away all movement and comment, and Clement
Attlee was like a man trying to make himself understood in an
airless void as he sought permission to have the House suspended

until six o'clock, when a very upset Winston Churchill spoke of 'this melancholy and bitter conclusion' and Jimmy Maxton seized what he obviously thought and hoped was a moment of monarchlessness to advocate a republic. This was nothing against Colonel Wedgwood's inspired lack of tact when he said that though 'tomorrow they would take the Oath to the new King but if they sometimes raised their glass to "the King across the water", who shall blame them?' which brought ministerial cries of 'Oh!', as well it might.

Mr. Gallacher the communist was surly and said that it had all been too much for him and that, anyhow, he had known about Mrs. Simpson for over a year. And Mr. Buchanan of the Independent Labour Party and Member for the Gorbals, exploded. 'If he is a tenth as good as you say, why are you not keeping him? Because you know he is a weak creature. You want to get rid of him and you are taking the step today.'

*

The Crown passed from him as he sat at luncheon with Winston Churchill at precisely 1.52 p.m. This was the moment when the Clerk of the Parliaments droned 'Le Roy le veult' to the Abdication Act. And so Edward was prince again and free. His tremulous happiness was in marked contrast with that of his companion, who was near to tears and murmuring Marvell. The last hours were precipitous with poignant functions. There was a broadcast to make. His mother—and many other people—begged him not to make it. 'Do please take my advice,' pleaded Queen Mary. But of course how was she to know that the whole awful joy of his late action was that he never need take advice again? The Director of the B.B.C. himself arranged the broadcast from Windsor Castle, earning from *Punch*:

> *How doth the Busy B.B.C.*
> *Improve the Shining Hours?*
> *By adding to its Glorious Reith*
> *Another Bunch of Flowers.*

The broadcast was kindly received rather in the way a curtain speech is received. The drama was at an end. Satiety had been reached—some thought over-reached—and the chief actor who had held the stage for ten amazing days seemed to lose all significance as he stepped from his wonderful trappings. Earlier in the day Churchill had tapped out with his walking stick the elegiac lines,

He nothing common did nor mean
Upon that memorable scene

and there was, too, something of the scaffold about the deliberately amateur speech, with its commendation of his mother and his heir and the subtle manner in which he forgave his enemies by pretending that they did not exist. Only a few yards away lay the body of Charles I and it was asking too much of Winston Churchill to forget the fact when he helped another small sad King to make his farewells. The greatest subconscious emotion the broadcast stimulated was probably to remind the remnants of the lost generation that their youth, too, was over. The living symbol of their reaction was middle aged. *The Times* itself said so.

A few hours later the Prince, created Duke of Windsor on the spur of the moment, sailed away in the destroyer *Fury* and went to stay with the Baron Eugene de Rothschild in Austria. Sixty other castles were reputed to have been put at his disposal. Nothing was done to hasten Mrs. Simpson's divorce absolute and the couple had to wait until May 4th before they were reunited. They were married in circumstances which all the art of Constance Spry and Mainbocher could not redeem from shabbiness. A North-country clergyman, the Reverend R. Anderson Jardine, ran the gauntlet of his bishop to perform the ceremony and the final snub arrived with Walter Monckton in the form of a letter from George VI telling his brother that his title of H.R.H. could not be extended to his Duchess. This little action ruined the day. Edward was then forgotten. Perhaps Royalty, having to spend so much of its time fountaining honour and magnanimity over its inferiors, has to be indulged on the rare occasions when it turns on the cold tap over its equals.

The new reign was refined and correct without being in the least stuffy. Queen Mary loomed over it, her stature so increased by her recent stoicism that even physically she gave the impression of being ten feet tall. The new consort dismissed the vague epithet of 'charm' and swiftly established herself as enchanting. Her racy culture and quite staggering personality took everybody by surprise, not least her relations, and soon the memory of svelte little

suits was obliterated by daring finery. The King's slight inco-
herency endeared him immediately to a nation which has never
quite trusted conversational ease in men and his very real goodness
surprised and delighted everybody. They were crowned on May
12th, for it was thought that quite enough things had been changed
over the past six months without altering the Coronation date. The
evidences of his brother's reign, the shortest for 453 years, were
tactfully scanty. Some very attractive stamps had been issued but no
general coinage. The only pillar-box with the cypher ER was at
Ilford.

As for the Duke and Duchess, they became homely, so it is
believed. Nearly thirty years may have sanctified their union but has
only deepened their enigma. Their tragedy has the polish of an old
Lubitch film. Looking back on it we know our hearts should feel
more and our senses be entertained less, for this *was* a King and this
was 'the girl for whom he gave up his Throne', as they said. Perhaps
the key to the sadness is that it is not communicable and the version
which throbs in our ears from the distant thirties retains the chic
melancholy of 'These foolish things. . . .'

'And would your life have ever been the same if you had broken
it off?' asked Ernest Simpson. 'I mean could you possibly have
settled down in the old life and forgotten the fairyland through
which you had passed? My child, I do not think so.'

CHAPTER TWELVE

The Crucible of Grief

'This was the Spain which at the beginning of April 1939 looked to General Franco as the man who would forge a united nation in the crucible of grief.'

Spain BY SALVADOR DE MADARIAGA

THE truly romantic gesture is never histrionic. It is always a passionate action taken with a realistic end in view. Don Quixote had very sound motives for charging his windmill, and the thousands of young men from all over the world who swept into Spain when the forces of General Francisco Franco appeared to threaten the second stage of the Leninist millennium were not out for adventure. The thinking part of the International Brigade, and it was the predominant part, was made up of the last people on earth who were likely to thrill to the brave music of a distant drum. Most of them were old enough to have heard the indecent sound of chivalric pretensions being exploded in Flanders, and all were young enough to be cynical about military politics. Worst of all and in alarming contrast to the Spanish in either camp, they possessed an exalted concept regarding the sanctity of human life. Yet the battle noises from Spain in the summer of 1936 produced in these voluntary soldiers spiritual reactions which would have shocked Wilfred Owen and pleased Rupert Brooke. Terribly articulate, their pockets stuffed with literary broadsides, their blood on fire, they left their 'singing feasts', as Spender called their passive literary activities, and went to face the grim testing of their teachings.

There was, in the rich innocence of their muster, a naïve idealism only equalled, perhaps, by that of the Children's Crusade. It was not their intention to seek ritual death in a Spanish domestic holocaust. They had accepted the doctrine of the long view and they related all the good and bad in the world to opposing elementary principles governing Right, which was wrong, and Left, which was right. In Britain Right and Left were new words in the political language and like the rest of Britain's party nomenclature, they didn't mean what they did abroad. Their over-simplified use by the intelligentsia was much to blame for what happened when the comrades landed in Spain. For there it was discovered nothing tallied, neither love, death, God nor government, with what these terms meant—even in the broadest sense—outside Spain. As for 'Left' and 'Right', they were used by the sumptuously elaborate Spaniards as a kind of Iberian pidgin in order that they might make some political communication with the hordes of foreigners who had gate-crashed their private revolution.

The basic error was the assumption that Spain was roughly at the same stage of political and emotional development as the rest of the Europeanized world. It was not. Nor did it wish to be. It was Spain, a vast terracotta annexe of burnt highland stretching out like a flag from the Pyrenees to Africa. For a short while during the sixteenth and seventeenth centuries, it had, by practising an unnatural extroversion and backing up its conquests with a uniquely cruel concept of Christianity, become the greatest power on earth. Its decline was swift and absolute, and, by the Spanish themselves, apparently unmourned. They relished the subtleties of insulation. They resisted change and resisted it so completely that in places like Andalusia the traveller from London or New York in the 1930's could see men and women still living in the direct tradition of Roman serfs, and observe, in the Carlists, a reactionary movement which, if it had its way, would have taken the country back to the traditions of Queen Isabella and medievalism. In no other country would such a movement have had the faintest effect. It would have been equivalent in Britain to Norroy and Ulster King-of-Arms heading a back-to-the-Plantagenets party. Yet it was Carlism, with its motto 'The King Christ, and the Holy Virgin', which provided Franco with one of his best military forces.

A further shock was Spanish Christianity. The members of the International Brigade were in many cases too Christian for their own peace of mind. They came mostly from liberal backgrounds where Christian socialism or Jewish liberalism had been put into practice in one way or another for more than a century and while they had self-consciously shed the divine aspects of these faiths in their obvious forms, they were frequently never quite sure whether it was the Red

Dawn or the Light that lighteth every man which illumined their conscience and had brought them to fight the darkness of fascism. The British atheist is the most apologetically considerate man in the world and British anti-clericalism is practically non-existent. As for the British churchman, he goes to church as he goes to the bathroom, with the minimum of fuss and with no explanation if he can help it. The fighting intellectuals and the simpler comrades who had in some cases left the dole queue or modest jobs to serve in Spain in a great modern Theban band held together by comradely love expected to find similar Marxist-Christian ambivalent confusions among the Republicans. They knew about the gloomy *Pietà* complex of Spain, of its dark gold cathedrals and churches where the blood-streaked Christs gleamed and the Virgins wept tears of real pearls, of the rapturous processions at Seville and the sinister glory of the hierarchy. This was 'Spain' just as the *corrida* was Spain. The initial shock as they journeyed into this huge strange land was to see its churches burning, hear its priests being executed and watch ordinary people apparently thankfully piling their personal religious aids, statues, holy pictures and rosaries, on to bonfires. Quite what the Catholic Church was in Spain it seemed impossible to say but, except in the Basque country, it was quite obvious that it had little in common with the Catholic Church anywhere else. This was one of the first jolts to the preconceived image; the second was very terrible.

By far the worst of all the old Spanish customs the International Brigade volunteers and idealists had to endure, and this whether their internationalism was for or against Franco, were the judicial murders carried out daily by both sides. At the close of the war it was estimated that more than *800,000 people had been executed*, which was just exactly double the number of those slain in actual battle. These executions crippled and deformed the original impetus which had led many people in the International Brigade to take up arms. Already their Communism was giving place to a broader form of protest, which was eventually to become the militant anti-fascism which challenged the appeasement policies of Chamberlain and Halifax, and which was to destroy the huge pacifist movement built up by George Lansbury and others. Now their whole civilized outlook was outraged by the mannered barbarities of the Spanish peasant who behaved exactly as did his counterpart during the

reign of terror of 1792 in Paris. What escaped the foreigners in
Spain was the fact that to countless Spaniards of all classes it *was*, in
effect, 1792. There was no awareness of slipping back into a dark
past; Spain had ignored the ideas of modern Europe or hadn't even
felt them. It fought its Civil War with, to the observer, a pointless
and disgusting agony which was as stylized as the agony in Greek
drama. German sadism and Anglo-Saxon masochism were equally
affronted and bewildered by it. A young German serving with the
Requetes, the Carlist-Falange unit, surprised his Spanish officer by
showing excitement at the thought of shooting a prisoner and begging with shining eyes, 'Let me do it, *please* let me do it!' The more
so as the prisoner was also a German, though fighting on the other
side. The Spanish firing squads and those who set them in motion
performed their rites with a cool fatalistic efficiency, and if the
victims happened to be Spanish too an equally fatalistic acceptance
of the situation was usually returned.

The motto of the Spanish Legion was *Viva la muerte!* and throughout Spain the foreign writers and artists who had gone to fight
fascism found themselves repelled, mesmerized, fascinated, sickened
or aesthetically intrigued by the cult of death. For some it was the
end of the whole adventure. Auden, who had gone to Spain as a
stretcher-bearer in an ambulance unit, came home after a very short
visit of which, said Stephen Spender, 'he never spoke'. Arthur
Koestler's death sentence and the weeks of horror which followed it
as a handful of prisoners were quietly taken away from their cells
each evening to be shot, and described in one of the first and best
books to come out of Spain, *Spanish Testament*, published in 1937,
emphasizes the emotional dilemma of the twentieth-century
European trapped in this strange Iberian time-check. From his
bench in the Seville Prison he was like a man waiting for the tumbril
in a world which journeyed past his predicament in trains and planes.
He recognized that the intercessors who finally saved him from the
small pile of twitching bodies in the midnight yard of Seville Prison
were not people from another country, but from another century.
For the unsophisticated volunteer, like Stephen Spender's friend
Jimmy Younger, the position was nightmarish.

The heart of the matter was that international Fascism and
international Communism had raced to support a purely national
insurrection where neither was welcome, though both were grudg-

ingly used. Fascism recognized its error early on in the war and thereafter callously took advantage of the situation to try out its bombers. Communism remained hopeful to the end. Stalin and the Republican Premier, Dr. Negrin, who was not a Communist, were mysteriously in league concerning a vast transfer of gold from the Bank of Spain to Moscow—over £65 million of it. The Rebels started with nothing but were never embarrassed about funds because outside capitalist Fascism saw to that. The Government started by making Russia its trustee and discovered that even when the piper is paid with his own money those who are holding the kitty can still call the tune. This was only one of the uncomradely disillusions experienced by the anti-Francoists. There were countless more and all were to be crowned by the final infamy of the Hitler-Stalin Pact. Few wars, if any, were fought where so much unsullied personal idealism contended with such a morass of political depravity. And all the time the blood of the young poured out, not so much on battlefields but between the grubby cobbles of backyards, behind bullet-speckled walls on which contending posters flapped and in the bullrings themselves in mass *aficionada* as the machine-guns waved to and fro.

The Spanish Civil War was the great event which utterly changed, by means of a mysterious chemical power, all the political and ethical ideas of democracy in the mid-thirties. Its catalytic property was not obvious for some time and it came as something of a revelation to those who were so profoundly influenced by it that while it made changes in others which in some instances amounted to a political *volte face*, it made no change in itself. Burdened by the best and worst of international patronage, Spain spilt its blood in its own inimitably shocking way, and, what was more, forced its lovers and exploiters to do likewise. If the rebellion had taken place in 1931, as it could have done had King Alfonso defended his throne, the Republicans would probably have won, but the world itself would have watched.

The King had made a series of mistakes, none of them surprising in a man who had received more or less the same education as Philip II. He came to the throne as an attractive but quite fantastically imperious boy of sixteen in 1902 and from then he moved like the glorious central figure in a great pavane, the grave adulatory music forever in his ears and with all his actions circumscribed by an antique protocol which was cold and gorgeous. He reigned surrounded by army officers and priests. 'If,' wrote Salvador de Madariaga, 'King Alfonso had been entrusted in his early years to Don Francesco Giner, Spain would probably have become a peaceful and contented nation.' But instead the King shut his mind to the ideas drifting in from the Atlantic and through the passes of the Pyrenees into Spain, as did most of his subjects. Liberalism, even the classical sort propounded by the best European philosophers in the past, was screened from the King by his advisers as if it was an infection. He was a civilized man of action with the most exalted conception of himself and examples of his pride were legendary. He could lead Queen Ena through an avenue of ambassadors without acknowledging one of them or showing any sign that he had even seen them. He spoke in the second person singular always. His ministries drifted bitterly like the winds in Toledo. There were over thirty governments during the first years of his reign, each of whose administrations averaged a little over seven months. The failure to govern constitutionally led him to the strong man solution and General Primo de Rivera was appointed his Mussolini. The General called himself Dictator quite unblushingly. He trusted in his own omnipotence, he gagged the Press, brooked no criticism and suspended what democracy there was. The strange Spanish Church, which had for centuries drawn back from its ordinary pastoral duties and which endured a neurotic fear of the common people, was given mandates for directing all education and for exacting servile obeisance. With these measures and many more like them, all anathema to a nation as eccentrically individual in matters of religion and politics as the British, the Dictator sought to preserve a *status quo* which would have struck Ferdinand and Isabella as rather old-fashioned. It was too much even for the Church and for the Army, which gained some benefit from these ideas, and the Dictator fell. The people were not deceived. They knew this time it was not the power behind the throne which had brought about this brief tyranny, but the throne behind the power. Accordingly they swept through the enormous squares of Madrid shouting, 'Down with the King!' In a bizarre way there were hints here of what might have happened to Charles I of England had Buckingham lived until the months preceding the Cromwellian War.

On March 16th, 1930, Primo de Rivera died in Paris, broken-hearted it was supposed. That year Republican committees were secretly set up in all the great cities of Spain. Among those who scattered Republican propaganda from aeroplanes was a good-looking young pilot named Ramon Franco, whose brother, a dressy little army officer, was then serving abroad. The King had the greatest difficulty in forming a government and had to resort to the indignity of seeking his ministers in prisons. On April 12th, 1931, the municipal elections were held and, except for Cadiz, all the great cities of Spain put in Republicans. Two days later the Republic was actually proclaimed in some cities amidst scenes of delirious happiness. On that day, too, the late dictator's chief accomplice, General Sanjurjo, declared for the Republic and when the King heard this he abdicated. The British Press made it sound like the last hours of Louis XVI and Marie Antoinette at Versailles, but in actual fact the departure of the Spanish Royal Family took place in conditions of the utmost courtesy. The Monarchy had died, the Republic had been born and there wasn't a spot of blood to be seen anywhere.

What happened after this has never been better or more succinctly described than in the manner in which Salvador de Madariaga describes it in *Spain*, the fairest and one of the few wholly authoritative books to come out of the immense literary maelstrom stirred up by these events.

'The history of the Republic is in its essence the history of this inner struggle—of the centre, to exist; of the two extremes, to prevent it from gathering substance and momentum. In the end, the extremes won and Spain was plunged into the most disastrous civil war of its history. The international importance which this war came to acquire, and the active intervention in it of two Fascist and one Communist States, have tended to obscure the fact that in its inception and in its essence the Civil War was above all Spanish. These Spanish origins and aspects of the Civil War must be stressed in order to understand it adequately even as an episode in the European civil war of which it was the prologue.

'Why did the centre fail—fail not merely to govern but even to be born? First and foremost because of the unyielding and absolute nature of the Spanish character. This is the psychological root-cause of all Spanish troubles. It determines all that happens in Spain, and explains the periodical failures of Parliamentary government and

8

periodical rises of dictators. . . . By nature, the Spaniard gravitates to the farther end of his thought, just as the Englishman gravitates to the near end of it—for thoughts are tricky things, feels the Englishman. So, while Englishmen who think differently are nevertheless always within sight and hearing of each other and of the parting of their ways, Spaniards are always out of each other's mental reach and must shout to each other, and always run the risk . . . of mistaking a pipe for a revolver.'

For the next five years the Republic tremblingly endured. Disorder abounded. There were strikes, land-seizures, murders, church-burnings and countless confusions caused by amoral social activities indulged in by anarchic peasants to whom a mild form of brigandage was second nature. The Left and the Right moved warily, like two enemies trying to assess the strength and whereabouts of each other in total darkness. Both were tense with nervousness, keyed up and likely to explode by the most feathery brush with the other side. While these small committed factions waited for the big bang, a very large uncommitted section of the population took advantage of the turmoil to take what remained of the law into its own hands and settled private scores. Anarchy, the Spanish national pastime, flourished. The contrasting and very ambitious Rightist leaders emerged, Gil Robles and Calvo Sotelo, and at the same time the Spanish Foreign Legion and large numbers of Moorish troops crossed to the mainland. Terrible rumours reached Madrid of the Moors being let loose in the Asturias, a mining province with strong Leftist sympathies. The Moors and the Asturians were ancient traditional enemies and with what seemed to be *carte blanche* from their Nationalist leaders the Moors were taking a dreadful revenge on the miners, castrating them and torturing them.

The war was very near now and arrangements had already been made with Mussolini for military aid for the Right. Calvo Sotelo now spoke plainly for the Fascists and monarchists. He was a neat dark man whose businesslike speeches were flat, cold and arrogant, and in marked contrast to the flowery urbane oratorical elegance of President Azaña. The Government clung wildly to caution, like a straw. Although their activities were brazenly exposed, the leaders of the Right remained free, though romantic firebrands, such as the handsome and amusing Jose Primo de Rivera, the son of the fallen dictator and the founder of the Falange, were locked up. It was noticeable after the war that not even his political opposites spoke ill of this young man, who died by the firing squad. He was a mixture of Valentino and matador in the popularity sense and Oliver Baldwin was much amused to find the courtyard of his prison thronged by cars belonging to fashionable women who were filling his cell with flowers.

After May Day, 1936, the Right and the Left began their power-ful and dangerous simplification of politics. The gloves were off and the labels were on. Thus countless thousands were to die by the crudest and most inaccurate rule of thumb. Everything hung poised while a nation made up of 85 per cent of poverty-stricken peasants and 15 per cent of upper crust made plans to settle their differences. They were not the differences of the Fascist-Communist thirties but of all the time-locked Spanish centuries. Hitler was too ignorant, Mussolini too inflated and the British Left too ecstatic to realize this.

On July 13th, 1936, Calvo Sotelo was murdered. Gil Robles, until then his enemy in the same camp, at once claimed him as a martyr. Military revolts broke out in Seville, Cadiz and many other places. The revolts appeared at first to be autonomous but they were touched off by the arrival on the mainland of a little-known army officer from the Canary Islands, General Francisco Franco. The General was the Governor of the Canaries and the Commander-in-chief of the forces there. When the Civil War broke out he imme-diately assumed leadership of the rebels. To prove that Right-wing Britain was as concerned with Spanish affairs just as immediately as the intellectual Left it is only necessary to add that General Franco's sudden aeroplane flight from the Canaries to Morocco was facili-tated by the reactionary Douglas Jerrold, who obtained the plane, and that the General's flight from Morocco to the Spanish shore was taken care of by Major Hugh Pollard, an amateur adventurer who might have come straight from the pages of Dornford Yates. General Franco's pilot was also English, a man called Bebb, and the Caudillo also had the pleasure of the company of Bebb's eighteen-year-old daughter Diana as he flew in to preside over the incomparable tragedy about to unfold itself on the high Spanish plateau. He established his Nationalist H.Q. at Burgos. The legitimate Government held Madrid and rallied its support from there. It extended its friendship until it embraced, first the Socialists, then the Basque Nationalists and finally the Communists.

The effect abroad was electric. British poets and American novelists were fired with literary passions of a kind which no occurrence had produced in their own countries for many years. Where British writers were concerned, particularly, there was a breakthrough into a fervent emotional nakedness scarcely known in English literature since before their own civil war and the aftermath of its long legacy of restraint. The candour was inspiring and it led men to leave everything and fight what they believed to be ideas that would lead to a new Dark Age. Their noble militancy made Musso-lini's old-fashioned territorial ambitions in Ethiopia look trumpery in the extreme in comparison.

The great dress rehearsal for the events of 1939–1945 began with the actors emerging from the wings in some odd costumes and, also, in some vague comprehension of their rôles. The German soldiers and airmen who had been lounging around Spain in their thousands disguised as tourists and commercial travellers thankfully climbed back into their uniforms. Young British Right-wing sympathizers, such as Peter Kempe, a twenty-year-old Cambridge graduate, went the whole romantic hog and got themselves up in all the stylish elegance of the Requetes, tasselled forage cap, jack-boots, knee-hugging breeches and a vicious switch created by the Spanish, with their fine regard for the conjunction of passion with pain, out of a bull's pizzle. This initial magnificence was not to last for long and soon the Nationalist troops were wearing green trousers pulled in at the ankles and green serge blouses, the forerunners of British battle-dress. The practical lessons learnt by both sides during the Spanish Civil War were too innumerable to mention but they included such economies as seeing that prisoners dug their own mass graves before being executed, anarchist tricks that were later to prove invaluable to the Resistance Movement in France, Norway, Holland and elsewhere, propaganda warfare, terror bombing and even the invention of the Fifth Column.

The immediate response in Britain to the outbreak of the Spanish Civil War was a swift and definite retreat into strict neutrality by all parties. Ever since the advent of Hitler the Government's policy had been that of the man busy stamping out such sparks and brands of his maniacal neighbour's bonfire as should drift into his garden.

There was never the ghost of an attempt to dowse the bonfire itself or restrain the incendiary neighbour. Out of such rooted cravenness bloomed the dead nettle of Munich and the policy of non-intervention. The Non-Intervention Agreement was signed by Britain, Italy, Germany, Russia and various other European countries towards the end of August, 1936. It gave both amusement and strength to Hitler and Mussolini, whose armed forces were being afforded the most realistic manœuvres any soldiers, sailors or airmen could wish for. And it allowed the Soviet Union to cash in on the sentimentality of the West and use thousands of liberal idealists instead of party members as cannon fodder, and to reap the political rewards of youthful martyrdoms which, all unsuspected by the victims and those who believed in them, were regarded in Moscow with blatant cynicism. Non-intervention was shameful and cowardly but it was not injudicious. . . . The alternative, after all, was World War II. And in 1936 only office-less Jeremiahs like Winston Churchill believed that such a conflict was inevitable. The Government itself made only the smallest concessions to such an inevitability, though privately it was buying time for all it was worth. Nothing was too costly, certainly not honour, to placate the Dictators for another year or two, and this long before Germany led in the arms race. The price of time soared higher and higher. The few months' respite between Munich and September, 1939, cost the Prime Minister his pride, Britain its self-respect and Czechoslovakia its existence.

Not the least reprehensible thing about the Non-Intervention Agreement of August, 1936, was that it by-passed the League of Nations, and this alone made it clear that it had far more to do with convenience than with morality. The Labour Party endorsed it at its annual conference, held that year at Edinburgh, though it added a proviso that it only did so on the condition that there was strict non-intervention on *both* sides. Nothing could have been worse than this agreement, for Hitler not only recognized in its urgent placatory tone the timidity of the democracies but also the triumph of his own strength. He interpreted non-intervention in Spain as the amber light for his Juggernaut, and he began to roll across the freedom of Europe. Both he and Mussolini were noticeable more *exalté* and poised, assured and daring. The effect on the British Government was the opposite. It became more and more unsure of itself and

presented to a disgusted world a disgusting spectacle from which the
self-respecting felt bound to dissociate themselves. Anthony Eden
and Duff Cooper resigned.

Non-intervention was a Godsend to the Spanish Nationalists and
General Franco was quick to realize it. It meant that the army of
foreigners which had swarmed into Spain from nearly every
country in the world under the auspices of various national Communist parties, would now have to withdraw. Russia saw this, too,
and the ink of her signature on the Agreement was scarcely dry
before she recanted on the grounds that, as others were violating it,
she felt morally free to send help to the Republicans. Only six days
later, on October 29th, 1936, the Labour Party also went back on its
non-intervention decision out of sympathy for Russia. Thus was
born the great ethical rather than political division. On the one hand
there was the nervous appeasement of Neville Chamberlain, the
grotesque 'Gentleman's Agreement' of 1937 in which Italy and
Great Britain promised each other not to do anything which might
upset the *status quo* in the Mediterranean and on the other hand
there was an ever-increasing force which despised the Government
for its pusillanimity, but which remained restrained in its criticism
because of the prospect of World War II.

The outlet for these frustrations was Spain. To be there made
honest men feel clean again. At home all was bewilderment as
Conservatives found themselves obliged to support neo-pacifist
policies which made them deeply uncomfortable and Left-wing
idealists moved straight from pacifism to war-mindedness. The
Press was openly pro-Republican and went to town on atrocity
stories, giving on the whole an unfair view since the appalling
cruelties described had little to do with either Fascism or anti-
Fascism and everything to do with the peculiar nature of Spanish
violence. *The Times* stayed as neutral as it could. Exultant and thrilling above the bloody journalism was the surging, bugle-like poetry
and prose of Spender, Auden, Lorca, MacNeice, Roy Campbell,
John Cornford and George Orwell. It was word over all. A whole
consort of pipers was leading the simple working men from their
homes in the Welsh valleys, the depressed areas of the Clyde and
Tyne, and the backstreets of London to a land from which 543 of
them were never to return.

The strength of the various International Brigades was uncertain at the time. Salvador de Madariaga has recorded that in Paris one could hear that they consisted of 70,000 men and of 5,000 men from eye-witnesses describing them within a hundred yards of each other. The final estimate of the British volunteers is 2,762, of whom 543 were killed and 1,763 were wounded. Douglas Hyde sours this nobility by the following unsavoury anecdote taken from his party recantation *I Believed*.

'The events in Spain were a challenge and a showdown. Here was the war and fascism against which we had been warned, already beginning in one corner of Europe. . . .

'All over Britain and right across Europe, recruits to the Party came thick and fast, the sensitive intellectuals, the troubled and disillusioned pacifists, and solid working-class and trade-union types who had distrusted us in the past.

'When a Welsh section of Spanish Medical Aid was formed I at once organized a meeting to raise cash for a Welsh ambulance. I asked all my Left Book Club members to prove their sincerity by giving it active support. The platform of the meeting was solidly lined with clerical collars. . . .

'Our first ambulance left within a few weeks for Spain. With it went the Welsh national secretary as driver and I took his place. In the months that followed I worked as I had never worked before. . . . I showed the propagandist film *Defence of Madrid* at each meeting.

'The sacrifices were huge. At a meeting in a village near Bethesda I had an audience entirely composed of working folk . . . at which I Dutch-auctioned a Spanish militia man's hat and a militia girl's scarf.

'Two men made the final bids for the first. When I knocked it down to the purchaser he handed up an unopened pay-packet. . . . At great London meetings men and women were throwing on to the platform their wedding rings. . . . The widespread, often quite un-reasoning and almost instinctive hostility to do with Franco's Spain, which still survives to this day, is a tribute to our achievement.

'Often at my meetings I would get volunteers for the International Brigade. . . . More often than not they were lads with no political background at all. Some never came back and I, and others working in the cause, felt we owed it to them to work even harder.

'The communists went to Spain for quite different reasons from those of the non-communist. We saw it as a chance of learning the art of insurrection . . . to get experience at the barricades, to learn to use the modern weapons of death and destruction for the cause of communism.

'Every communist party in the world sent numbers of its members there to obtain experience . . . the rank and file in the early days died in very great numbers. Too many died, in fact, for the Party's liking. It was not intended that Party members should be slaughtered wholesale. Dead men could make no contribution to the fight for Soviet Britain.

'So I and others doing similar work were dissuaded from sending out any more Party members. When cannon fodder, above all else, was needed, one Party organizer's job was to go around the Thames Embankment in London at night looking for able-bodied down-and-outs. He got them drunk and then shipped them over the Channel.

'They sobered up in Paris, were dined and primed, then made drunk again. Paralytic, they went over the Pyrenees and, when next they were sober, they were already members of the British Battalion of the International Brigade. . . .'

The foreign volunteers who had come to help the Republicans began to arrive in Spain during September, 1936. Soon they were being backed up by Russian arms, guns, tanks and planes. General Franco, for his part, had his 'spontaneous' assistance from those who intended to save mankind from the Red terror at hand when the revolt broke out. By the spring of 1937 there were more than 30,000 Germans in Spain and 80,000 Italians. Mussolini was the first to end the farce of pretending that these considerable armies were anything other than help for the Spanish Right on an extremely practical scale, and after victories at Malaga and elsewhere during the summer of 1937 he sent his troops congratulatory telegrams in the most open manner. This was thought at the time to be great perfidy, though in a sense it was honest. And, anyway, it had all been arranged, not months, but years before. As early as 1934 the Spanish monarchists had been promised Italian help by the Duce. And in the winter of 1936 the monarchist Antonio Goicoechea was in Rome making arrangements with Mussolini and Marshal Balbo for Italy's military assistance in a civil war which was shortly to be organized in Spain. Gil Robles had also been observed visiting a Nazi congress in Germany and the dashing Jose Primo de Rivera's jaunt to Berlin, where he was treated like a prince, was hardly a secret. These elaborate arrangements between their upper-class countrymen and international Fascism could not have had any profound effect one way or the other on the ordinary Spaniard though, whose politics were insular and parochial and violently personal. They would have found the long view beyond them. It would have puzzled them rather than pleased or angered them that one of the rewards Hitler demanded in return for his help was Spanish iron ore so that he could keep his munition factories at full blast in preparation for the Second World War.

Another bitter diversion was caused by persistent rumours that Trotsky had arrived in Spain and was living in Barcelona. This Trotsky talk, ignorant and superstitious, was to have terrible consequences as it gave blood-thirsty peasants a convenient jargon for destroying those who refused the main labels. 'Trotskyite traitor', the illiterate judge would intone and two or three minutes later the ubiquitous rifles would crack in the near distance. The Germans took a great interest in the moral confusion caused by the skilful dissemination of lies and sent their experts in this field to study the effect. They also sent members of the Gestapo. But nothing invented by the Nazi lie-machine could approach the tragic and horrific nature of the truth. At least the foreign soldiers were free of the ultimate pain of knowing that they were killing their own neighbours and relations. And stark incidents like the destruction of the little town of Guernica, the 'Holy City of the Basques', made all the fanciful inventions of the propaganda touts sound like dirty jingles.

General Mola may have been responsible for this crime. The Basques had been a profound irritation to him and he had often threatened them. But it was carried out by the Condor Legion of the Luftwaffe, which arrived over this small cultural centre at half past four on the afternoon of April 26th, 1937, and systematically reduced it to blood and dust. The population of nearly seven thousand was almost wiped out. As Lidice was to do in the near future, Guernica concentrated the indignation of the world. Lord Robert Cecil called it 'the most savage act in history' and artists such as Picasso and poets everywhere recognized this obscene act as a milestone of human evil. After Guernica anything was possible. The Nazis were at first bewildered and then made nervous by the

8*

universal denunciation of this deed. The obloquy exceeded anything they had previously experienced, which was saying something. They launched counter-accusations at the tops of their voices but this time the big lie fell flat, and nobody believed that the Reds had committed this atrocity merely in order to defame the Right. The world Press continued to harp on atrocities and so reduced their impact. Eventually it required an effort of will to be as appalled as one felt one should be. Journalists everywhere, in their sincere efforts to discredit the Right or the Left, caused suffering to be a glut upon the market of feeling and conscience, and debased the coin of agony.

After Guernica there were increased demands for intervention but the louder the insistence, the less the appeasement Government of Britain seemed to hear it. Basque children arrived and their presence brought the entire Spanish tragedy home to ordinary men and women as nothing else could have done. British merchant shipping was sunk by German and Italian submarines as private owners ran the blockade for a brave mixture of charitable and commercial reasons. The continuous insult and outrage offered to Britain by the Dictators made the dogged complacency with which the Government accepted the rotten fruit of its Non-intervention rule appear incredible even to its nominal supporters. By the end of 1937 no intelligent person could condone an official policy of cowardice masquerading as prudence while the morality and law of centuries was going down like nine-pins on the European mainland. Those who saw these things in all their grim clarity committed themselves with the unreserved intensity of ancient saints to halting them. Careers were abandoned, money discounted, personal comfort and convenience ignored and nothing allowed to matter except the extermination of the political Black Death virus called Fascism which was infecting the world. Britain and the Empire became divided into two obdurate factions one of which urged war and the other, peace at any price. National disunity had seldom been so complete and had the Führer possessed any real psychological intelligence where the British were concerned he would have seen two aspects of phlegmatism which, should they ever be reconciled by a national emergency, might produce a halt to any man's ambitions. Spain had its lesson for him as well as for his storm troopers, only he failed to see it.

The Spanish Civil War ended officially on March 26th, 1939. Some thought that it could have ended much sooner if Russia had been able to bring herself to abandon her incredible day-dream of a Soviet Spain and not kept the fighting going artificially, long after its true impetus had run down. Franco had won because Hitler and Mussolini had helped him, said the friends of the Republic. The Republicans lost because they became the cat's-paw of the Russian Communist Party, said both the Left and the Right.

The truth was less obvious, and, like so much else, wholly Spanish. The Civil War was a struggle between a disciplined professional army, which was aided and abetted by Right-wing elements in the State and Church, against a number of highly individualistic Iberian countries each simultaneously engaged in agrarian revolutions which threatened the general administration of what was virtually a small continental empire. The error of the British in particular was to equate Aragon, Catalonia, Navarre, Andalusia, Valencia, Asturias, etc., with English counties, when in fact they were tiny egocentric *nations* with acute ethnic, religious and cultural divisions. The error the world was to make was to believe that these multiple insurrections were entirely linked to the main chain of events belonging to the first third of the twentieth century, when their political climate was the last third of the eighteenth century.

Daladier and Chamberlain recognized the Franco victory with an alacrity which was entirely despicable. But nothing the appeasers said or did now could surprise their critics. Only a month before Chamberlain and Halifax had been in Rome where they had been forced to raise their glasses in a toast to 'His Majesty King Victor Emmanuel, Emperor of Ethiopia'. The Labour Party was shocked at the official acceptance of Franco, though in fact only four days previously Chamberlain had vaguely indicated in answer to a question on this point that no change in Britain's attitude to Franco was contemplated.

All this, and so much more besides, threw the intellectual Left into an orgy of amateur politics. But they, too, were losing their brilliant impetus and in a strange way they knew it. The ground upon which they had constructed their eloquent yet simple house of universal brotherhood was eroding on every side. During the six months' breathing space which separated the profound Spanish adventure and World War II they found time for elegiacs. They needed to see life through human relationships again. Death too. Spain had taught them that to see it any other way was madness. And thus they celebrated their experiences, in the old quiet Bloomsbury tones of the individual, not the mob. Auden did it best.

> On that arid square, that fragment nipped off from hot
> Africa, soldered so crudely to inventive Europe,
>   On that tableland scored by rivers,
> Our fever's menacing shapes are precise and alive.
>
> Tomorrow, perhaps, the future: the research of fatigue
> And the movements of packers, the gradual exploring of all the
>   Octaves of radiation;
> Tomorrow the enlarging of consciousness by diet and breathing.
>
> Tomorrow the rediscovery of romantic love;
> The photography of ravens, all the fun under
>   Liberty's masterful shadow;
> Tomorrow the hour of the pageant-master and the Musician.
>
> Tomorrow for the young the poets exploding like bombs
> The walks by the lake, the winter of perfect communion;
>   Tomorrow the bicycle races
> Through the suburbs on summer evenings; but today the struggle.
>
> Today the inevitable increase in the chance of death;
> The conscious acceptance of guilt in the face of murder;
>   Today the expending of powers
> On the flat ephemeral pamphlet and the boring meeting.
>
> Today the makeshift consolations; the shared cigarette;
> The cards in the candle-lit barn and the scraping concert,
>   The masculine jokes; today the
> Fumbled and unsatisfactory embrace before hurting.
>
> The stars are dead; the animals will not look;
> We are left alone with our day, and the time is short and
>   History to the defeated
> May say Alas but cannot help or pardon.

from Spain by W. H. Auden

CHAPTER THIRTEEN

He Thought He Was Right

Where all the waking birds sing 'Heil'—
They tell me—in Bavarian woods
Lifting their tiny claws meanwhile
From underneath their leafy hoods
To greet the Leader as he toys
With vegetarian repasts
And Nazi girls and Nazi boys
In unison sing counterblasts.

What wings are these? What sound of Hope?
A phoenix or a turtle dove—
A kingfisher—a phalarope—
Dropping to earth from heaven above?
With Europe's prayers to aid his flight,
With all the people's loud acclaim,
Having his luggage for the night,
The Premier of England came . . .

EVOE

'*Ich bin von Himmeln gefallen.*' ('You could have knocked me down with a feather.')—The Führer, on hearing that Mr. Chamberlain wished to come to meet him.

MUNICH remains a hideously incised political indictment for which, twenty-five years later, there still does not exist a Rosetta Stone. What did happen? Why did it happen? And, most baffling of all, *how* could it happen? It was a dark deed done in the limelight. No other great twentieth-century treaty-signing possesses such an unparalleled documentation. The men of Munich are, in most instances, conspicuously reasonable human beings and not all of a kind. For the most part they resolutely refuse to transform themselves into the least kind of monster and thus they regularly frustrate their biographers. Roy Jenkins, wearily but watchfully coming to the end of yet another fat book about them, finds himself little the wiser and confesses it. 'The appeasers, whether diplomats or politicians, appear as a collection of neatly dressed men who rarely venture out without their overcoats in September. . . .'

And this, shallow though it may sound, is honest in its way. Chamberlain, Halifax, Hoare, Simon, Runciman and Daladier, Geoffrey Dawson the editor of *The Times* and all their friends in places high and low—the 'friends' who shut their hearts against Chamberlain when, *in extremis*, he called on them to rescue him during the Norway Debate—these men are patently not vile. But what are they if they are not vile?—that is their enigma. They peer astutely from miles of film and Press photographs; they have offered up, not only their official papers but their diaries. Yet nothing jells. It is as if they were saying, 'That is all you know, and all you need to know'.

Perhaps it is because of this that the eye turns from the baffling broad design and seeks relief and entertainment in the wealth of fascinating close detail. In the words of a contemporary song, it is, 'How did he look?' How did Jan Masaryk look, for example, when, sitting in the gallery of the House of Commons, he heard the packed chamber burst into tumultuous joy and throw its order papers into the air in ecstasy because a note had arrived from Hitler to say that with Britain and France's help he was willing to carve up Czecho-slovakia without a war? How did Hitler look, a monster from whose monstrousness the ordinary intelligence has been forced to shy away, with the result that this repellent creature is fast on the way to becoming a comic sideshow in the political chamber of horrors, the yelling carpet-biter instead of the thrifty Austrian dwarfed by a mountain of children's shoes at Belsen? But, most of all, how did Neville Chamberlain, scapegoat extraordinary, look? Well, he looked good, as the Americans say.

By now, of course, the detail has got us and we succumb to some of the most evocative lumber known to history. Vaguely, as we turn it over for the thousandth time, we hope to find the solution. Umbrellas, jackboots, swastikas, Super Lockheed 14 aeroplanes, the nettle danger, the flower safety; Miss Unity Mitford bobby-soxing the Führer, defunct Heston, Spitfires, Hurricanes, Wagnerian eyries, Anderson shelters, the ironically named Coventry Climax fire trailers and Coventry Victor portable pumps, Siebe Gorman's gas-masks, Bexhoid window adhesive, the black-out rehearsals, the building of the Maginot Line; all the trappings of prudence and the gear of shame. Munich, in fact, is so well furnished that it comes as something of a shock to find that it echoes so hollowly. Munichists— they are a special race of political historians who must eventually find themselves in the same predicament as the Schoolmen—argue round and down and for and against, but eventually they are brought to a halt by the inscrutable. Those who set out to bait the appeasers find that critical teeth can never get a firm grip on those excellent winged collars. Those who set out to explain them end up by having a sphinx on their hands.

'One day,' says Hugh Trevor-Roper, 'a good book will be written about them. It will examine the social and psychological springs of their action and success. Why, for instance, was its emotional content so different between England, where appeasement was a positive creed, and France, where it was a vulgar necessity? Which social group, in general, supported it? What part was played by "imperial interests"—"Milner's Kindergarten", the "Round Table" etc.—and why? How far was appeasement in Europe the continuation in a new form and in new circumstances, of an old mystique?'

Here there seems to be a finger pointing in a promising direction. Could it be possible that the men of Munich sensed that the only way out of the brutal impasse was for the Fascist mystique, at its zenith in the midsummer Germany of 1938, to be met by an opposing mystique? Or was Neville Chamberlain simply in full spiritual retreat from the loathsome twentieth century and was he privately determined to confront the sordid dictators with the whole armour of a nineteenth-century Christian liberal English gentleman? The pity, of course, was, it was not his own other cheek he turned for the blow.

On September 29th, 1938, the appeasers bought-off the criminal government of Germany by 'giving' it Czechoslovakia, a country of complete independence with an ancient history and a modern reputation for having made a success of democracy. The story is not at all brief in spite of the notoriously few hours it took to force the deal through. It is a story of great dramatic reliability from start to finish, it bristles with anecdote, it allows endless opportunity for every kind of philosophical aside and it lures the critic of politics on from article to chapter, from chapter to bloated volumes. The morality of the Dreyfus affair divided France for a decade but it is likely that the 'morality' of Munich must divide Europe for ever.

See then, not another theory, not the moment of truth or un-truth, whichever it was, but the odd historic scene *en passant*. And remember that as the deed was done it was endorsed not only by the Conservative Party and *The Times*, but nearly all the civilized world, with Prague a notable exception.

First the German city, hurriedly be-flagged for the occasion with roof-to-pavement black sheets bellying in the wind and crooked crosses everywhere, the heraldry of the new knighthood. Munich is a holy place; it was here that the saviour was rejected. It cannot forgive itself. An item of its propitiation is the Führerhaus, a manic-Doric temple recently erected for the furious god. This is where Hitler waited for Mr. Chamberlain, this is where Ribbentrop brought the Prime Minister of England by the back streets from Munich aerodrome. It was all rather down to earth after the airy flights of Berchtesgaden or even of Godesberg, where the Führer had taken both Mr. Chamberlain's hands in his to draw him affectionately up the steps of the Dreesen Hotel, the same steps down which he had hurtled four years ago to arrange the Night of the Long Knives. But the Prime Minister is sanguine.

There are two dictators, two appeasers and two foreign minister-ing disciples. They sit two and two, Chamberlain with Hitler, Mussolini with Ciano, Daladier with Ribbentrop. The four arm-chairs and the huge cane sofa make three sides of a square which is completed by a polished granite and steel fireplace in which two unlit logs cross each other. No Keitel this time, as at Godesberg, when he was seen shamelessly driving through the streets in an open coupé clutching a rolled map of Czechoslovakia as tall as himself. Only an interpreter. There are silk-shaded lamps. They make the great nude head of the Duce rosy. The Duce's military peaked cap lies upside down on a cabinet behind him. A chaplet should warm those cranial canals revealed by his baldness and down which the thick Italian blood appears to rush into a pouchy chin held at an artificial angle for heroism's sake. Mussolini has just conquered Abyssinia and the British Government has officially recognized the victory. He is Caesar. Hitler has, in March, joined Austria, his homeland, to the Fatherland. He is Siegfried. Mr. Chamberlain has two secret sheets of Downing Street writing-paper in his pocket. He is the Angel of Peace. M. Daladier has nothing beyond a frantic desire to get back to Paris as soon as possible. He is tepid. Ciano gleams. He is virile. Ribbentrop, panda-eyed, fidgets. He is sulking. It is not fair that Mr. Chamberlain should reap the thanks of the world for the Führer's unprecedented magnanimity regarding the Sudetenland. This is why he brought him to the Führerhaus by the back streets.

Was Mr. Chamberlain charmed in some way by Hitler? It wasn't as impossible as it sounds now—thousands of non-Germans were. Might that be the answer? No. Only three weeks previous to Munich Chamberlain had written, in a private letter, 'Is it not positively horrible that the fate of hundreds of millions depends on one man, *and he is half mad*?' So he knew. So he was, in fact, consciously placating a maniac. This is an important thing to remember when it comes to the two sheets of writing-paper and the millennial commotion they caused. They, however, were Mr. Chamberlain's own staggering piece of abracadabra for both the short-lived brilliance and lasting ignominy of which he alone was culpable. The dismembering of Czechoslovakia was a very different matter. He had a mandate for this such as few politicians had enjoyed for any matter at any time. Only two men in the Commons the day before had shown real antagonism. Churchill had sat quiet and still and Eden had walked slowly out. Everybody else went wild—in spite of the presence of Queen Mary, who sat in the gallery looking down at the happy scene. The Prime Minister had been wafted to the German shore in his Super Lockheed 14 on gusts of unadulterated love and he was to land at Heston the following day in a climate of pretty near pure adoration. The King sent the Lord Chamberlain to bring him to the Palace, where he was the first commoner to receive balcony honours. The cheering crowds were greater than at any time since the Armistice. The sashes of Downing Street were thrown up to let in the bouquets, the presents, the ululating gratitude of the West End. It was, while it lasted, a vast triumph such as few men have ever experienced.

The good man and the bad man had come to terms. How? If the good man had not become bad, nor the bad man good, how could they come to terms? Justice is not elastic. The point is that it was made expedient at Munich, though nobody questioned such expediency for days afterwards. Relief ran ahead of logic. But when relief died its cowardly death and the country came to its senses, the earlier self-congratulation was only exceeded by the new self-disgust. What had the Prime Minister done? He had given Hitler what he had sternly refused him only seven days before at Godesberg—and for which refusal he had been cheered to the echo as a moral man. He had signed away a fat rind of provinces all round the edges of the Czech state and all that country's chief defences. But worst of all he had established a terrible precedent. It would be Poland next. Again, where was the logic? The statesmanship? Never mind the charity. Where in all this lies the rational line? If any one of these things exists, it remains unearthed. The myriad lines of approach to the drama of Munich refuse to be synchronized. An essential fragment of the story is lost or cannot be identified. Hence, all that has so far been written about the Appeasers remains gnomic. Suspecting this, exhausted by it, perhaps, the Munich apologists sheer-off into absorbing relevancies of place, time, people and national and personal pathologies. The last two at least, from this safe distance, are good for a bitter laugh.

While Germany was giving itself to sunburnt Aryanism, to manly hymns and the blond view of life at the tenth Nazi Congress at Nuremberg, Britain, of all places, was going through a brief panic season brought about by the threat of aerial warfare. Even the experts quoted half a million casualties on the first day as the minimum carnage. The inexpert, who read H. G. Wells as a prophet and not as a proto-science-fictionist, were even wider of the mark and quite a large part of the explanation for the rapturous welcome which they gave to the Prime Minister at Heston on September 30th was due to the fact that hundreds of thousands believed he had personally stayed the rain of death from the skies. The country's Henny-penny complex, from which it recovered completely by the time the bombs did fall, began to show itself round about the period of the *Anschluss* crisis. As the war clouds gathered, as August, the war-month, drew near, the fear of bombing worked itself up to an overwrought crescendo. Normal anti-raid preparations, instead of re-assuring people, merely certified fear. The ruination of most of London's parks and gardens, sacred places at the best of times, by slit-trenches was a distinct psychological shock. Children massing at stations with name labels and gas-masks round their necks left a taste of intense resentment in many minds still powerfully influenced by the concept of the League of Nations and the dream of pacifism. The disappearance of façades behind sandbags, and the first extensive black-out test, carried out over the Midlands and East Anglia, perturbed people deeply, as did the lists of reserved occupations, the twenty-five million handbooks on national service, the sudden intrusion by the state into private life and all the semi-amateur scuttling and burrowing by the authorities as they sought to put the country on a defensive footing, and was in general detested. In 1938 nobody wanted to go to war. In 1939 everybody did.

Chamberlain knew this. He was sure of it. It gave him the authority for his next action. At one o'clock in the morning, while the appeasers and the dictators waited on the draftsmen, who had taken away the map of Czechoslovakia to change it, the Prime Minister played his lone hand. Turning to the Führer, he suggested another little talk. Hitler 'jumped at the idea' and soon the two of them, plus an interpreter, were in Hitler's private flat. They talked about Spain and South Eastern Europe, then the Führer grumbled about losing 50,000 men in Spain and then Mr. Chamberlain put his hand in his pocket and drew out his masterpiece, a typewritten Anglo-German truce in duplicate. Would Herr Hitler sign? Would he sign now? '*Ja, ja*,' the Führer was muttering as the interpreter interpreted; he was obviously surprised to his wits' end. They signed. Mr. Chamberlain kept one of the sheets of paper and gave the other to Hitler. A few hours later, the Prime Minister climbed out of his plane at Heston, transfigured with success, and holding something white aloft. He read it.

'We, the German Führer and Chancellor, and the British Prime Minister, have had a further meeting today, and are agreed in recognizing that the question of Anglo-German relations is of the first importance for the two countries and for Europe.

We regard the agreement signed last night, and the Anglo-German Naval agreement, as symbolic of the desire of our two peoples never to go to war again. . . .'

And from the window in Downing Street, he, the man who normally shunned the histrionic gesture, borrowed Dizzy's words to enchant the delirious concourse yet further—'This is the second time in our history that there has come back from Germany to Downing Street peace with honour. I believe it is peace in our time.'

This was the pinnacle of appeasement. From its unprecedented height the Prime Minister was to fall to a depth of abuse and opprobrium rarely known in public life, and all in a few months. His colleagues in appeasement drifted to their graves with 'Munich' stamped on them like a felon's brand-mark. All except Lord Halifax, who lived long enough to write his own Munich apologia, and young Lord Dunglass, who grew up to be Lord Home and a foreign secretary among the nuclearists. The sensational backcloth remains. Benes calling down to the sea of faces in Wenceslas Square, 'Have no fear. . . .' Yet a hundred thousand were to die. Hitler telling his massed followers in the Sports Palace, Berlin, 'When this problem is solved, Germany has no more territorial problems in Europe.' The Duce saluting the statue of Augustus. The flight of the Jews to Palestine. . . .

In Germany the mood was very different. For those with a taste for bronze knees and the well-drilled bay, *Sieg heil! Sieg heil! Sieg heil!* it was intoxicating. The manhood of the Fatherland wheeled and counter-wheeled across the land. There were immense army manœuvres involving a million men which made all Europe tremble and there was the Nuremberg rally itself, and the *Parteitag*, when 40,000 youths, 'sunbrowned and steeled' in the Führer's phrase, swept across the vast arena singing,

> *Germany suffers no longer,*
> *The Führer came as the orderly of God and made it free.*
> *Blood is stronger than enemy power*
> *And what is German must belong to Germany!*

The Hitler Youth, even the cynical had to admit, presented a matchless picture. What was more to the point so far as Nazi mysticism was concerned, they also presented a lump in the sentimental German throat which throttled all criticism. When they wheeled by the box containing Göring, Goebels and Hitler, the Führer screamed, '*Heil, mein Arbeitsdienst!*' and was answered with a sound like all the elect of Valhalla—'*Heil, mein Führer!*'

There followed the barbaric chanting, regular as if it had been timed with a metronome, by the entire Nazi company. In the evening there was Wagner in the opera house with tiers of jewelled women and stout blond men rising with hypnotized precision as the costive little figure strutted into his box, then Tannhäuser . . .

Siegfried, processions in Vienna to lay wreaths on the spot where the murderers of Dr. Dollfuss had been hanged, the review of the storm troopers in the Luitpold Arena, the bringing back to Nuremberg of the regalia of the Holy Roman Empire, the ecstasy and the sado-sexuality, the exaltation and the first all-out pogrom.

In Paris, in as subtle an affront to the raucous apotheosis of the new Germany as could be imagined, the French were entertaining King George VI and Queen Elizabeth during a state visit which was a marvel of beauty, civilized feeling and taste, and probably the most exquisite occasion of its kind in modern times. They were also racing to finish the Maginot Line, a string of 17,000 concrete forts behind which stood the entire German people in arms.

These preoccupations and diversions soothed some. 'They have gone away. Some of them are on the grouse moors and some are visiting the continent . . . but as they are gone, nothing very serious is likely to happen. . . . So when I read that the Home Secretary, good man, is walking about on the beach at Southwold in canvas shoes and an open shirt, that Mr. Chamberlain has left for an unknown destination in Scotland . . . I rejoice,' wrote Arthur Bryant on August 13th. The very same month, Sir Ian Hamilton, lulled into euphoria by the views of Berchtesgaden, declared, 'You cannot imagine anything warlike being planned here.' And a whole month later, on September 10th, Arthur Bryant was still able to write in a typically 'decent' English way, 'As quite a number of well-informed people seem to suppose—I hope and believe quite wrongly—that all mankind is shortly to commit suicide over the troubled affairs of Czechoslovakia,' he wonders 'if the Sudeten-German crisis of 1938 will mean as little to our descendants . . . as the many Danubian crises of the nineteenth century. . . .' This was published two days before Hitler's final speech at Nuremberg on September 12th when Whitehall and Downing Street were jampacked with anxious people and crowds filled the churches to pray for peace, yet it contained the germ of sentiments which could have given the Prime Minister one of his most criticized lines.

'How horrible, fantastic, incredible, it is that we should be digging trenches and trying on gas-masks here because of a quarrel in a far-away country between people of whom we know nothing . . .' he said in a broadcast to the nation. His detractors seize on this as an instance of his callousness but it is really an instance of his naïveté.

It is the remark of an unsophisticated man for whom Czechoslovakia really was a far-away country. He was merely saying truthfully and personally what the average Englishman thought of Czechoslovakia—only, as Prime Minister, it was not his place to hold such unsophisticated views, any more than it was his place to believe that Hitler's signature, extracted with all the guile of the autograph hunter when its giver was in a good mood and presumably worn out from the excitements of thirteen hours' hard bargaining which had brought him the Czech nation, could assure 'peace in our time'.

CHAPTER FOURTEEN

The Dove

I am sure this Jesus will not do,
Either for Englishman or Jew.
WILLIAM BLAKE

EASILY the most terrifying thing which can happen to any political party on the threshold of its first real power is to find itself saddled with a saint. Mercifully for politics and tragically for mankind, such things are rare. Between 1924, when King George V braced himself to send for Ramsay MacDonald, and 1935, when Ernest Bevin martyred him in full view of the annual party conference as cruelly as only he knew how, the Labour Party found itself with a Saint George with far more dragons and chivalry to his credit than the national hero ever had. Was the Labour Party delighted with this flesh and blood moral capital? Of course not. Political parties like it to be naturally assumed that they have a soul just as they prefer it to be assumed that they have a programme. The last thing they want is a big noisy old man too stupid to appreciate the occasional divergencies of policy from probity.

George Lansbury had no fear, no conceit, no interest in money, no chip on his broad shoulder, no puritanism and no doubt at all that Blake's 'Jerusalem' vision of England would one day find its place amongst the Government's measures in the Gracious Speech from the Throne. The worst thing which could be said about him was that he could be silly, and naturally this was said quite often. It was said most by those too spiritually illiterate to understand the subtle connection between silliness and goodness. After all, who could be sillier than St. Francis? Or General Booth? Or Lord Russell? Not that the Labour Party wasn't proud of Lansbury; it was. It had to be. It was immeasurably in his debt. It was he who had provided its dignity in the early days, its heart when Beatrice Webb was icily theorizing and its virtue when Ramsay MacDonald ran about London in search of duchesses. Never once did Lansbury, in all his long, overworked life, take an unprincipled short-cut to a political objective.

He was the son of a railway navigator or 'navvy' and lived nearly every minute of his life in Bow Road, yet the natural patrician element in his character gave him a noticeable social ease and whenever he shook hands with the King (with mutual chumminess) or with Lady Astor's guests at Cliveden (to their amusement) or with the endless crocodile of Cockney supplicants shuffling through his front room (to its near-adoration), the English class structure would wobble uncertainly. He called himself an East Ender and never moved from Bow after a single disastrous attempt to settle in Australia during his early twenties, but in fact he was a countryman, born in a tollgate cottage on a lonely Suffolk road near Halesworth. He retained the high colour and brilliant pale eyes of the East Anglian, though none of the countryman's aloofness and restraint. He was gregarious. Humanity seethed, pullulated around him and he loved it. There were twelve children of his happy and candidly sensual marriage. There were workhouses, prisons, rallies, marches, congregations, emigrant ships, hospitals, parks, Parliament, palaces and they were all full of people. Reformers are always said to love people, though often what they love is tidiness. Lansbury never sacrificed human happiness to hatred of litter or to lawn-worship. Everywhere he went he broke down fences. Spiritually and idealistically, the flowers were there to pick—particularly if one happened to be the nit-headed inmate of an L.C.C. orphanage. The Victorians had made public property sacred and public money holy. Lansbury refused to be impressed. Parks and institutions were social abstractions and were there for the convenience of mankind. He genuinely loved his neighbour as himself and by so doing he introduced an unmanageable element into political life for which his party was most ungrateful.

The Lansburys came to the East End in the sixties when George was a small boy. Bow and Poplar were then stridently English, with scarcely any Jewish or other foreign elements. The smoke-blackened streets were packed with illiterate multitudes through which jaunted the boisterous racing cavalcades on their way to Epsom. The working-class population, undocketed, stunted,

Crookshankian, stayed alive through sheer bird-like ebullience. The Lansbury children enjoyed this human tumult and sharpened their wits on it. Miracles occurred. While the neighbours were being scorched into salvation by Mrs. Booth's terrifying hellfire oratory the young Lansburys had the extraordinary good fortune to encounter the Oxford Movement in the saintly though scrupulously aesthetic person of the Reverend J. F. Kitto, a man of the utmost taste and goodness who delighted his gaudy congregations with his Anglican pageantry. Mr. Kitto's influence on George was profound. He provided a window through which the gawky East End youth could stare at the fields of the earthly paradise. To begin life by being on nodding terms with the angels is not a bad training for a working man whose duties would include occasional visits to Buckingham Palace. Mr. Kitto's Christianity was quite unconstricting. It left George spiritually sensuous. It gave him the eagle-view of mortal affairs and a heavenly vision which naturally put any reward earth might offer among the booby prizes. On top of this spiritual lead George possessed striking human advantages. He was tall and handsome and very strong. He had a deafening voice and a command of the affection of others which would have been dangerous in a lesser man. He was not so much one of nature's gentlemen as one of nature's royalty. In any primitive society he would unquestionably have assumed the chieftainship. As he grew older his moustache and his sideburns met in a beautifully barbered loop of beard which divided his face, making it look as though it were visored. His dandyism, once assumed, stood still all his long life at blue serge, white linen and brightly polished boots. His expression was tranquil and sentimentally benign but those who tried to break through it, expecting to find a kind of pliant Sunday-school-superintendent cosiness, encountered a steely strength.

In 1880 Lansbury married Bessie Brine, a very pretty girl whose father, albeit that he was descended from James Brine the Tolpuddle Martyr, made it no secret that he considered his new son-in-law beneath him. George was twenty and Bessie was nineteen. In 1884 they succumbed to the immigration touts and sailed for Australia, taking with them their three babies and George's twelve-year-old brother. The nightmare of the emigrant ship was only succeeded by the nightmare of what awaited them at Brisbane. As soon as he could collect enough money together George returned home to breathe

fire and thunder at the callous colonial authorities who were shipping thousands of trusting, simple people into conditions which were
outrageous and indecent. The colonists tried to silence him by calling
him workshy but George, who was later rather sadly to confess that
he was entirely free of 'the gift of laziness', let fly in one of his social
fabric-renting tirades which finished off his enemies and caused his
local M.P., who was present, to suggest that he stand for Parliament.

Someone else who was beginning to notice the benevolent but
raucous George was H. M. Hyndman, who was the friend Karl Marx
had left behind in England to lead the 'glorious revolution', should it
occur. Hyndman, who always drove to his soap-box in Hyde Park
exquisitely dressed in a frock-coat and top-hat to rouse the rabble,
provided Lansbury with the entrée into late Victorian radicalism.
In no time at all the £3-a-week worker for a Whitechapel timber
yard was meeting William Morris, the Webbs, the absurdly vain
John Burn, kind Ben Tillett and, eventually, Lenin himself. He also
met Shaw and the dazzling H. G. Wells, though brotherliness met
its Waterloo here. G.B. and H.G. found George embarrassing and
emotional, and he found them too clever by half. Their incompati-
bility was one of the earliest instances of the schizophrenic cleavage
between heart and head which has played havoc with British
socialism ever since.

In 1895 old Mr. Brine died and George took over the timber yard.
He was thirty-six and the intensification of his political activities and
the added fillip of being an employer instead of an employee made
him feel keen to start turning the world upside-down. His method
was a dramatic, though never egotistical identification with each
social problem. He thrust his good-looking person and boisterous
arguments into a series of brilliant *tableaux vivants* which instantly
reduced wordy radical theorizing to a workable reality, and Bumble-
dom to horrified silence. Dickens had exposed the workhouse system
but all that had happened was that those who enjoyed looking could
look. Lansbury destroyed this 'charitable' voyeurism, threw out the
monstrous entertainers and rehabilitated their victims, the paupers.
The Prince of Wales, apprehensively presiding at one of Lansbury's
meetings during the nineties, called to discuss the extraordinary
problem of the many thousands of innocent people virtually imprisoned in orphanages and workhouses, handed round cigars and
nervously referred to the question of underclothes. 'Certainly they

need those, just like you and I do,' George boomed at him severely.

In 1904 Lansbury made an important new friend—Joseph Fels, a Jewish-American millionaire who had made his pile out of Fels-Naphtha soap. Fels used to tell his critics, 'I shall go on making as much money as I can: and I will use it to prevent people like you and me being allowed to do so any longer.' The beginning of Mr. Fels's perverse policy was the founding of the Vacant Land Cultivation Society. When Keir Hardie introduced Fels to George, George didn't like him a bit at first. It was the camel and the eye of the needle all over again. But eventually rich Mr. Fels managed to wriggle through into the socialist heaven, where his unerring business sense proved to be a godsend. Lansbury and he became very close friends and the soap profits could be said, as Raymond Postgate, Lansbury's son-in-law, has remarked, to have altered the whole course of world history. For had it not been for a £500 donation, the Russian Social-Democratic conference which took place in London in 1907 might never have been concluded, nor might its delegates ever have got home. As this was the meeting at which Lenin the Bolshevik carried the day against Martov the Menshevik there is no knowing what vast issues hung upon Mr. Fels's modest sub. Was there a bat's squeak hint of the wrath to come that the soap merchant should require some moral assurance that it was a good cause before he advanced the money? It was a very trivial sum to him, after all. But saying, 'I must first consult my almoner,' Fels went to Lansbury and so Lenin was able to leave for Russia with his mandate for the Revolution.

Lansbury then began to use the soap profits for buying up derelict farms and turning them into little self-sufficient agricultural colonies for some of the human rubbish he rescued from Poor Law. The biggest of these colonies was Hollesley Bay, a wild and beautiful farm on the Suffolk coast which was eventually to edge its way into literature as Brendan Behan's borstal.

In 1910 Lansbury put up for Parliament and beat his waspish Tory opponent, L. S. Amery, by 863 votes. Lansbury was fifty-one and so encumbered with office that it was hard to see how he would be able to take on this latest and greatest one. His reputation was settling down to that of the patriarchal tribal chief of magical goodness. The Bow Road house saw a ceaseless procession of visitors, from the youthful Nehru to aged costermongers. Between meetings,

Lansbury wrote all his own correspondence in a laborious self-taught hand and read everything which came into the house in the way of printed matter in the rather impressed and wasteful manner of one who was aware of an endless process of self-improvement. His energy was only exceeded by his kindness.

The year 1912 saw the first really big strike of the century and it tempted Lansbury to gather up his scattered reforms and to declare war on the class structure. But some antiquated notion of gallantry caused him to place himself wholly at the service of women's suffrage instead. He had the Victorian's mystic worship of women. But while the Pankhursts and the Pethick-Lawrences found him useful, they didn't want their somewhat stylish campaign too closely linked with Lansbury's proletarian activities. They constantly reminded Lansbury of their 'lady' status and when he virtually gave away his parliamentary seat as a courtly gesture to publicize their political plight, they scarcely thanked him. It taught him a lesson. The ladies would have been astounded that he should have taken it all to heart so. 'But the *cause*, Mr. Lansbury!' Christobel would have screeched.

In 1913 Lansbury became editor of a new newspaper, the *Daily Herald*. It was a case of the amateur genius. He had no experience of journalism and his writing was very hit-or-miss, but his editing was brilliant. The *Herald* started as a strike sheet and the first edition sold 13,000 copies. Most of those who contributed to it weren't socialists at all but simply used it as a platform for their personal literary anarchy. The suffragists used it shamelessly. Someone said that it contained the noblest aspirations and the basest adjectives in the English language. There were moments of high comedy such as when the wistfully Priapic Frank Harris was brought all the way from the Riviera by poor Ben Tillett to help edit it. Harris said that he would edit it according to Christ's teaching but when he learnt what the salary was he soon changed his mind. The *Herald*'s tone was spiteful and harsh but running like a thread of gold through all the journalistic ballyhoo was Lansbury's faith in the doctrine of love and its *deus ex machina*, universal socialism.

The First World War wounded the *Herald* grievously. It had neither the money nor the professionalism to get war news like the rest of Fleet Street and it shrivelled up into a skimpy weekly. As its pacifism developed, so did its distinguished contributors drop away. As the carnage mounted, and with it the necessary jingoism to make it acceptable, the *Herald* began to take such a dangerous anti-war line that plans were made to suppress it, though this never happened. Instead Lansbury had breakfast with Lloyd George at which the wily Prime Minister told the Cockney saint that he knew Haig was a butcher who massacred soldiers uselessly, but he wasn't able to do anything about it *because of the Conservatives*.

The *Herald* was now read by many thoughtful people who were far from being socialists because it was the only newspaper whose information was undistorted by blood-lust and chauvinism, and because George Lansbury, seen in the context of men like Bottomley and Northcliffe, stood out like a rose in a sewage bed. But still nobody recognized in Lansbury's ideals a perfectly valid and workable form of Christian politics—that is, until it was too late and pacifism began to sweep through the rank and file of British socialism. When more than 17,000 people crushed in and about the Albert Hall to hear Lansbury welcome the Russian Revolution in March, 1918, a less sentimental view had to be taken of him.

The war ended at last and on March 31st, 1919, with a fat kitty of some £200,000 collected from the unions and co-operative societies, the *Daily Herald* was re-born as a daily. The reactions of scores of young demobbed intellectuals against the repellent journalism of the Tory Press during the fighting years brought the *Herald* more dazzling talent than it had room for. There were regular contributions from Rose Macaulay, E. M. Forster, Aldous Huxley, Walter de la Mare and Robert Graves. In 1919 the *Herald*'s vigorous intervention did much to avert an Anglo-Russian war and Bonar Law was urged to consider the prosecution of the paper. A memo was circulated to all commanding officers in the armed forces ordering them to burn the *Daily Herald*, 'with as little publicity as possible', should it ever arrive at their camps, which led to a leader in free-verse by Osbert Sitwell which began,

> *The* Daily Herald
> *Is unkind.*
> *It has been horrid*
> *About my nice new war.*
> *I shall burn the* Daily Herald. . . .

In 1920 Lansbury went to Russia, the brief-lived and hopeful

Russia of Lenin and the nascent Revolution, as different, as Raymond Postgate has said, from the Russia of Stalin as was the Empire of Bonaparte and Fouché from the France of the Convention. Lenin and he chatted in a cold little room in the Czar's palace. They both thought that it would be only a matter of months before all the socialist groups in the world would merge with the new Soviets in a thankful tide of brotherly love. When Lansbury returned home he tried to tempt all the varied British socialist organizations to join the Internationale *en bloc* and he put the idea before the annual Labour Party conference. The motion was massively defeated and the political isolation of Lansbury began.

It was easier said than done. Lansbury's post-war position in the Labour Party had become so extraordinary that any direct action taken against him at once assumed sacrilegious and patricidal associations. To avoid these feelings, which ranged between the deepest blood-guilt and mere bad taste, the Party began to isolate him, leaving him alone on his own little island, from which he radiated his unflinching message of mountain-moving love. It became the custom to treat Lansbury with an almost ceremonious respect and this soon turned into veneration.

Towards the end of 1923 Stanley Baldwin, the Prime Minister, held a general election, the result of which was: Conservatives, 258 seats; Liberals, 158 and Labour, 191. The Liberal Party, to the very real terror of the country, used its dying strength to turn out the Tories and put the Socialists in. The sensation throughout Britain was indescribable. The upper classes found the prospect of railway-men and Scottish peasants in Downing Street hilarious and sufficiently bizarre to be in keeping with the wildness of the decade. But the middle classes, with whom the Royal Family was morally identified, were genuinely frightened. Baldwin and the King clung together in an unconstitutional *status quo* in their effort to postpone Nemesis. The Socialists were affronted by this and Lansbury, whose resonant voice had no difficulty in penetrating the Palace, was heard reminding the King that this kind of interference had ended with Charles I. As he had also, on another occasion, spoken of the King as 'George Five' and was notorious for his friendship with Lenin, the Court believed that Lansbury's—of all people—was the voice of bloody revolution. The King hung on and hung on until he could decently do so no longer. Then, putting on a red tie, he sent for

Ramsay MacDonald. The relief was as great as it was mutual. The King met a courtly, handsome old Highland goat and the new Prime Minister met a tetchy, kindly little royal papa. In no time at all they discovered a subject of profoundly shared interest and were able to settle one of the most pressing questions which had occupied His Majesty's mind above all else when the Labour Government became a reality—would it wear court dress when it came to kiss hands? Most certainly, said MacDonald, who, as Malcolm Muggeridge later remarked, could hardly wait to get into his.

MacDonald offered Lansbury the Ministry of Transport, a non-Cabinet post. Lansbury believed that this was entirely the King's doing; he wasn't going to have somebody in the Cabinet who boomed threats about cutting off his head. Lansbury was bitterly disappointed and refused the offer. The first Labour Government was neither exhilarating nor competent. Its efforts to play down its early ardour by a display of pin stripes and winged collars made it merely frowsty. Eventually it was witless enough to allow itself to be toppled by a letter in the *Daily Mail* signed by Zinoviev, which told the British Communist Party how to control the British Labour Party and thus start an armed revolution. This letter was almost undoubtedly a political hoax *de luxe*, but MacDonald fell for it, and so the Government fell because of it.

The Zinoviev Letter was yet one more factor in the isolating process which went on around Lansbury after the war. There were those amongst his colleagues who took care not to stand too near him for fear that his particular brotherhood-of-man redness might brush off on to them. And even those of his friends who saw his beliefs in the best Christian sense realized that they were hardly the kind of thing one could go to the country with. But if they had been able to see beneath what they thought was little more than Lansbury's dated socialist-Christian sentimentality and recognized the daring idea growing there they would have had genuine cause for alarm. For Lansbury was moving towards an absolute acceptance of the great untried doctrine of Christian pacifism, something which every sound Anglican knew was a notoriously unworkable part of the Faith. But to Lansbury it was the key. All through the twenties, as the stench from the trenches was gradually superseded by the smell of despair as the dole queues multiplied, he mulled over the thrilling possibilities of a political application of Christ's rule of non-violence. In 1926 he was absorbed in it and the General Strike passed him by. In August of that year he took his wife to Russia. He wasn't well. He talked to Trotsky and was fooled by the beginnings of Stalinism. He even went so far as to ask himself why he wasn't a Communist. The answer, as he later realized, was that in applied Christianity he had all he needed to change the world. By 1928 the 'respect' which was fast becoming the custom for people of all classes and parties to offer him reached its apogee. In fact he was immobilized by it; like a Roman policeman at Christmas he couldn't move for tributes. The Labour Party, since it could hardly do less, elected him its Chairman and he poured into its sour councils and anaemic blood the old heady hopefulness. In 1929 the Party won the election against the Conservatives by twenty-nine seats and once again the Liberals held the balance of power.

Lansbury, who was now seventy, knew that he wasn't wanted in the Cabinet and pretended he didn't care. He said he thought it would be nice if they made him an ambassador and sent him to Moscow. Instead, he was made First Commissioner of Works, one of the smallest departments in the Government to carry Cabinet rank. He was to look after parks and palaces. To add to the joke, a flashy young upper-class assistant called Oswald Mosley was allotted to him. Nor did the comedy cease there, for no sooner had this been announced than Ramsay's great wail of but-what-shall-we-wear-when-we-go-to-see-the-King was heard in Downing Street. Blue serge, said Lansbury. And brightly polished boots. Knee breeches, said MacDonald. And the great issue raged. While unemployment spilt over into millions and Germany became a land of sick and dying children because of the Geddes vindictive squeeze-until-the-pips-squeak policy, the first action of the first socialist Prime Minister of Great Britain on taking office was to work himself up into a paddy because the man in charge of the tulips in Regent's Park and the flagpole at Windsor wouldn't wear fancy dress.

Lansbury might have been forgiven if he treated the Office of Works as a sinecure but this wasn't his way. He used this curious appointment parabolically. He tore down miles of railings and the people flocked in—to tear down the gardens, said *The Times*. Nothing happened. All through 1930 he busied himself with what was in effect a miniature of how he would deal with dreary official-dom versus the natural pleasures of the world, were they in his

Photo: *Radio Times Hulton Picture Library*

'I think that we ought to take heart . . . that those who enter upon this colossal struggle have to admit that force cannot settle anything.' ——GEORGE LANSBURY.

The year of Appeasement. Neville Chamberlain arriving at Downing
Street for a Cabinet meeting, January 1938.

power. He carved his *credo* on the unlikely material offered to him and to the astonishment of his colleagues, who thought they had silenced him, it worked. He built the Lido by the Serpentine and allowed mixed bathing. 'Grotesque and horrible', shuddered *The Times*, whose correspondents concerned themselves to an astonishing extent with the ending of the male privilege of swimming in the nude. Lansbury merely said, 'I should myself not object to men and women bathing in a state of nature if what are described as morality and public opinion would allow me to give permission.' After this *The Times* probably had no option in calling the handsome, pure-minded old Minister of Works the 'Caliban of the Parks' and the other papers carried shocked descriptions of the bare arms and legs of young Londoners. A body without the least official backing set itself up as the Parks Purity Police and issued a report of such morbid salacity that Lansbury forgot his restraint and blasted it out of existence.

All the business about the parks brought him into considerable contact with the King, who, as Ranger, expected to be consulted on everything. Their meetings were odd. They were both men who had made a religion of family life. Each had, for more than half a century and in his different way, been conditioned by the hyperbolic respect of his fellow creatures. And each had, beneath his cultivated hierarchic façade, a racy pre-Victorian unshockable knowledge of humanity. Each, too, was confused by the generally understood class issues. The King, simply by fact of being King, was forced to reflect in public a great many *bourgeois* virtues which could not have any place in his private life, while Lansbury's approach to life was assured and in its way, aristocratic, and particularly so when he was at his most ostentatiously plebeian. To appreciate the full meaning of this one has only to measure him against Ramsay MacDonald. A courtier, worried about one of Lansbury's time-oblivious audiences with the King, crept in to find the two old men sitting side by side 'like charwomen' and the King saying indignantly, '. . . but they called it a minor operation, Mr. Lansbury, and they opened me from *here* to *here*'.

All through 1930 unemployment soared, while the Government did nothing. Worse, Philip Snowden the socialist Chancellor began to talk like the meanest-minded financier. Wall Street and Threadneedle Street were slimy with slump and the younger unemployed

9

began to walk out of the sordid towns towards the hills and moors. *Wandervogeling* became the great craze. There was a great burst of hiking, camping, sunbathing and youth hostelling and Lansbury became much identified with fresh air. In 1931, although it might have been thought impossible, the economic crisis grew worse. Plans for reform, including a quite reasonable one by Oswald Mosley, were frustrated by the sheer lassitude which the disaster generated. Montagu Norman, the bearded, sinister and supremely arrogant Governor of the Bank of England, who was as near to being an E. Phillips Oppenheim character as to make no difference, began to take a scandalous hand in national affairs, treating cabinet ministers like clerks and quite often disappearing for personal reasons for days on end while the nation waited.

By June 1931 unemployment reached the two and three-quarter million mark and Philip Snowden told a shocked country that the British Government was virtually bankrupt. Savings of £96 million had to be made at once and £66 *million of this would have to be got by cutting the dole*. Almost at the same moment that Snowden announced this the great Kreditanstalt bank in Austria failed and had to close its doors, and cold fear swept through Europe. After scores of meetings and what might be called 'non-meetings', the Labour Government resigned. Only not quite. Calling all his old colleagues together one notorious Monday morning, Ramsay MacDonald shattered them with the news that although *they* had all lost their posts, *he* had not. The King was going to let him form a National Government with Stanley Baldwin and Herbert Samuel. And so Lansbury left his unlikely niche at the Ministry of Works. His office had been brief and there would be no more of it. The only thing by his hand to reach the Statute Book during a long lifetime of public service was a bill to safeguard the ancient monuments of Britain.

Ramsay MacDonald's abandonment of his colleagues was no more than the inevitable sequel to what had been slowly and obviously happening to him for years. One of Saki's characters remarked of a young adventurer 'that he had sprung from the people, but he hadn't sprung far enough'. By the ruthlessness with which he forsook his friends in their blackest hour it was obvious that MacDonald wasn't going to risk having such a thing said of him. Lansbury, who was not without the inspired malice of the saintly, said of him that he had 'reaped the harvest of his apostasy'—which Thomas Jones called 'a cruel verdict'.

The Economy Bill was passed, the Gold Standard was abandoned and, crowning horror, there was insubordination in the Royal Navy of such proportions that it was prevented from going on manœuvres. In October there was the famous 'Coupon' election in which the Labour Party's seats were decimated, only forty-six socialists being returned. Nearly everybody supported the coalition. George Lansbury was the only cabinet minister to retain his seat, and so he became Leader of the Labour Party. His task was unenviable. He had to sit on the Front Bench like God's Good Man and act as a kind of sublime corrective to the abysmal shortcomings of his Party when it had known power. He represented political decency and hope to the now three million unemployed. There were those who found him anathema—Winston, for instance, who occasionally abandoned his hod at Chartwell to drop a brick at Westminster. He and Lansbury clashed scurrilously. 'Hold your tongue!' the old man would boom, and Winston was heard mumbling furiously something about 'a perfect cataract of semi-coherent insults from the so-called head of the so-called opposition. . . .'

The National Government discovered a new way to chop the dole estimates—the Means Test. No one seemed to appreciate what this cost in terms of simple human dignity. Ramsay MacDonald got better and better looking, and vaguer and vaguer. He and Lansbury headed the processions which swept to and from the House of Lords on great occasions. They made a fine couple. On one such trip Ramsay turned to his old colleague and whispered, 'George, do you feel your age now? I do. I do not always know what I mean to do. . . . Often I am speaking and *I have no idea how the sentence I am saying should finish. . . .*'

In 1932 Japan attacked China and the Government refused to back the League of Nations' proposed boycott in the form of economic non-co-operation with the aggressor, so inaugurating the appalling policy which was to lead straight to the Second World War. Cripps and Attlee, both brilliant men and true, but devoid of platform magic, now began to close upon the venerable Lansbury. The three made a strange bridge which stretched from Tolstoy's humane romanticism to the new Fabianism of G. D. H. Cole and Harold Laski. The bridge was slight and idealistically precarious.

There was no room on it for MacDonald, Clynes, Snowden or even Miss Bondfield; nor for many another Labour brother who had lost his head when shown the political heights. Although the world of 1932 was as black as black could be, Lansbury, red-faced and good as an archangel between Attlee and Cripps, his pallid disciples, experienced a new surge of his old vision. And it gave all three a formidable energy, just when energy was needed. Fascism, as compulsive and as exciting as sex to those with a taste for it, had crossed the Channel and was percolating down from the dinner tables of country houses to sinks in the East End. Soon, Lansbury and his friends found themselves having to defend the most elementary civil liberties. They became watchdogs and took to questioning everything which took place in Parliament and the Press.

In 1933 Bessie Lansbury died and later that year George broke his thigh falling off a platform at Gainsborough Town Hall. But as he had absolute certainty that he and Bessie would meet again in a Thaxted-like Heaven full of country dancing and Mr. Kitto's spiky gaiety, and as his accident carried with it no superstitious portents, he was able to proceed to the final and most extraordinary phase of his life with equanimity. His illness had a similar sentimental impact on the country as that of the King's a few years earlier and brought him the kind of popularity most politicians would give their right arms to possess. The masses had become a trusting sparrow in his fatherly old hand and first to the amusement and then to the consternation of the Labour Party he soothed the people with lullabies of Peace.

Popular pacifism in 1933 tended to be treated by the authorities like popular anything else. It was just a craze, like playing yo-yo or 'all this hiking', and it would die out. But this didn't happen. Even when the Oxford Union, on February 9th, voted by 275 votes to 153, 'that this House will in no circumstances fight for its King and Country' it was thought that the phase had merely taken a typically undergraduate turn. But soon after this Peace began to create havoc at the hustings. At a by-election at East Fulham the pro-armaments Tory was roundly defeated by a destroy-all-the-weapons Socialist. Also, quite ordinary people who weren't supposed to know much about such things were making a great fuss about the Government's failure to back the League's policy towards Japan. On January 30th of this strange year Hitler became Chancellor of the

Reich and on March 28th, to the annoyance of practically everybody, Winston thanked God publicly for the French army.

On October 14th, the Disarmament Conference, which had begun the year before, was resumed and the delegates patiently waited for Hitler's signature. Instead, it got a telegram telling it that Germany was not only withdrawing from the Conference but also from the League itself. Hitler had taken a risk but nothing happened. The French didn't seize the Ruhr and the Poles didn't seize East Prussia. So he took this to mean that in future he could do what he liked, and it became merely a matter of how long it would suit his convenience to prepare for the Second World War. This terrible inevitability was not—*could* not—be accepted by a Europe only fifteen years away from the carnage of the Western Front. The sheer obscenity of the idea made people look around for some untried alternative, and so doing they saw George Lansbury and the League of Nations. Both were immediately deified. 'Leaguomania' became a cult and Lansbury became a saviour.

In October, 1934, Canon Dick Sheppard of St. Martin-in-the-Fields invited people to write the following words on a postcard and send it to him:

I renounce war and never again will I support or sanction another, and I will do all in my power to persuade others to do the same.

And so was born the Peace Pledge Union which, by June 1936, had over a hundred thousand male members. The foundations of the Peace Pledge Union had been laid a year earlier, on June 27th, 1935, when the results of an enormous Peace Ballot gained by a nation-wide house-to-house canvass were announced. This ballot had been organized by a body called the National Declaration Committee, headed by Lord Cecil and it was in league with the League. The answers to the five questions asked all came down massively on the side of Peace and as the Ballot had the approval of $11\frac{1}{2}$ million votes it made a record as the greatest private referendum ever held. The Peace Ballot of 1935 marked the pinnacle of thirties pacifism and at the same time revealed the limitations of the League of Nations. This nation-wide knocking on doors and beating of breasts quite drowned the sounds from German dockyards, where the *Scharnhorst, Gneisenau, Bismarck* and *Tirpitz* were being laid down.

The Labour Party held its annual conference that year at the

Dome in Brighton. The main debate, which was the longest debate in the Party's history, was on the resolution calling on Baldwin's National Government to support the League in preventing Mussolini from attacking the medieval African kingdom of Abyssinia for no other reason than to make a Roman triumph. Stafford Cripps opposed the resolution because he distrusted the League, which he called 'the international burglars' union' and also because he thought sanctions against Italy would involve Labour in a capitalist war. He was now deeply committed to Lansbury's vision of universal brotherhood and he wasn't going to do anything which might precipitate working people into conflict with each other for the sake of such things as money or militarism. When Lansbury rose to make his great speech against the resolution he was given an amazing reception. Affection seemed to rush at his dignified old body from all sides of the huge room, the entire conference rose to its feet and sang 'For he's a jolly good fellow' and Lansbury, all unaware that this warm embrace concealed the kiss of death, was encouraged not only to give his reasons for not supporting the resolution but to make his speech an occasion for his personal *apologia pro vita sua*. It was superb. It was the best and most thrilling argument for applying the great doctrine of Christian pacifism to statecraft ever heard on a political platform. The Conference was mesmerized by the transparent fidelity of the old man and when he at last sat down its love for him rose in storms of applause.

One man didn't clap. When, at long last, there was silence, this man lumbered up to the front of the room, and those that watched saw, as he did so, the platform of hope slowly turn into a scaffold. Executioners are not called upon to be kind, considerate or even just. Only efficient. Ernest Bevin was this pre-eminently. He saw the Labour Party soothed into silvery happiness by its saint and the sight made him sick. The aspirates flew, the awkward flesh rolled in fury and the small sagacious eyes glittered. He sneered at Cripps, he cocked his snook at the Blake-like hopefulness and slowly but surely he brought the bludgeon of his wrath nearer and nearer to the holy one. And there, in full view of the great movement he had helped to found and at the zenith of his moral influence, George Lansbury was martyred.

'It is placing the Executive and the Movement in an absolutely wrong position,' Bevin roared at the deathly pale Lansbury, '*to be hawking your conscience round from body to body asking to be told what you ought to do with it. . . .'*

For minutes after the uproar which followed, Lansbury's bewildered eyes swept the sea of faces as he waited for at least one single soul out of all the vast concourse which had clapped him so short a time since to stand up in his favour. No one did. He had preached his faith and he had died his death: there was to be no resurrection. Though sickened by what it had seen, the Party wasn't so enfeebled as not to be able to rally to expediency and the resolution in support of sanctions against Italy was carried by 2,168,000 to 102,000. Lansbury then rose and the Executive let him shuffle past without a glance, without a gesture. All except Herbert Morrison, who suddenly leant forward and took his hand and murmured something about 'standing by your beliefs'.

The next day Lansbury resigned from the Leadership and Major Attlee took his place. The Tories, enchanted and exhilarated by the fact that the Socialists had slaughtered their greatest vote-collector, immediately announced a general election, with the result that the National Government was formidably strengthened, the League of Nations was thrown on the junk heap and Italy was 'allowed' Abyssinia.

And so the cowards-in-Cabinet tottered on towards the abyss. And so, too, did George Lansbury, who now seemed to be ageing daily. He had four more years to live. He had practically no money, never having bothered to claim his ex-cabinet minister's pension and being vague about most other money matters. The house in Bow Road continued to be full of letters and people. He wrote a lot of flaccid journalism for magazines like *John Bull* and the literary process somehow contrived to turn the noble heart-warming oratory into a sentimental mish-mash which could only appeal to the very simple or the very charitable. He had an enjoyable, energy-giving row with Sir John Reith. And when news of the rigged Trotskyite trials filtered out of Russia, he faced up to the failure of Stalinist communism. The issues of the Spanish Civil War were such as to make any man question pacifism and Lansbury never quite allowed himself to understand them. As the Second World War drew nearer and nearer, he continued to repeat the truism that the causes of war were financial, and he pressed for an economic peace conference. Now that he was reckoned 'harmless' he was allowed unusual privileges both inside and outside the House for speaking his mind. He could not see the mixture of condescension and courtesy which existed behind this attitude towards him and believed that he was making some kind of come-back. And this rather pathetic assumption renewed much of his old pre-Bevin verve and set him on a last Quixotic crusade.

In 1935 he had lent his name to a pacifist group called the Fellowship of Reconciliation which was run by a number of Christian pacifists which included Dick Sheppard, Canon Raven and Percy Bartlett. The idea of the Fellowship was explained by Lansbury in a letter to *The Times*. Certain people should undertake personal 'embassies of reconciliation'. But the unfortunate thing was that, when it came down to brass tacks, Lansbury was the only ambassador who turned out to be *persona grata*. And so, at seventy-seven, and with released doves swirling about him wherever he went, he toured the United States in the oratorical circus which the Americans call a lecture-tour. His message was nothing less than the message of Boyd Orr ten sickening years later, that the over-fed countries must share their food and wealth with the under-fed countries and that there should be world-help committees.

He followed up this American triumph by a round of visits to distinguished European social democrats and liberals like Leon Blum, Van Zeeland and the famous old socialist Prime Minister of Denmark, Thorvald Stauning, who belonged to the age of socialist giants like Jaurès and Liebknecht, and who, like Lansbury, was rapidly becoming a morally displaced person. Of course, all these leaders spoke peace, peace—who didn't? Even Hitler mouthed the word for talismanic effect. Lansbury took train after train and went from frontier to frontier, full of excitement, full of hope. But when he came home the Commons laughed at him—only in its best jolly way, of course—but even when they yelled, 'Go and tell that to Hitler!' he took the banter gamely.

The Government was now forfeiting its decency piecemeal and men like Lansbury no longer had to even pretend that they were dealing with 'Right Hon. Gentlemen' other than in the mere convention of the phrase. The latest and most beastly concession to the Nazis was the suspension in Britain of the age-old right of asylum. The number of victims added to the gas chambers by this smug policy will never be known. Only what were called 'special cases' were admitted and Lansbury showed an almost comic invention in deluging Sir John Anderson with his 'special cases'. How many lives the old man saved by this personal effort is something else which will never be known. Nor was Lansbury the only man in Parliament to draw in his skirts before the mess of expediency which was to lead to Munich. Eden, Cripps and Duff Cooper all shrank with disgust from the official line.

'I think my work for the Party, as a party, is finished. I see life ever so much broader than in the days gone by. . . .' Lansbury wrote to Stafford Cripps. And like D. H. Lawrence in another context, he added, 'The Party nearly chokes me: I want to shout out *against* them.'

He went to the Foreign Office and half-demanded, half-requested that it should make arrangements for him to meet the Führer. The meeting took place in Berlin on April 19th, 1937. Lansbury was accompanied by two Quakers, Percy Bartlett and Corder Catchpole. Their appointment with Hitler was for one o'clock on Monday. On Sunday they all went to pray at the Friends' Meeting House, while the world's Press reporters buzzed outside, fascinated by the impending conjunction of light and darkness. Lansbury entered the lion's den alone, except for the interpreter, Herr Schmidt, and a nervous Foreign Office man. They were together for two hours and the Führer demanded, for what must have been for him a charade in the Austro-Hungarian manner, the privileges attached to a 'private meeting', which meant that no statement would be released. Lansbury honoured the Führer's wishes and no full account of what took place exists. There was a platitudinous outline of common courtesies. Hitler was restrained and didn't shout or bite the carpet. Lansbury's disingenuous thumbnail sketch of him was that he was 'a mixture-dreamer and a fanatic, that he appeared free of personal ambition, that he wasn't ashamed of his humble start in life, that he was a vegetarian and lived in the country rather than in town, that he was a bachelor who liked children and old people, and that he was obviously lonely'. 'I wished,' added Lansbury, 'that I could have gone to Berchtesgaden and stayed with him for a little while. I felt that Christianity in its purest sense might have a chance with him.'

The following day was Hitler's birthday and rather than watch a

9*

Krupp's benefit make its way along the Unter den Linden Lansbury and his friends turned their attention to the Berlin slums. There the poor folk and children besieged them with parrot cries of Peace! The visit caused a great sensation all over the world and was praised or condemned in the most extravagant language.

After Berlin, Rome. Count Grandi arranged it. About eight weeks later, on July 8th, Lansbury went to talk peace with Mussolini. Dick Sheppard saw him off at Victoria Station. He was greeted at Rome by an army of reporters and photographers and was taken straightway to the Palazzo Venezia, from whose balcony the Duce made his Caesarean announcements. Mussolini's customary manner of receiving human beings was to remain seated behind an heroic desk at the far end of a great room, the idea being that the supplicant would mislay his resolution while crossing the formidable intervening floor-space. But when Lansbury was shown in, damp and tired from the long train ride, Mussolini hurried to the door to meet him, saw that he was exhausted and immediately arranged another meeting to take place when the old man had rested. He seemed to affect the Duce like a truth drug. The Dictator spoke English. Lansbury told him that 1935 was no time to be building empires and Mussolini was puzzled. How was it right to build them in 1835 and not right in 1935? Lansbury, who had been wandering round Rome's Christian monuments, lectured the Duce severely on Love. The Duce listened and listened. But when Lansbury had the temerity to point out that it was the Nazarene and not the Julian family which dominated the Eternal City, it was too much. Saying, 'Good night, we must do the best we can', he once more walked the length of his megalomaniac's audience chamber and showed Lansbury out. He stayed in Rome for a few days, swamped by the beautiful Italian children all screaming, 'Peace! peace!' and returning their Fascist salutes with the Boy Scout salute. He talked to Marconi, who was old and disillusioned and most upset, like Colonel Moore-Brabazon, that such a marvellous invention as the aeroplane should have been turned into a horror weapon by the militarists.

He returned home to hear Winston urging the Government to arm at once and to accuse it of having lost the years that the locust hath eaten. Baldwin said that he had no mandate for rearmament, to which Winston replied, 'The responsibility of ministers for the public safety is absolute and needs no mandate.' Everybody was

reading a lively *exposé* of the Tories called *Guilty Men* and plans
were being made to distribute gas masks. Lansbury listened to the
clamour for a while and then packed his bags and set off for Prague,
for Warsaw, for Vienna. In each capital it was the same, best
manners in front of the old man, glib concurrence with the idea of
Peace as a desirable abstraction, then fun with the children.
Lansbury was far from being a holy fool but he did have a genius
for dragons' lairs. As he approached, hard-bitten careerists, tyrants,
and monsters would automatically rummage about in their sub-
consciences for fragments of human decency and youthful idealism.

On March 7th, 1936, Hitler marched into the Rhineland.
Germany's arms expenditure had reached the terrifying figure of a
thousand millions a year while the United Kingdom's figure was a
mere £186 millions. To increase this Chamberlain proposed a
patriotic tax called the National Defence Contribution (NDC) on
business people. The City at once called this 'socialism' and was
furious—so furious that N.D.C. was never tried. In March, 1938,
Hitler invaded Austria and in August that year he mobilized for the
descent on Czechoslovakia. Chamberlain at once flew to Berchtesgaden to talk to Hitler and returned with 'Peace in our time'.
Lansbury, like the vast majority of people, saw Munich as a triumph.
He was now the President of the Peace Pledge Union. When the
end came, on September 3rd, 1939, he went to the Commons and
acknowledged the crushed olive branch and the crippled dove.

'The cause that I and a handful of friends represent is this
morning going down to ruin. But I think that we ought to take
heart and courage from the fact that after two thousand years of
war and strife, at least those who enter upon this colossal struggle
have to admit that force has not settled and cannot settle anything.'

A few months later he died and soon afterwards the bombs
of the 'Mixture-dreamer' obliterated number 39 Bow Road as
thoroughly as eleven and a half million pacifists were obliterating
their pledges.

CHAPTER FIFTEEN

The Destruction of Neville Chamberlain

'O! What a fall was there, my countrymen'
Julius Caesar

ON May Day, 1940, the first day of a week which was to see one of those hermetic processes of history in which the codes and conduct of an epoch are sealed away, the Leader of the Opposition, Clement Attlee, by private notice, inquired of the Prime Minister when it would be possible for him to make a statement on the position in Norway. 'Tomorrow,' said Mr. Chamberlain. The House then went on to discuss such imperative matters as sheep on the Kentish farms being frightened by low-flying aeroplanes, unemployment in the hardstone industry, Scottish hotels which charged naval officers an extra threepence for a cup of coffee, the reduction of unemployment on the island of St. Helena, fraudulent solicitors, the condition of Aldershot slaughterhouse, the plight of hackle-makers in Dundee and whether quack medicines should be advertised in stamp-books. All this and more having been aired if not settled, the House then went on to debate the novel but extremely inadequate proposals put forward in the first war-time budget. Sir John Simon had presented this on St. George's Day. He had put sixpence on income tax, bringing it up to 7s. 6d., but as he had done this once before the Press was deprived of its jolly joke—'Simon the tanner'—and so had to make what it could of the Chancellor's interesting levy which he intended to put on sales, and which was to be called 'purchase tax'. As well as these taxes, everybody with an income of more than £1,500 was to pay surtax, beer was to go up by a penny a pint, whisky was up by 15s. a gallon and letters were to cost 2½d. This last tax was thought to be the worst. Everybody insisted that it was immoral and brutal because, due to the war, families were scattered all over the place, and it amounted to a tax on the affections. Finally, Sir John said that there would be a tax on war fortunes— after the war.

ˈˈThe war had now been in progress for 240 days, though progress was hardly the word for the profound *status quo* of the Siegfried and Maginot Lines. At home the black-out had been exalted to a degree where it had become a kind of tyranny. Maintaining its perfection became a wholly absorbing preoccupation for a large part of the population. It was called the Bore War and the Phoney War, and, as a cool but beautiful autumn drifted into a bitter winter and the winter into a perfect spring without a hint of carnage, Mr. Chamberlain was sufficiently heartened to declare that Hitler 'had missed the bus'.

The false peace was an unutterable personal solace to him. He was not the kind of man who could take a detached view of agony. A battle was not 'a battle' to him; it was a thousand bereavements; countless hurts of body and mind. The deaths and suffering of sailors, soldiers and airmen haunted his sleep. He was seventy-one years old and, as day followed day, and still the blood-bath held off and the great Western cities, which so many people thought would by now have been Wellsian infernoes, awoke intact, there grew in Mr. Chamberlain's breast the faintest of all faint hopes that by simply declaring war France and Great Britain had out-bluffed the Führer, and that Germany would destroy her own leaders in her own time. And without outside help. Nothing that Hitler had done annoyed him so much as the fact that this dreadful man had forced him, Neville Chamberlain, the man of peace, to go to war. But having gone to war he discovered a mysterious situation which did not compel him to make war. Thereafter, what seemed like a dilatoriness unparalleled even by Ethelred the Unready was really the nerve-rackingly deliberate policy of the British Prime Minister as he faced the greatest raider of all time. And such was the general relief that the horrors of the First World War were not being repeated that the do-nothing attitude of the Premier had a far greater support than might have been supposed at that time. Many people began to dislike Hitler more for having tricked poor Mr. Chamberlain than for having raped Poland. It did not seem unduly strange that he should have come to the microphone on September 3rd, 1939, so seething with personal disappointment and private irritation that his announcement of the second half of the terrible twentieth-century tragedy was a mass of 'I's' and 'me's' and 'my's'.

'You can imagine what a bitter blow it is to *me* that all *my* long struggle to win peace has failed. Yet *I* cannot believe that there is anything more, or anything different, that *I* could have done . . . everything *I* have worked for, everything *I* have believed in during *my* public life, has crashed into ruins. There is only one thing left for *me* to do; that is to devote what strength and powers *I* have to forwarding the victory of the cause for which we have to sacrifice so much. . . .'

He had no sooner finished speaking than the sirens wailed in scarifying derision and the cool blue sky over London filled with barrage balloons whose tethered silken spheres glittered delight-fully. While the world took cover, the Churchills climbed out on to the roof of their house to see what was going on. Nothing was going on, and with everybody feeling a bit of a fool the shelters emptied. Thus, from the very beginning of hostilities the precedent of peace in war was established and Chamberlain succumbed to its tentative charms. 'To carry the spirit of peace into war is a weak and cruel policy; a languid war does not save blood and money, but squanders them.' So said Macaulay. Neville Chamberlain had a mandate for finding out whether this statement was true which was unsurpassed in the political history of England, and he intended to exercise it.

'It may be, but I have a feeling that it won't be so very long. There is a widespread desire to avoid war, and it is so deeply rooted, that it surely must find expression somehow. Of course the difficulty is with Hitler himself. Until he disappears and his system collapses, there can be no peace. But what I hope for is not a military victory—I very much doubt the feasibility of that—but a collapse of the German home front. . . .'

He hoped we would not start bombing 'unless they begin it'. He deplored that 'we have to kill one another just to satisfy that ac-cursed madman'. And he told the Archbishop of Canterbury, 'You will understand how hateful I find my personal position. I simply can't bear to think of those gallant fellows who lost their lives last night in the R.A.F. attack, and of their families. . . .' Six weeks after this he said, 'How I do hate and loathe this war. I was never meant to be a war minister, and the thought of all those homes wrecked with the *Royal Oak* makes me want to hand over my responsi-bilities to someone else.'

Added to this extreme personal revulsion for those duties which

now belonged to his great office and from which he continued to
pray that a miracle might release him, there was the further embarrassment of the Labour and Liberal parties' refusal to join any
government which he headed. All three parties were agreed on the
necessity of stopping Hitler but the lack of coalition led to a marvellous dissipation of national strength which heartened fascists
everywhere. To the undisguised relief of the entire country, Chamberlain had given Winston Churchill the Admiralty, the post he
had held in the First World War. He had also given him a seat in
the Cabinet. The two, so disparate, men worked together in surprising harmony and this was a small compensation for the greater
political divide. Not the least instance of Churchill's genius was his
tact during the first eight months of the war, when the tragic de-
featist attitude of his chief was not only in exasperating conflict with
his own views, but produced in the country at large a climate of
despair which, when the time at last came, needed all his passion
and eloquence to dispel. Hence the Sophoclean grimness of the
'blood, toil, tears and sweat' speech delivered as a sad, stark truth,
and not as parliamentary histrionics.

But this speech was still an age away from the autumn of 1939.
Only five weeks after he had declared war on German fascism,
Neville Chamberlain received, in three days, 1,860 letters beseech-
ing him to stop the war. Sir Oswald Mosley, on the eve of his in-
ternment, concurred with these correspondents and humanely
advised the Government 'to make peace now, with Britain unde-
feated and unexhausted'. Between these pacific extremes there
began to exist a quite unwarrantable hopefulness that the whole
unexciting business would soon peter out. Evacuees swarmed back
home and everywhere there was tedium, purposelessness and ennui.

The chief obstacle to this sweet complacency was Churchill. On
October 1st he made his first war-time broadcast and the country
heard the strangely authoritative orotund diction with a certain
cautious interest. In November he came to the microphone again
and although in this speech he paid fulsome tributes to Chamberlain
and insisted, in spite of much gossip to the contrary, that he and the
Prime Minister saw eye to eye, it was obvious to anyone able to hear
between the lines, as it were, that there could be no sharper division
than that which separated the thinking of these two men. Although
Churchill was sixty-four in 1939, his years in the wilderness with

trowel and easel had left him with his political vigour intact. He was, both physically and mentally, in astounding contrast to most of the Cabinet, who were grey with office. There is something peculiarly invigorating in having one's predictions proved right—even if they happen to be one's worst fears justified—and the Cassandra of the thirties had every reason to crow, 'I told you so!' Only he was too busy to do this or even to attend the House as often as he would have liked to have done. While what Chamberlain called 'the twilight war' continued and soldier and civilian alike kicked their heels, the First Lord of the Admiralty worked furiously.

New wars must recollect the precedents set by old wars but must not be bound by them. One of the things recollected by Churchill in 1939 was that Norwegian territorial waters were mined in 1917 and that they would have to be mined again if the blockade of Germany was to be of the slightest use. On November 19th he reminded the Cabinet of this. He also reminded it that huge trans-portations of Swedish iron ore were being made via Narvik, a port high up on the 1,000-mile Norwegian coastline. Neither Narvik nor Norway itself seemed at all important at that time to Churchill's colleagues and nothing was done. All Churchill's insistence could not make them think otherwise. Yet there was to be something almost occult in his correct guess that Norway held a very special significance in the German grand strategy. While everybody con-centrated upon the stalemate in France, he thought continually of that vast rake-like coast where the sea slipped into countless secret fjords.

Narvik is an outlandish place in which to wind up an era and a trading document is a dull kind of literature across which to write 'finis' as an epoch, with all its hopes, vanities and concepts, dies. Germany's munition factories had to have iron ore from Sweden. In winter it was fairly simple. The ore could be shipped from the far north of Norway and carried for over a thousand miles in the safety of Norway's territorial waters. When Churchill made his plan to mine the waters and put a stop to this trade, the Foreign Office immediately stepped in with a reminder of Norway's neu-trality, something which had meant nothing to Hitler.

On November 30th Stalin attacked Finland and so great was the moral outcry that such a huge power should make war on such a minute one that the British Government got together a special

contingent of soldiers with ski-ing experience and would have sent
them to Finland's aid—except that both Norway and Sweden, each
in fear and trembling of Germany who was now Russia's bizarre
ally under the terms of the Ribbentrop-Molotov pact, refused to
allow them passage. So the Finnish aid brigade, like nearly every
other brigade in the British Army, kicked its heels while, to the
pleasure and amazement of the Allies, the Finns gave the Russians
a single-handed thrashing. Narvik, after this, as Churchill said,
suddenly took on a sentimental value. It became famous as the
gateway which led to these Finnish Davids who were slinging a new
pebble called the Molotov Cocktail at the Red Goliath and bringing
him low with it.

Christmas came and went and found the Allies and their enemy
still glumly lined up with scarcely a shot fired. The United States
watched with a detachment which was fast deteriorating into cold-
ness. At home, the extent of the war effort and the sense of crisis and
immediacy can be assessed by the fact that at the beginning of 1940
there were still over a million unemployed men shuffling through the
labour exchanges. Early in January Chamberlain sacked the sensitive and extraordinarily intelligent, though unconventional, Leslie
Hore-Belisha from the War Office and put in his place the rather
usual Oliver Stanley. Industry sagged. The moral fervour which had
backed the Government's ultimatum to the Führer on September
3rd evaporated. Early in the new year, a deathly complacency, which
would have been bad enough in peace-time but which when civilization was in greater jeopardy than at any other time since the Dark
Ages was either lunatic or criminal, blanketed Britain and France.
The B.E.F. alone appeared to be isolated from this 'sinister trance',
as Churchill called it, and prepared itself for fighting.

In February there was a vivid adventure in the perplexing
Scandinavian seas which once more jolted everyone's attention
back to Norway. H.M.S. *Cossack* boarded the *Altmark* and found
its hold stuffed with nearly 300 British merchant seamen on their
way to the Nazi prisons. The Norwegians had 'searched' this ship
and had declared that they had 'found nothing'. The rescue had a
certain boyish gaiety and it rallied the flaccid emotions of the
nation. Everybody enjoyed its Drake-like temerity while at the same
time they experienced, many for the first time, a sharp awareness
that this rescue of 300 seamen would not have happened had not the

First Lord and the Captain of the *Cossack*, Philip Vian, departed from the sacred letter of the law. From now on dismay and unease at the direction of the war began to affect the country. The Prime Minister and his colleagues still exacted a glowing respect but under this rosy surface there was a deep-seated malady which no amount of individual gallantry could dispel.

In March, after a fight which had stripped the Red Army of its mythology, Finland collapsed, an event which brought the Führer and the Duce hurriedly together at the Brenner Pass. What now? Was the boredom to be broken? The sudden uncertainty trundled the British and French governments into some kind of lugubrious preparedness and, at last, on April 8th, as rumours accumulated of Germany's plans to capture Scandinavia and thus make sure of the Swedish iron, Churchill was at last allowed to carry out the plan to mine Norwegian waters. It was done very early in the morning of that day. And that same evening Hitler invaded Denmark and Norway. Oslo, a city of 300,000 people, was taken by fifteen hundred Germans marching through its hypnotized streets to a brass band. The King and government fled to the north and a Major Vidkund Quisling was to enjoy a fortnight's heady power as the Führer's satrap and some kind of immortality when his name went into the dictionaries as a synonym for 'traitor'.

At home, scales fell from eyes, woolly party loyalties were discarded and dear old British tolerance evaporated. If the socialists and liberals would not serve under Chamberlain, then a prime minister would have to be found whom they could—and must— serve under, for party politics were a luxury the nation could no longer afford. Lloyd George, the veteran director of World War I, now made it his business, and none too feelingly, to sever Churchill from Chamberlain, and showed himself far from averse to a bit of butchery in the process.

The Norwegian campaign rapidly went from bad to worse and as it did so the basic disastrousness of Chamberlain's war leadership escaped from the Press and parliamentary 'respect'. Still thinking in personal terms, he saw this as ingratitude, even as insolence. He faced up to the icy criticism and the mounting dislike with dignity. The dark, bright eyes in the exhausted face flashed challengingly at the constant abuse. His own integrity he knew to be inviolable and that was all that mattered in any prime minister. Even his enemies

granted him integrity and because of it they might have done their
best to deprive him of power considerately as well as constitutionally.
But in the mid-spring of 1940, with the new barbarism at the gates,
there was no time for niceties. The sinewy old man was hustled
along by the uproar of events until, on May 7th, the showdown was
enforced by the Commons in one of the greatest debates in its
history.

*

The House was packed. Barry's fine chamber which had just a year
to go before the Luftwaffe destroyed it on May 10th, 1941, had never
witnessed a more dramatic occasion. The sense of great theatre
could not be separated from what was about to take place and even
before Neville Chamberlain rose, at 3.48, the atmosphere was
unbearably tense. The Peers' Gallery was crowded and the Distinguished Strangers' Gallery contained the massed ambassadors
and ministers of the United States, Russia, China, Argentina,
Belgium, Brazil, Egypt and many other nations. Chamberlain made
a quiet grey entrance and was accorded a ritual cheer from his own
backbenchers. The normality of this barely had time to reach him
before it was drowned in catcalls. 'The man who missed the bus!'
and 'Resign!' were howled in his ears. The intensity of the attack
appeared to rock him, as though he had received a physical blow,
then a disdainful strength reasserted itself and he came bravely on.
Looking shocked but far from frightened, he began to speak, his
own anger and the anger of the House feeding on each other, so that
the big Gothic room became suffocating with latent tumult.

He praised the courage of the soldiers, sailors and airmen in
Norway as they retreated from position to position.

'No doubt the news of our withdrawal from Southern Norway
created a profound shock both in this House and in the country,' he
said. 'And abroad,' reminded somebody sharply. 'All over the world,'
cried another voice. He tried to continue but his words were lost in
the baying of, 'They missed the bus, they missed the bus!' The
Speaker was furious and said he would not allow it, and this brought
a mocking silence. This silence grew crippling as Chamberlain's
words ran into a querulous spate of self-justification and even self-
pity. The disappointment of the Norway campaign unconsciously
took second place to the Prime Minister's personal disappointment.

He tested the apparently shamed-into-docility mood of the House by reminding it haughtily that the Debate was a concession. This didn't please the House at all. He went on, bleakly, 'We cannot help it, but in this Debate we are giving hostages to fortune. Our military advisers have told us in very solemn terms of the dangers of holding such a discussion . . .' and when he summed up legitimate criticism as bickering he guaranteed that the backs of his enemies would be arched to the greatest extent of their spite. His speech ended in an earnest appeal for co-operation. He sat down looking thin and ill and burning-eyed.

The next speech, delivered by Clement Attlee in a flat, rather yapping tone, was coldly destructive. There was actual cruelty in the way he made the events of the present grow out of the mistakes of the past. His presentation was remorseless.

'It is not Norway alone. Norway comes as the culmination of many other discontents. People are saying that those mainly responsible for the conduct of affairs are men who have had an almost uninterrupted career of failure. Norway follows Czechoslovakia and Poland. Everywhere the story is "Too Late". The Prime Minister talked about missing buses. What about the buses he and his associates have missed since 1931 ? They missed all the peace buses and caught the war bus. The people find that these men who have been consistently wrong in their judgement of events, the same people who thought that Hitler would not attack Czechoslovakia, who thought that Hitler could be appeased, seem not to have realized that Hitler would attack Norway. They see everywhere a failure of grip, a failure to drive. . . .'

And then, the dry voice now positively arid with feeling, '. . . we cannot afford to have our destinies in the hands of failures or men who need a rest. They have allowed their loyalty to the Chief Whip to overcome their loyalty to the real needs of the country.'

The tone was thus set. The great debate was as yet in its opening stages but the level of execration was already high and would require thought and skill if it was to be maintained. Normal inter-party sniping was out-classed and the tired old man who was Prime Minister and whose death was so near braced himself for the inhumanity of it. The fake calm of the winter had allowed him to steal away to Chequers and immerse himself in Flaubert and Shakespeare's comedies, and to embellish his dream of peace further. He

listened to Sir Archibald Sinclair thrashing the Government as
though it were some kind of loathsome monster instead of the little
group of decent men he had watched taking its place on the Front
Bench for years, and he could not understand it. Following Sinclair,
Sir Henry Croft, in an indignant attempt to restore Chamberlain's
cracked image to its honourable true-blue state, made the fatal
mistake of attacking the Press for its gloomy exaggerations. He
attempted to reduce the Norway débâcle to a conventional military
reverse. He refused to see that it was a lightning victory by the Nazis
which had, only four short weeks after the arrival of the fifteen
hundred men in Oslo, infected the entire climate of democracy.
It took Colonel Wedgwood to eliminate this kind of 'facile optimism', as he called it. His words missed his audience's heart and
went straight to the pit of its stomach.

'For myself, I think that the country is in greater danger than ever
it has been before in my life; and, at such a time, I am not prepared
to bother about who is to blame for anything . . . the Fleet can save
us from starvation . . . it cannot save us from invasion. Has the
Government not yet prepared any plans to combat the invasion of
this country?'

These words were the first to be heard on such an unmentionable,
unthinkable, though probable event. They drew everybody together as Colonel Wedgwood continued with, 'We are living in a
new world, and this is a new war, the end of which may be the utter
destruction of the British people.' Chamberlain listened, appreciat-
ing the 'new war' but quite uncomprehending the 'new world'. He
seemed to be visibly shrinking; the morning clothes and gleaming
collar were a cast keeping his fragile body in some kind of decent
shape for its ordeal.

A good British divertissement was then caused by the astonishing
and not unalarming sign of Admiral Sir Roger Keyes bearing down
on the House in the full-dress uniform of Admiral of the Fleet.
Blinded and agog, it heard him indict the Chamberlain régime in
what was a *tour de force* of accusation. Salvo after salvo blasted the
Government, bringing its feeble rigging down in festoons. The
Norway excuses were blown to smithereens. The House heard him
with more than one kind of amazement. How had such a famously
bad speaker grown so undeniably eloquent? Sir Roger, who knew
his limitations, had been very depressed that his awkward oratory

would destroy the force of what he had to say. But after having
sought Harold Macmillan's advice he had written out his speech in
full and rehearsed it thoroughly. What the House was hearing was a
superb recitation, a brilliant party-piece. He said that Norway was a
little Gallipoli and this analogy let him arrive at the real point of
why he was making a speech at all. Medals and lace blazing, he
turned to the Government Bench where, silent up to now, except
where a Naval question had required a formal departmental answer,
sat Winston Churchill. Glaring at him, Sir Roger said in a distinctly
challenging voice, 'I have great admiration and affection for my
right hon. Friend the First Lord of the Admiralty. *I am longing to
see proper use made of his abilities.* I cannot believe that it will be done
under the existing system. The war cannot be won by committees....'

The Debate was now racing towards its gruesome climax and at
three minutes past eight, after nearly four and a half hours of
denunciation against which the Government's passionless defence
had proved useless, Leo Amery rose to his feet to administer the
coup de grâce with a blunt Cromwellian sword. His action had all the
careful premeditation of a dagger-thrust by an inspired assassin,
and he had been preparing for the kill ever since he heard Chamberlain addressing the 1922 Committee the previous November. Two
hundred Conservatives had gathered on that occasion, all of them
aching to have their chief, for whom they had the famous Tory
affection, freed once and for all from the moral slime of Munich.
They waited eagerly to hear him wipe the Party and himself clean
of the sneers and smears of appeasement. But, as Amery was to
confess to his diary, all they got was 'a city councillor's speech'.
There followed the dismissal of Hore-Belisha. By April a number of
Tories were so worried by the sheer nervelessness of their Government that they took the unprecedented step of setting up a 'watching
committee' under the chairmanship of Lord Salisbury. Such a cabal
should have shown Chamberlain which way the wind was blowing.
When the great Debate became inevitable, so did the Tory revolt.

When Leo Amery rose to make one of the most famous speeches
ever heard in Parliament the House was nearly empty. Only ten
or twelve members still occupied their seats. Everybody else had
gone off to look for food or to join friends in the Library to release
the tensions of the day in talk. Amery was so depressed by this that
he nearly decided to put off the crucial part of his speech until the

following day, but Clement Davies, realizing that such a plan might fracture the extraordinary momentum which alone could topple Chamberlain from his perch to which he seemed stuck fast with righteous quicklime, persuaded Amery to go ahead. While Amery stalled for time, Davies hurried out of the chamber to collect an audience. It was like a conspiracy. Members returned to their places in dribs and drabs. Then, with a sixth sense that something unique was about to occur, they came thronging back. All the time, Amery was speaking and speaking well, but still not saying anything which justified the arrested air. When he reached the bitter essence of his speech the House was massed around him.

There are few sights more quelling—a cannibal banquet, perhaps —than one Tory slaying a fellow Tory for the good of the country in the parliamentary arena at Westminster. Against such fury the rage of the Opposition is the cooing of doves. There had obviously existed a hope that Chamberlainism might be tactfully and pain-lessly sloughed, but when it became clear that flaying alone would rid the Party of it, there was no hesitation in wielding the knife. Amery could not be expected to enjoy such an operation. Unlike Churchill or even Eden, he had been closely connected with Chamberlain all through the thirties, though he had been among the first, when war became inevitable, to ignore the sanctity of the Whip. 'Speak for England!' he had shouted as Chamberlain rose to tell the House that Hitler had attacked Poland, and at that time Chamber-lain had. But on September 3rd and all too frequently afterwards he had spoken for himself under the illusion that he was England. His genuine grief and sensitivity made these utterances acceptable for a time. Some day, somehow, there must be victory. Morality ordained it.

Amery could not accept this. 'This afternoon, as a few days ago, the Prime Minister gave us a reasoned, argumentative case for our failure. Making a case and winning a war are not the same thing. Wars are won, not by explanations after the event, but by foresight, by clear decision and swift action.'

Then, stage by stage, Amery went over the calamitous Norway landings to expose to view the country's excellent land and sea forces being hobbled time and time again from taking full, leading strides against the enemy by the policy of the Government. The House listened in deep silence.

'We cannot go on as we are,' said Amery at last, and this the House interpreted as a plea by the speaker that when the moment came it was to show no mercy. Those who counted England first and Chamberlain second must turn down their thumbs. 'There must be a change in the system and the structure of our government machine. This is war, not peace. The essence of peace-time democratic government is discussion, conference and agreement; the Cabinet is in a sense a miniature Parliament. The main aim is agreement... to secure... to compromise, to postpone, to discuss. Under those conditions there are no far-reaching plans for sudden action. It is a good thing to let policies develop as you go along and get people educated by circumstances. That may be or may not be ideal in peace. It is impossible in war. In war the first essential is planning ahead. The next essential is swift, decisive action. We can wage war only on military principles. One of the first of these principles is the clear definition of individual responsibilities—not party responsibilities or Cabinet responsibilities ... and the proper delegation of authority. ...'

And so on and so on. It struck at the pathetic uselessness of the 'our brave lads' approach. It ruled out of order 'my disappointment' and all those trudging 'steps' which His Majesty's Government were for ever on the verge of taking. Chamberlain was not present to hear the axes eating into his plinth, he had other engagements to fill. Sir Edward Spears likened Amery's relentless attack to volleys fired into sandbags.

The culmination of the speech which destroyed the Government was high theatre. Amery, a squashed little man with the minimum of presence, suddenly seemed, to the hallucinated eyes and strung-up nerves of the House, to loom over Parliament like a monolith. There was a moment of hesitation on his part and a suggestion of unbearable strain on the part of everybody present. He was afraid of overdoing it and they were afraid that some fatal last minute injection of gentlemanliness might prevent him from doing it at all. In his autobiography he wrote, '. . . I could only dare to go as far as I carried the House with me. To go beyond the sense of the House ... would be not only a fatal anti-climax, but a fatal error of judgement. I was not out for a dramatic finish, but for a practical purpose; to bring down the Government if I could.' He achieved both.

Suddenly irrevocably committed and wholly assured, he declaimed the terrible words with which Oliver Cromwell dismissed the Long Parliament.

'You have sat too long here for any good you have been doing. Depart, I say, and let us have done with you. In the name of God, Go!'

There were further speeches that evening—nearly three more hours of them—but those which continued to defend the Government were pallid, as suited apologiae for a corpse. At about half-past eleven M.P.s went home through the blacked-out streets above which the searchlights fingered the stars.

*

Officially, the Debate was but a third over. It was a tragedy in three acts. The next day, 8 May, saw the excited and exultant atmosphere of the previous evening reduced to one of nervous consternation. The small hours of the night had brought home to everybody the terrible crisis which faced the country and the not unenjoyable turbulence of the previous day had given place to a huge restless disquiet as members crushed into their places on the benches until the House was packed almost to suffocation.

Nothing could have been more ironical than the Speaker's first duty, which was to announce the death of George Lansbury, although, in the tributes which followed, many people were able to rid themselves with decency of the remnants of their pacifism, throwing them gracefully into the grave of this peaceful old man. Private Business and Oral Answers followed in tantalizing normality. The Youth League of Sierra Leone, sugar, excursions to Holland, a dance band's contract with the B.B.C.—it could hardly have been more inconsequential if it had been devised by a satirist for *Punch*. The Speaker seemed to go out of his way to lend all the pomp he could to these preliminaries. While Rome burned he made Ellen Wilkinson re-phrase a too tartly put question. When Mr. Pethick-Lawrence asked why preference was to be given to unmarried men under forty for jobs as assistant potato inspectors there could only be a glazed respect for the monstrous imperturbability of the Commons and, with elbows and knees jammed into each other like players in a vast pin-striped scrum, its members listened politely.

It was particularly dreadful for Neville Chamberlain—almost

like conducting a quiz programme from the scaffold. He replied
gamely when he had to. He looked more shrunken than ever and his
thin throat was now no more than a straggling collection of veins
which did not look as if they had strength enough to support the
restless head.

A trifle after four o'clock Herbert Morrison rose to continue what
he described as 'an exceptionally grave and important debate'. He
was tough but guarded. Obviously the Tories could not be turned
out *en masse* as in normal times. The Government had to be discredited—was discredited—but Winston was part of the Government. The baby must not disappear with the bath-water. 'I will
sing the praises of anybody who is instrumental in winning the war,'
he declared. This indicated that there were to be exceptions but if
the baby, square and glowering, heard, then he showed no sign. He
sat perfectly still among the disgraced men who he alone seemed to
remember were still his colleagues. Morrison went on to quote
damagingly from a speech by Chamberlain which had got itself
printed in the *Listener* only two days before.

> 'Today our wings are spread over the Arctic. They are sheathed
> in ice. Tomorrow the sun of victory will touch them with its
> golden light ... and the wings that flashed over the great waters of
> the North will bear us homewards once again to the peace with
> honour of a free people and the victory of a noble race.'

When members burst into laughter, Morrison was sharp. The
quotation had not been selected for their amusement, he scolded.
It was an illustration of the delusion which gripped the Government. Soon he was to heap his stony tribute on the pile of indictment, taking care, as was observed by everybody, not to bruise
Winston.

'... is it the case that the right hon. Gentleman the First Lord of
the Admiralty is being used as a sort of shield by the Prime Minister
when he finds it convenient to do so? I am quite aware that the
Prime Minister has great confidence in the First Lord. ... But it
appears to me that when the Government are in trouble ... they
tend to bring the First Lord into the shop window. ...'

Churchill heard this with intense distaste. The rope ladders from
the band-waggon were dangling about his ears and it was obvious
that he was expected to scramble aboard gratefully. He made no

move, said nothing, but was noticeably engrossed in the stupendous implications of the emerging situation.

It was in the few sentences he spoke after Herbert Morrison's demand for a vote of confidence that the Prime Minister made his worst mistake of the entire Debate. The weeks of mockery in the Press and the unprecedented attack of the last few hours had goaded him to a state of bewilderment.

'I accept the challenge!' he cried petulantly. 'I welcome it, indeed! At least we shall see who is with us and who is against us, *and I will call on my friends to support us in the Lobby tonight.*'

A single second's thought, and this gaffe might have been bitten back. But broken hearts and smarting eyes have little use for prudence. Only feeling remains. No one in the House that day was to give a damn for feeling. There was 'feeling', presumably, in the image of iced-up wings melting in the golden light of victory, but what else was there? The House was ruthless. It fell on the 'friends in the Lobby' phrase grimly, like a sleuth on a slip of the tongue. There were to be no concessions for nervous fatigue, age or even decency. All that mattered was to crush narrow Party loyalties. Speaker after speaker seized on the unfortunate phrase and it boomeranged back on to the patchy white head of the Prime Minister time and time again.

Lloyd George made a profound impression. The old war director of 1917 had broken his retirement to be present and was one of the few men in the House who did not seem overawed by the ponderous events. The world, he suggested, hadn't come to an end—yet. He was derisive about the Norway strategy and silenced a Government supporter with, 'You will have to listen to it, either now or later on. Hitler does not hold himself answerable to the Whips or to the Patronage Secretary.' He grew inexorable, and the House cringed under the sourness of the truth.

'We promised Poland: we promised Czechoslovakia. We said, "We will defend your frontiers if you will revise them". There was a promise to Poland, to Norway, and to Finland. Our promissory notes are now rubbish on the market.' On and on he swept but when he, too, held out a helping hand to Churchill with, 'I do not think that the First Lord was entirely responsible for all the things that happened there [in Norway]', it was brushed away in no uncertain terms.

'I take complete responsibility for everything that has been done by the Admiralty, and I take my full share of the burden,' growled Churchill. It was a warning to any other Chamberlain-slayer who felt like patting the First Lord on the back with his knife-free hand. But it didn't worry Lloyd George in the least.

'The right hon. Gentleman must not allow himself to be converted into an air-raid shelter to keep the splinters from hitting his colleagues,' he said, not at all abashed. This, too, was a guide to the House on how to deal with Winston. Chamberlain's party loyalty was to be grabbed at and thrown back in his face, even when it was no more than a slip of the tongue. Winston's was to be ignored even when he meant it. Lloyd George ended his speech with the cruel advice, 'I say solemnly that the Prime Minister should give an example of sacrifice, because there is nothing which can contribute more to victory in this war than that he should sacrifice the seals of office.'

A lot of skirmishing followed this. Aneurin Bevan wigged the Deputy Speaker for his partiality and a Mr. Lambert reminded Lloyd George that he had walked behind him into St. Margaret's, Westminster, on Armistice Day, 1918, and heard him declare before God and the congregation present that 'This is the war to end all wars'. Mr. Lambert then went on to deplore the beastliness of the debate and to praise his friend, the Prime Minister, to whom everybody was offering violence. Why, he said, 'I listened in the early days of the war to a gentleman named Lord Haw-Haw. He tried to sap our confidence. That is what is happening today. Dr. Goebbels could not have done better than the House of Commons has done.'

At 6.34 Sir Stafford Cripps rose and began to say something about the previous speaker's case for maintaining the present Government in office, when he was interrupted by Mr. Lambert with, 'It was the other way about. I have asked *you* to come *in*'.

'He has asked,' amended Sir Stafford bleakly, 'that the Government, substantially under the same leadership, should have certain accretions, that the Mad Hatter's tea-party should have another session, and he fails to realize that you cannot identify the leadership of a particular government with the interest of the country. He takes the view apparently that it is better that the leadership should remain . . . intact, whatever its effect may be upon the chances of victory. . . .' And then, in sentences which mounted until they reached a flood-tide of obloquy, he attacked Chamberlain, ending with, 'I never thought that I should be present in the House of Commons when in a moment so grave a Prime Minister would appeal on personal grounds and personal friendship to the loyalty of the House of Commons. I trust that those revealing sentences which he spoke will show that he is unfit to carry on the government of the country.'

For Duff Cooper this was all a great personal vindication of a very different kind, but he forebore to crow. He, too, made Agag-like circumlocutions round the brooding First Lord. A patriot of the classical kind, he showed real anger with the timidity which was, with every likelihood, about to cost the country its freedom.

Chamberlain's friends now began to thrust out their helping hands too wildly, with the result that the Prime Minister was pushed further and further into the mire. Sir George Courthorpe's 'help', for instance was a case in point. 'Thank God, we are led by a Prime Minister who is not easily rattled!' cried Sir George. And Mr. Brooke went so far as to see in the sorrowful crumpled figure on the Government Bench 'a cool judgement and a fiery hatred'. One would have needed to have been a saint to accept such tributes in the spirit in which they were given.

A little past nine o'clock A. V. Alexander began to speak, gently working his way towards the delicate problem of Winston Churchill. Members listened to him with hearts in their mouths, as though he was walking across a minefield. He had heard Churchill speaking at Manchester as long back as January. He had heard him implore the country not to be taken in by the phoney war and to turn to self-sacrifice. 'There is not a week, not a day, not an hour to be lost!' Churchill had said. It made no sense at all then. Alexander was half-way through his speech when Churchill, who had presumably left the chamber to eat his dinner, returned to hear a whole string of questions about the Navy's part in the Norway failure.

Alexander's speech took over an hour and it was well past ten when Churchill rose to wind up the Debate in a slaughterhouse atmosphere of murdered reputations, glassy eyes, flayed dignity, wounded susceptibilities, bleeding hearts, butcher's ferocity and crushed careers. Nothing so Tudor had been seen at Westminster for centuries, no scene was less inviting. But it was no time to show fastidiousness. In marked contrast to the political carnage all around him, Churchill was singularly unscratched. Not only not tired, but bright and fresh. Not swayed by all that had gone before, but calmly in control of himself. At first he spoke moderately—almost casually. He put a few people in their places with jolts which made them appreciate the difference between legitimate criticism and hot air. Mr. Alexander had asked him about twenty questions; he would answer the principal ones. When Sir Roger Keyes dared to interrupt he replied, 'I am sure that my hon. and gallant Friend is always accurate . . . but that is not the point I am discussing now.' He did all he could to salvage the Chamberlain Government from its disaster, taking on himself every bit of responsibility possible. He was witty about the popular reporting from Norway—'In the brown hours, when baffling news comes, and disappointing news, I always turn for refreshment to the reports on the German wireless.' And, when at last he wound up with a not very virulent denunciation of Labour for forcing a division, the House divided, most of it exultant again, but cautiously so.

The division itself was a kind of political fratricide and even the moral certainty behind their actions could not conceal the outward shame of those Conservatives who found themselves in the Opposition Lobby. Shifty eyes and blushes met the Labour and Liberal grins. But the choice was sticking by the old man who, God knew, meant well, or the survival of democracy. When the figures were announced, and the Government's usual majority of 200 was reduced to 81 there was bedlam. The Speaker's voice was drowned in shouts of 'Resign! Resign!' It was a war-cry, the first ever heard since September 3rd. Chamberlain heard it and looked transfigured by it. As the hurly-burly subsided they watched him stiffen, rise, turn and make his way out of the House. His movements and his appearance were tragic and considered, as though he was remembering who he was and how he usually acted as he strolled out of the Commons. He was not humiliated by the exposure of his weakness. He knew no weakness. He was stunned by what he saw as an incomprehensible treachery and it was to face the blow of this that a mask of aloofness and pride settled over his features. He left behind him much true pity but no remorse.

The next day he invited Attlee and Greenwood to Downing Street and asked them to join him in the construction of a National

Government and a few hours later he received the answer. Labour would serve in a National Government, but not *his* National Government. He had expected this and long before the Socialist reply came back he had given Churchill's name to the King. That evening he made his farewell broadcast in a brave, dull little talk which flopped plaintively into clichés nobody could object to. Fine language was for others to concern themselves with now.

The speech barely held its own amongst the deafening news which shook the world on May 10th. Hitler had invaded Belgium, Holland and Luxembourg. Belief in one's self begins as a venture and ends as a habit, and on the very morning that the German avalanche rolled across the Low Countries, Neville Chamberlain had sufficiently recovered from his parliamentary mauling to make a last attempt to retain power, and was only persuaded not to think of such a thing by Sir Kingsley Wood. There followed an intensely polite little scene in which Halifax and Churchill waited for the Prime Minister to choose between them. Halifax settled the matter by withdrawing on the grounds that as a peer it would be difficult for him to keep in touch with the Commons.

And so, at six o'clock on May 10th, 1940, Winston Churchill drove the short journey from the Admiralty to the Palace and, 'acquired the chief power in the State, which henceforth I wielded in ever-growing measure for five years and three months of world war, at the end of which time, all our enemies having surrendered unconditionally or being about to do so, I was immediately dismissed by the British electorate from all further conduct of their affairs'.

Thus ended the week of the great Debate, the week a world died and a world was born. The birth pangs were terrifying. Brussels was bombed, Rotterdam was set in flames, as the Blitzkreig shook Western Europe. Roosevelt lashed isolationism and the United States battle fleet massed at Hawaii. In the Low Countries, the B.E.F. raced to meet the German armies and to endure the victory-in-defeat of Dunkirk—now less than three weeks away. When the Commons met again, on Monday 13th, it was to hear Churchill, who now seemed to have been in power for years for so much had happened in so few short hours, rasping his *De Profundis*.

'I would say to the House, as I have said to those who have joined this Government, "I have nothing to offer but blood, toil, tears and sweat. . . . We have before us an ordeal of the most grievous kind. We have before us many, many long months of struggle and suffering. You ask, what is our policy? I will say: it is to wage war. . . . You ask, what is our aim? . . . it is victory".'

A List of Sources

(See also *Bibliography* and *List of Periodicals*)

The following is a list of the sources (excluding those already given in the text) from which the extracts quoted in this book are taken:

(13) 'I came back from the line at dusk . . .' is from 'The Origin of the Unknown Warrior's Grave' by the Rev. David Railton, published in *Our Empire* magazine.

(15) The poem 'Mother's advice and Father's fears' is from *The Woman of 1926* by Jacques Reval.

(18) 'Pale hands, pink-tipped . . .' is from *Four Indian Love Lyrics* by Laurence Hope, music by Amy Woodforde-Finden (Boosey & Co., 1903).

Chapter 2 (*passim*). The speeches by Jix are quoted from *Jix, Viscount Brentford* by H. A. Taylor (Stanley Paul, 1933).

(31) 'Come to Britain and lead the gay life' is by A. P. Herbert (*Punch*, later included in *A Book of Ballads*, published by Ernest Benn).

(32) 'Since he cannot round up the brewers . . .' is taken from 'Jix', an article by A. G. Gardiner in the *Daily News*.

(50) 'Sunday is what the lawyers call a *dies non* . . .' is from an article by Harold Laski in the *Daily Herald* (1931).

(52) 'Is it not a travesty . . .' is from a letter from Lord Blanesburgh dated 4 February 1926 in the B.B.C. archives.

(58–59) 'The idea that the middle classes . . .' is from a letter by Sir Richard Terry in the B.B.C. archives.

Chapter 4 (*passim*). Extracts from Lawrence's letters are taken from *The Letters of T. E. Lawrence*, edited by David Garnett (Cape, 1938), *The Mint* by T. E. Lawrence (Cape, 1955), and *The Home Letters of T. E. Lawrence and His Brothers* (Blackwell, 1954).

(68–69) Sir Winston Churchill's speech was later published as the Preface to *The Home Letters of T. E. Lawrence and His Brothers* (Blackwell, 1954).

(77–78) 'A clean-cut blond . . .' and 'Lawrence, also fresh from the works . . .' are quoted in *Lawrence the Rebel* by Edward Robinson (Lincolns-Prager, 1946).

Chapter 5 (*passim*). The autobiographical fragments are taken from an essay contributed by Amy Johnson to *Myself when Young*, edited by the Countess of Oxford and Asquith (Muller, 1938).

(84) 'A brave naïve *déracinée* . . .' is from *The Mist Procession* by Lord Vansittart (Hutchinson, 1958).

(105) '. . . they for a time took . . .' is from *Axel's Castle* by Edmund Wilson (Scribner, 1931).

(108) 'Georgian poetry was dead . . .' is from *The Sign of the Fish* by Peter Quennell (Collins, 1960).

(109) 'There is no one in politics today . . .' was quoted in *Communism and the British Intellectual* by Neal Wood (Gollancz, 1959).

(120) 'Just a Smack at Auden' from *The Gathering Storm* by William Empson (first published by Faber & Faber, 1940).

(120) 'From all these events' is from *Collected Poems* by Stephen Spender (Faber & Faber, 1945).

(124, 129, 131–2) The cables which passed between the Australian Board of Control and the M.C.C. appeared in *The Times* (January 1933) and *Wisden Cricketers' Almanack* (1934).

(125–6) *The Times* fourth leader appeared on 19 January 1933.

(127–8) Letter from Lord Buckmaster to *The Times* (21 January 1933).

(129–30) Letter from R. A. Lyttelton to *The Times* (24 January 1933).

Chapter 8 (*passim*). Extracts are quoted from the full account of the trial of the Rector of Stiffkey, published in *The Times* during 1932.

Chapter 9 (*passim*). The account of Ellen Wilkinson's part in the Jarrow march was drawn from her book *The Town That Was Murdered* (Gollancz, 1939), *Hansard*, *The Times*, the *D.N.B.*, the *Daily Herald*, etc.

(197) ? (Hardinge letter). Quoted from *A King's Story* by H.R.H. The Duke of Windsor (Cassell, 1951).

(204) Mr. Baldwin's speech to the Commons is quoted from *Hansard*, November 1936.

Chapter 11 (*passim*). Extracts are taken from *A King's Story* by H.R.H. The Duke of Windsor (Cassell, 1951) and *The Heart Has Its Reasons* by the Duchess of Windsor (Michael Joseph, 1956). Also from *The Times*, December 1936; *Hansard*; etc.

(226) 'On that arid square . . .' is from 'Spain' by W. H. Auden in *Collected Short Poems* (Faber & Faber, 1950).

(227) 'Where all the waking birds sing Heil!' by 'Evoe' (E. V. Knox), published in *Punch*, 21 September, 1938.

(229) 'One day a good book will be written . . .' is from a review by Hugh Trevor-Roper in the *Observer*, 1963.

(235) Quotations from articles by Arthur Bryant in the *Illustrated London News*, August–September, 1938.

Chapter 15 (*passim*). Extracts are quoted from *Hansard*.

(277) '[I] acquired the chief power . . .' is from *The Gathering Storm* by Sir Winston Churchill (Cassell, 1948).

Bibliography

Aldington, R., *Portrait of a Hero—but . . .*, Heinemann 1950.

Allen, F. L., *Only Yesterday.*

Amory, C. and Bradlee, F., *Cavalcade of the 1920s and 30's*, Bodley Head.

Angell, Sir N., *After All*, Hamish Hamilton 1951.

Annual Register.

Auden, W. H., *Collected Shorter Poems*, Faber and Faber 1950.

Auden, W. H. and Isherwood, C., *The Ascent of F6*, Faber and Faber 1939; *The Dog Beneath The Skin*, Faber and Faber; *Journey To War*, Faber and Faber 1939; *On The Frontier*, Faber and Faber 1938.

Auden, W. H., and MacNeice, L., *Letters From Iceland*, Faber and Faber 1937.

Barker, G., *Collected Poems*, Faber and Faber, 1957

Bennett, J. W. Wheeler-, *History of The Times.*

Bennett, R., *A Picture of the Twenties*, Studio 1961.

Bolitho, H., *King Edward VIII*, Eyre and Spottiswoode 1937.

Borkenau, F., *The Spanish Cockpit*, Faber and Faber 1937.

Boveri, M., *Treason in the 20th Century*, Macdonald 1962.

Bowers, C. G., *My Mission To Spain*, Gollancz 1954.

Broad, L., *The Abdication*, Muller, 1961.

Brook, C., *Devil's Decade.*

Broad, L., *Winston Churchill*, Hutchinson 1956.

Campbell, R., *Lorca*, Bowes 1952.

Cecil, Viscount, *A Great Experiment.*

Churchill, W. S., *The Gathering Storm*, Cassell 1948.

Cockburn, Claude, *Crossing the Line*, MacGibbon and Kee 1958; *In Time of Trouble*, Hart-Davis 1956.

Cole, G. D. H. and Postgate, R., *The Common People*, Methuen 1956.

Collier, B., *Heavenly Adventurer*, Secker 1959.

Collis, M., *Nancy Astor*, 1949.

Cooper, D., *Old Men Forget*, Hart-Davis 1953.

Crewe, Q., *The Frontiers of Privilege*, Collins 1962.

Crockford's Clerical Directory.

Cross, C., *The Fascists in Britain*, Barrie and Rockliff 1961.

Cruikshank, R. J., *Roaring Century*, Hamish Hamilton 1946.

Dalton, H., *The Fateful Years*, Muller 1957.
Dangerfield, G., *The Strange Death of Liberal England*, 1936.
De Madariaga, S., *Spain*, Cape 1942.
Dictionary of National Biography.
Documents in the Library at Westminster Abbey.
Dorman, G., *Fifty Years Fly Past*, Forbes, R. 1951.
Eden, Sir T., *Durham*, Hale 1952.
Eliot, T. S., *The Sacred Wood*, Methuen 1953; *The Waste Land*, Faber
    1940.
Encyclopaedia Britannica.
Ensor, D., *I Was a Public Prosecutor*, Hale 1958.
Feiling, K., *Life of Neville Chamberlain*, Macmillan 1946.
Fitzgerald, M. F., *Hubert Edward Ryle*, Macmillan 1928.
Gardiner, A. G., *Certain People of Importance*, Cape 1926.
Garnett, D. (Ed.), *Selected Letters of T. E. Lawrence*, Cape 1952.
Gibbons, S., *Cold Comfort Farm*, 1932.
Gibbs, H., *The Masks of Spain*, Muller 1955.
Goldring, D., *The Nineteen Twenties*, Weidenfeld and Nicolson 1945;
    Odd Man Out, 1935; *Roaring Twenties*.
Graves, C., *The Bad Old Days*.
Graves, R. and Hodge, A., *The Long Week-End*, Faber and Faber 1950.
Greenwood, W., *Love on the Dole*, Cape 1933.
Guedalla, P., *The Hundredth Year*, 1940.
Haldane, C., *Truth Will Out*, 1949.
Halifax, Lord, *Fulness of Days*, Collins 1957.
Hamilton, C., *Modern England*, 1938.
Hamilton, M. A., *Remembering My Good Friends*, 1944.
Hamnett, N., *Is She A Lady?* Wingate 1955.
Hampson, J., *Saturday Night At The Greyhound*, Eyre and Spottiswoode
    1950.
Hansard.
Harrisson, T. and Madge, C., *Mass Observation.*
Henson, H., *Retrospect of an Unimportant Life.*
Hyde, D., *I Believed.*
Johnson, A. C., *The Making of the Auden Canon*, 1957.
Jones, T., *Diary With Letters*, Oxford University Press 1954; *Lloyd
    George*, Oxford University Press 1951.
Kempe, P., *Mine Were of Trouble*, Cassell 1957.
Koestler, A., *Spanish Testament*, Gollancz 1937.
Lansbury, G., *Looking Backwards and Forwards*, Blackie 1935; *My
    England*, Selwyn and Blount 1934; *My Life*, Constable 1928; *My
    Quest for Peace*, M. Joseph 1938.

Laver, J., *Between the Wars*, Vista Books 1961.

Lawrence, T. E. and Brothers, *Home Letters*, Blackwell 1954; *The Mint*, Cape 1955; *Revolt in the Desert*, Cape. *The Seven Pillars of Wisdom*, Cape 1955.

Lehmann, J., *The Whispering Gallery*, Longmans 1961.

Lewis, C. Day, *Collected Poems*, Cape, and Hogarth Press 1954; *The Buried Day*, 1960.

Lewis, W., *Doom of Youth* 1932; *Left Wings Over Europe*, Cape 1936.

Lindsay, D. and Washington, E., *Portrait of Britain*, 1851–1951, Oxford University Press.

Livermore, H., *A History of Spain*, Allen and Unwin 1958.

MacColl, R., *A Flying Start*, 1939.

MacDiarmid, H., *Lucky Poet*, Methuen 1943.

Macdonald, A. G., *England Their England*, Macmillan 1949.

Mackenzie, C., *The Windsor Tapestry*, Rich and C. 1938.

Maine, B., *Edward VIII, Duke of Windsor*, Hutchinson.

Marshall, S., *An Experiment in Education*, Cambridge University Press 1963.

Mollison, J. M., *Death Cometh Sooner Or Late*, Hutchinson 1932.

Montgomery, J., *The Twenties*, Allen and Unwin 1957.

Mosley, O., *Mosley, right or wrong?* Lion Books 1961.

Mowat, C. L., *Britain Between the Wars*, 1918–40, Methuen.

Moyes, A. G., *Australian Cricket*, Angus 1959.

Muggeridge, M., *The Thirties*, Hamish Hamilton, 1940.

Murry, D. Middleton, *The Necessity of Communism*, 1932.

Newsome, J., *In the Depressed Areas*, Blackwell 1936.

Nichols, B., *Cry Havoc!* 1933; *The Sweet and Twenties*, Weidenfeld and Nicolson 1958.

Nicolson, H., *Curzon: the Last Phase*, 1937.

Nicolson, H., *Life of King George V*, Constable 1952.

Nutting, A., *Lawrence of Arabia*, Hollis and Carter 1961.

Ogilvie, V., *Our Times 1912–1952*, Batsford 1953.

Orwell, G., *Homage to Catalonia*, Secker 1951; *The Road To Wigan Pier*, Secker 1959.

Oxford and Asquith, Countess of, *Myself When Young*, Muller 1938.

Parker, Eric, *The History of Cricket*, Seeley 1950.

Postgate, R., *George Lansbury*, Longmans 1951.

Priestley, J. B., *English Journey*, Heinemann 1934.

Quennell, P., *The Sign of the Fish*, Collins 1960.

Reith, Lord, *Into the Wind*, Hodder 1949.

Roberts, C. E. Bechofer, *Trial of William Joyce*, Jarrold 1946.

Roberts, P. E., *A History of British India*, Oxford University Press 1952.

Rolph, C. H., *Does Pornography Matter?* Routledge 1961.
Ronaldshay, Lord, *Life of Curzon*, 1928.
Rothstein, Andrew, *The Munich Conspiracy*, Lawrence and Wishart 1958.
Rowntree, B. S. and Lavers, G. R., *Poverty and the Welfare State*, 1951.
Rumbold, R., *The Winged Life*, Weidenfeld and Nicolson.
Schieldrop, E., *The Air*, Hutchinson 1957.
Sewell, J. E., *Mirror of Britain*.
Sieveking, L., *The Stuff of Radio*.
Sitwell, Sir O., *Left Hand! Right Hand!* Macmillan 1945–50.
Spears, Sir E., *Assignment to Catastrophe*, Heinemann 1954; *Prelude To Dunkirk*, 1949.
Spender, S., *Collected Poems*, Faber and Faber 1954, *World Within World*, Hamish Hamilton 1951; (Ed.), *Poems For Spain*.
Strachey, J., *The Menace of Fascism*, 1933; *The Theory and Practice of Socialism*, 1936.
Taylor, H. A., *Jix—Viscount Brentford*.
Templewood, Lord, *Nine Troubled Years*, Collins 1954.
Trewin, J. C., *The Theatre Since 1900*.
Upward, E., *The Mind in Chains*, 1937.
Vansittart, Lord, *The Mist Procession*, Hutchinson 1958.
Waugh, E., *Brideshead Revisited*, Chapman and Hall 1960.
West, R., *The Meaning Of Treason*, Macmillan 1952.
Whitaker's Almanack.
Who's Who.
Wilkinson, E., *The Town That Was Murdered*, Gollancz 1939.
Williamson, A., *Theatre of Two Decades*, 1951.
Wilson, E., *Axel's Castle*, Scribner 1931.
Wilson, S., *The Boy Friend*, Penguin 1959.
Windsor, Duchess of, *The Heart Has Its Reasons*, M. Joseph 1956.
Windsor, Duke of, *A King's Story*, Cassell 1957.
Winterton, Lord, *Fifty Tumultuous Years*, Hutchinson 1955.
Wisden Cricketers' Almanack, 1952.
Wood, Neal, *Communism and British Intellectuals*, Gollancz.
Young, G. M., *Stanley Baldwin*, Hart-Davis 1952.

Periodicals

British Weekly
Daily Express
Daily Herald
Daily Mail
Daily Telegraph
Daily Worker
Dominion
Evening News
Evening Standard
Illustrated London News
Left Book News
Listener
Liverpool Evening Express
Manchester Guardian
Melbourne Argus
Melbourne Herald

Nation
New Statesman
Nott's Journal
Observer
Our Empire Magazine
Punch
Queen
Sphere
Star
Sunday Chronicle
Sunday Times
Sydney Sun
Tatler
The Times
Time and Tide
Wireless World

INDEX

Date Due

Printed in the USA
CPSIA information can be obtained
at www.ICGtesting.com
LVHW012143281223
767414LV00038B/38